P9-AGO-791

SCOTT FITZGERALD:
The Promises of Life

SCOTT FITZGERALD:
The Promises of Life

edited by
A. Robert Lee

VISION PRESS · LONDON
ST. MARTIN'S PRESS · NEW YORK

Vision Press Ltd.
c/o Harper & Row Distributors Ltd.
Estover
Plymouth PL6 7PZ

and

St. Martin's Press, Inc.
175 Fifth Avenue
New York
N.Y. 10010

ISBN (UK) 0 85478 186 2
ISBN (US) 0 312 02423 1

Library of Congress Cataloging-in-Publication Data

Scott Fitzgerald: the promises of life

  (Critical studies)
  1. Fitzgerald, F. Scott (Francis Scott), 1896–1940—
Criticism and interpretation.   I. Lee, A. Robert, 1941–
II. Series: Critical studies (London, England)
PS3511.19Z844   1989   813'.52   88-26376
ISBN 0-312-02423-1 (St. Martin's Press)

© 1989 by Vision Press Ltd.
First published in the U.S.A. 1989

Printed and bound in Great Britain
at the University Printing House, Oxford.
Phototypeset by Galleon Photosetting,
Ipswich, Suffolk.
MCMLXXXIX

Contents

Introduction

by A. ROBERT LEE

> I can never remember the times when I wrote anything—
> This Side of Paradise time or Beautiful and Damned and
> Gatsby time for instance. Lived in story.
> —*The Notebooks of F. Scott Fitzgerald*[1]

Hard though it may be to recall, there was actually a time when Francis Scott Fitzgerald (1896–1940) seemed at genuine risk not only of dropping out of style but out of sight. Where during the 1920s he had shone like the very laureate of Jazz Age America, its literary golden boy if ever there were, to those who lived on through the Depression and World War II he gave every appearance of having inhabited a 'time when', some magic interlude or carnival which caused the age to resemble nothing so much as one unending Gatsby-like party. In a celebrated observation from his 'Echoes of The Jazz Age' (1931), it was a time of 'a whole race going hedonistic, deciding on pleasure'.[2] If at his too early death, the world had indeed moved on, then Fitzgerald could hardly avoid looking like the ghost of another age. To his fervent but small band of admirers he may well have been the acknowledged author of *The Great Gatsby* (1925) and stories as fine as 'Absolution' or 'Babylon Revisited', but he was also a burnt-out case as it appeared, a left-over from a more facile era who willingly enough had been felled by a combination of the publicity which had swirled about him, drink and the fatal blandishments of Hollywood.

Almost everything—and everyone—associated with Fitzgerald, accordingly, comes over as half-steeped in legend or gossip, both the man and his age seemingly borrowed as much from the pages of his own fiction as historical fact. In this, of course, Fitzgerald belongs in a long line of other American

7

writers made over into (and celebrated as) myth. Poe or Twain offer examples from among his predecessors, Ernest Hemingway, John Dos Passos and Thomas Wolfe from among his friends and contemporaries. Whatever else, then, Fitzgerald has not wanted for different and often competing versions of who or what he was. One version, however, perhaps rises above the rest. If once he had dazzled by his uncanny ability to capture the very image and energy of the Jazz Age—the Boom Times, the Babbittry, the self-denying ordinance of Prohibition, scandals like that of The Teapot Dome, the whirl of Flappers, Sex, Monied Glamour, Valentino and the Movies, he would also with time come to look like one of that age's prime victims, a perfect witness to his own fatigue and 'crack-up'. Even though, especially in his sad later years, Fitzgerald knew what had befallen him, he at the same time acknowledged his own persisting uncertainty as to the exact nature of his identity. Had he indeed, as he once asked, invented himself?

It is not too difficult, however, to summon up the highlights and better-known incarnations of Fitzgerald's career.[3] In the first instance, there comes to mind the comfortably born young Minnesotan, of Irish-American and Catholic stock, who would claim kin with Francis Scott Key of 'The Star-Spangled Banner' and who through the Key and McQuillan families would see both the strengths and the provincialisms of what in *Gatsby* he has Nick Carraway call 'my Middle West'. It was this Fitzgerald who stepped East to enrol as a student at Princeton first in 1913 and then a second time in 1916 and who took virtually all before him by his intelligence and charm, not to say abundant clean-cut good looks. At Princeton, too, he fell in with friends like Edmund Wilson and John Peale Bishop, stalwart allies in a life heady with success but also marked out by real pain and despair. Princeton also gave him access to the mores, albeit the affluent mores, of his generation, not exactly a *jeunesse dorée* yet at the same time something not far short of it (in an essay written in 1929 he would acknowledge that Princeton had become for him a 'myth', Nassau Hall and the Clubs as situated enrapturingly amid 'the loveliest riot of Gothic architecture in America'[4]).

Out of the same period, too, emerges 2nd Lieutenant Fitzgerald, the handsomely appointed Ivy League Officer (though he left Princeton without a degree), the fledgling writer who while stationed at Camp Sheridan, close to Montgomery, Alabama, would meet for the first time the 18-year old Zelda Sayre, the start of a romance which made the society columns with almost unchecked regularity. Discharged from the army in February 1919, Fitzgerald launched himself as never before upon a life in literature, working briefly for the Barren Collier advertising agency while beavering away at his stories and at the novel with which he would burst upon the scene, *This Side of Paradise* (1920). Mannered as it now looks, especially the girl-boy encounters and the novel's treatment of Catholicism, in the story of Amory Blaine Fitzgerald became the 'voice' of his generation. Or as *American Magazine* titled him in 1922, he had emerged as 'the Most Famous Young Writer in America'. If it is true as Fitzgerald once suggested that all his stories have 'a touch of disaster' in them, especially those concerning the lovely, the young and the wealthy, then the novel which followed, *The Beautiful and Damned* (1922), was utterly on key. Unfortunately its love-story of Anthony Patch and Gloria Gilbert too easily weakens into melodrama and a beginner's literariness. Not quite so, however, Fitzgerald's early stories, those first published in *Smart Set*, the *Post* and *Scribner's* and later in an array of up-market magazines, and which make up his two first collections, *Flappers and Philosophers* (1920) and *Tales of the Jazz Age* (1922). So momentous a literary bow heralded to all with an interest an American literary succession to the era of Henry James and Edith Wharton.

Running alongside the birth of Fitzgerald as author, be it as novelist or short-story writer, lies the birth of Fitzgerald as celebrity. First came the marriage with Zelda in April 1920 and the birth of their daughter Frances Scott Fitzgerald ('Scottie') in October 1921, then the socializing and parties and different sorties into Europe—mainly with rich glitterati like the Gerald Murphys and in such fashionable watering-places as the Riviera, Antibes and Montreux, and more dramatically than anything, Zelda's breakdowns which led to the first of her stays in a Swiss clinic in 1930 and which would continue on and off in various American sanitariums until her death in a fire in 1948. At their height, Scott and Zelda undoubtedly represented glamorous coupleship, both writers, both society personalities, both a kind of American cultural royalty. For observers of the 1920s scene in particular, an Edmund Wilson or H. L. Mencken or young Malcolm Cowley, Fitzgerald also takes a major part in the 'expatriate' story, a rising star with Hemingway at the court of Gertrude Stein and of the still greater presences of James Joyce and Marcel Proust. Despite the myths, neither Fitzgerald nor Hemingway were starving garret artists; rather they had steady dollar incomes from home, were on a spree, and took every relish in that most self-consciously 'cultural' of European cities, Paris. They both, let it be said, also got on with the serious task of writing, luminaries as may be of the fabled Lost Generation but also tough-minded professionals.

Quite Fitzgerald's best period has to be the year which led up to the publication of *The Great Gatsby* in April 1925. His letters to Maxwell Perkins, the marvellously helpful and shrewd editor he shared with Hemingway and Wolfe at Scribner's, show him as the fully engaged writer, excited at his own creation and self-disciplined in its making in a way he rarely was again. To follow the excisions, the changes, the different drafts and re-drafts of *Gatsby* as set forth in the Perkins correspondence, is to follow a 'novel' almost in its own right. One could make a comparison with Melville's 'Agatha' letters to Hawthorne or some of the Henry James notebooks. His letters to Perkins can also be matched with the letters he later wrote to Scottie, the letters of a devoted father to be sure but also a quite magnificent instance of a Guide to Reading, an affectionately devised literary education for a young woman coming into maturity.

It cannot be said that after *Gatsby*, in the fifteen years between it and his death, Fitzgerald simply fell into a gradual decline; rather it became a matter of successive jolts and lurches, disasters intermingled with great creative successes—though more through his stories than his longer fiction. Symptomatically, with *Gatsby* behind him, he fell more and more into the drinking, the rounds of parties and binges, whether in Europe or in Hollywood where he made his first visit in 1927. As he said of 1926–27, in a phrase which has lingered, '1,000 parties and no work'.

Yet he did continue to write stories and essays. Indeed, eventually there would be nearly 180 in all, each cast in the immediately recognizable Fitzgerald 'style', one so unaffectedly light of touch that often it was mistaken for inconsequentiality. They also, though it has not always been given recognition, exhibit his great skills not merely as some chronicler of the Jazz Age, or 'romance', or the manners of the American rich, but as a parodist, quite one of America's best satiric talents. Two further story collections appeared in his own lifetime, *All the Sad Young Men* (1926) and *Taps at Reveille* (1935), to be followed by the posthumous collections, *Afternoons of an Author* (1957) and *The Pat Hobby Stories* (1962). This latter volume, centred on Fitzgerald's alter ego figure, the Hollywood writer Pat Hobby, also reminds that he created other cycles or sequences—the Josephine stories (among the best of them, 'Emotional Bankruptcy' and 'A Woman with a Past') and the remarkable Basil Duke Lee sequence, which includes some of the very best writing Fitzgerald ever committed to print. Nor should mention be omitted of Fitzgerald's one dramatic effort, *The Vegetable*, which opened and closed in deservedly quick succession in November 1923, a political satire of sorts falling short on its own best ideas.

For the rest it was anything but silence, but at no time a clear line of imaginative succession to *Gatsby*. The stories continued, as did the essays, of different strengths and hues; Zelda's condition worsened—no doubt the obsession with dancing was in some way a key symptom—and she had a second major breakdown in 1932; Hollywood beckoned still more for Fitzgerald and especially in the form of Metro-Goldwyn-Mayer (to whom in 1937 he would be briefly contracted for no less than $1,000 per week); and in 1934 *Tender is the Night*, Fitzgerald's longest novel, saw publication. This latter has properly been seen as his major effort, though not his major triumph. It has a broader span and gravity than any of his other novels, but the well-known problems as to its right or best sequence bespeaks an unsureness. The themes could not have been more dramatic: the invalidism not only of Nicole Warren and Dick Diver as her doctor-suitor but of a whole generation in Europe and beyond turned 'psychiatric', schizophrenic, by both personal ravage and that of the Great War. Much of this and the life of monied expatriate life Fitzgerald handles decisively and even movingly. But the doubts about his overall mastery of the narrative persist. It has come under attack both for a failure of distance in the handling of its material and for a certain indulgence and crowdedness.

1935, and the five years up to the heart-attacks which brought on his end in 1940, have come to be known as the period of 'The Crack-Up'. We have, as prime testimony, his celebrated essay of February 1936, the 'breakage', the 'mortguaging myself physically and spiritually up to the hilt', as he called it, his version of himself as a piece of 'cracked crockery'. The irony of being able to formulate his own collapse with so assured a touch has not gone unremarked. Yet Fitzgerald's exhaustion, his trauma, cannot have been much other than what he describes. No doubt a lifetime's writing habits simply went into action. Then, too, the life he followed while living in different South Carolina and Baltimore hotels and residences—which he recalls with some irony in a number of the pieces in *Afternoons of an Author*—while trying to keep a watching brief on Zelda and giving way to his bouts of alcoholism make for a picture more bleak than hopeful. No doubt the move to Hollywood in 1937 and the liaison he began there with Sheilah Graham were the best, conceivably the only, options open to him. He needed both the cash and the love and companionship Sheilah Graham provided.

Not that it can be doubted that he had a genuine or continuing concern for Zelda, as his frequent visits to see her and his expressions of affection in his letters to Scottie both attest. Drink or not, too, and not just in his dry spells, he did continue to get work done. Not only did he turn out, often at derisory fees, his required quota of scripts (he did a stint for United Artists in 1940), but he had in hand *The Last Tycoon*, a novel which had it been completed and further revised might more readily have been regarded as far better than some last fragment shored up against his ruins. Different though it is from Nathanael West's *The Day of the Locust* (1939), it does share a great deal of West's ambition to capture the impact on human consciousness of the movies and the power of those in whose hands Hollywood had come to rest. Opinion on the whole has not favoured *The Last Tycoon*, but it assuredly does possess at least a residue of the qualities he attributed to his own life and work in a letter written to Scottie not twelve months before his death:

12

I am not a great man but sometimes I think the impersonal and objective quality of my talent and the sacrifices to it, in pieces, to preserve its essential value has some kind of epic grandeur.[5]

Fitzgerald's valediction bears closely, for certain, on his last novel. More arresting still, however, is how memorably it offers an epigraph to his entire career.

The great rehabilitation of Fitzgerald through the nearly five decades since his death is dealt with elsewhere in this volume, especially the scholarly and critical work which can claim a starting-point in Edmund Wilson's compilation *The Crack-Up* (1945). And be it in the journals, in the proliferation of full-length critical studies, in scholarly editions of the *Letters* and *Notebooks*, or in the series of major biographies, Fitzgerald has come increasingly into more complete focus, the human quantity and writer behind the legend.[6] In this respect, also, Fitzgerald has led another kind of fugitive or posthumous existence, his recurrence as a reference point in the writing of other authors. Explicit tributes there are in plenty. One only has to think, among others, of John O'Hara's in the Foreward to the 1953 reissue of *Appointment in Samarra* (1934) and his Introduction (1945) to *The Portable F. Scott Fitzgerald* ('our best novelist, one of our best novella-ists, and one of our finest writers of short stories') or of Ernest Hemingway's both in the slightly sour 'The Snows of Kilimanjaro' (1936) and in the portrait he gives of Scott and Zelda in *A Moveable Feast* (1964). But Fitzgerald has also, and on a most considerable scale, recurred as a 'fiction' in and of himself.

In the absolute first instance is Zelda Sayre Fitzgerald's depiction in *Save me the Waltz* (1932), often rightly judged a companion piece to *Tender is the Night*. In the pairing of David Knight and Alabama Beggs, Zelda projected with often wounding accuracy her version of the 'romance' and love-hate competitiveness of her marriage with Fitzgerald, a doubling in art as much as life. Zelda's novel also resorts to the same stuff of which Scott wove his own stories: the glamour, the love affairs and infidelities, the play of dream against waste and as always the parties. The other best-known portrait belongs to Sheilah Graham, a triptych in fact, first *Beloved Infidel: The Education of a Woman* (1958), then *College of One* (1967) and *The Real Scott*

Fitzgerald: Thirty-five Years Later (1976), tribute of a kind touched with gentleness and yet a no-nonsense grasp of Fitzgerald's human weaknesses as much as his creative strengths. Fitzgerald's Paris years make essential references back in two important first-person remembrances, as the newly arrived and married young writer in Gertrude Stein's *The Autobiography of Alice B. Toklas* (1933) and as the literary and bar sparring-partner of Hemingway and the rest in Morley Callaghan's *That Summer in Paris* (1963).

Historians of Fitzgerald's impact have also been keen to point out his different reincarnations in the fiction of others, most especially as the creator of *Gatsby*.[7] Among the more celebrated are Charles Jackson's anatomy of alcoholic decline *The Lost Weekend* (1944), Budd Schulberg's Hollywood saga *The Disenchanted* (1950), Raymond Chandler's landmark Philip Marlowe mystery *The Long Goodbye* (1954), Jack Kerouac's Beat classic *Doctor Sax* (1959), Louis Auchincloss's rags-to-riches 'business' novel *A World of Profit* (1968), Ron Carlson's pastiche Vietnam story *Betrayed by F. Scott Fitzgerald* (1979), and as an unabashed contemporary use of the Fitzgeraldian 'touch of disaster', John Irving's *The Hotel New Hampshire* (1981). But few Fitzgerald allusions have more sharply caught the attention than that of J. D. Salinger's Holden Caulfield in *The Catcher in the Rye* (1951). There, in Holden's 'I was crazy about *The Great Gatsby*. Old Gatsby. Old Sport. That killed me', a more recent adept at American vernacular can be said to pay his warm (not to say inventive) homage to a predecessor, one stylist's salute to another. Fitzgerald may in his own right have been a suitable case for fictional treatment, his life at once a cautionary tale and unfolding high drama. But for almost all these authors and others, he also elicits a peculiar sense of debt, his best art a strength to be learned from and in however different an idiom to be emulated.

The present collection offers a new round of Fitzgerald interpretation, six essays addressed sharply to the long and short fiction and three which assume an altogether more inclusive angle. In the opening essay, Andrew Hook argues for a subtler estimate than is usually given to *This Side of Paradise* and *The Beautiful and Damned*, Fitzgerald's first two novels as less documentaries of the Jazz Age young and rich than enquiries into the moral—and political—bases of human behaviour. My own essay looks at 'imagination' and *The Great Gatsby*, the meticulous process whereby the novel got written and the inspired imaginative 'distortion' whereby Nick Carraway discloses the transformation of Jimmy Gatz into Daisy's Knight Errant and Playboy of the Western World. Harold Beaver takes on *Tender is the Night* from a Jamesian perspective, Dick Diver and his world as 'portraiture' of a kind with that given to Isabel Archer. Robert Giddings in his account of *The Last Tycoon* ponders the relationship of Irving Thalberg to Monroe Stahr, Fitzgerald's portrait of a different kind of artist at a time when movies were about to become the dominant form of mass culture. Two essays are given over to Fitzgerald's short fiction. In the first Herbie Butterfield examines a selection of the work from the 1920s, a 'period' body of writing which yields quite some of Fitzgerald's best triumphs. Brian Harding pursues a similar compendium of stories, the *Saturday Evening Post* love stories, arguing for Fitzgerald as a writer infinitely weightier than some mere chronicler of 'romance'.

Of the considerations from a wider round of assumptions, Elizabeth Kaspar Aldrich pursues Fitzgerald's treatment of women in his fiction: the different transformations of and borrowings from Zelda to be sure, but also his debts to Poe in the depiction of woman as inspiration and icon. Historical consciousness in Fitzgerald has been an issue of some debate, not least his professed 'Marxianism' and his debt to Spengler. The latter, especially, is taken up in John Whitley's essay, an account of how Fitzgerald saw the signs hidden and revealed of the West's decline in the activity of his times. Lastly, Owen Dudley Edwards subjects Fitzgerald's Irish-Americanness and Catholicism to a broad sweep, a historian's analysis of the cultural shapings behind his fiction.

Much as Fitzgerald will probably always be most identified with the Jazz Age, at once its celebrant and its critic, his claims have come to be seen as infinitely more various. He was a major American stylist, as recognizably so as a Hemingway or Faulkner. In his strongest work, *Gatsby*, *Tender is the Night* and the great stories, he brought a genuine sense of history to his themes, be they those of romance, glamour, human fecklessness and breakdown, or loneliness. He could also call upon the keenest satiric powers, an unclouded shrewdness about self-delusion and egoism. Who, too, would deny the comic side to Fitzgerald, his ironic lightness of touch? Nor is it unfair to compare him with the mentor he most aspired to, Joseph Conrad, a radically different temperament for certain but one whose 'impersonality' he found it in himself to recreate when writing at his most inspired. Which is never to say that Fitzgerald was always successful. The flaws are plentiful and irritating. But he belongs in that select band of American writers who when he triumphs does so unforgettably and in an idiom wholly and for all time his own.

NOTES

1. Matthew J. Bruccoli (ed.), *The Notebooks of F. Scott Fitzgerald* (New York and London: Harcourt Brace Jovanovich/Bruccoli Clark, 1978), p. 159.
2. As reprinted in Edmund Wilson (ed.), *The Crack-Up* (New York: New Directions, 1941). The essay first appeared in *Scribner's Magazine*, February 1936.
3. I would like to acknowledge the sequence of biographies which set out Fitzgerald's life: Arthur Mizener, *The Far Side of Paradise* (Boston: Houghton Mifflin Co., 1951); Andrew Turnbull, *Scott Fitzgerald* (New York: Charles Scribner's Sons, 1962); Henry Dan Piper, *F. Scott Fitzgerald: A Critical Portrait* (New York: Holt, Rinehart & Winston, 1965); Matthew J. Bruccoli, *Some Sort of Epic Grandeur: The Life of F. Scott Fitzgerald* (New York: Harcourt Brace Jovanovich, 1981); and André Le Vot, *F. Scott Fitzgerald* (New York: Doubleday & Company, Inc., 1983).
4. 'Princeton', in *Afternoons of an Author: A Selection of Uncollected Stories and Essays* (New York: Charles Scribner's Sons, 1957).
5. Written 31 October 1939. Manuscript in the Princeton University Library. See also Matthew J. Bruccoli, *Some Sort of Epic Grandeur* (op. cit.).
6. These are footnoted in the Notes to the essays.
7. See, especially, Richard Anderson, 'Gatsby's Long Shadow: Influence and Endurance' in Matthew J. Bruccoli (ed.), *New Essays on 'The Great Gatsby'* (Cambridge, London, New York: Cambridge University Press, 1985), pp. 15–40.

1

Cases for Reconsideration: Fitzgerald's *This Side of Paradise* and *The Beautiful and Damned*

by ANDREW HOOK

1

Back in 1945, William Troy wrote an important critical article entitled 'Scott Fitzgerald—the Authority of Failure.'[1] Not of course—Mr. Troy insisted right away—that he was suggesting that Fitzgerald himself was a failure. Not at all. And here is why:

> he has left one short novel, passages in several others, and a handful of short stories which stand as much chance of survival as anything of their kind produced in this country during the same period.

Forty years later that strikes me as a good deal less than a definition of success. One short novel, passages in several others, and a few short stories, hardly amounts to the output of a literary giant. Indeed whatever his intentions, what William Troy has defined is in the end a record of literary failure. Achieving no more than this as a writer, Fitzgerald has to be seen as sharing in that experience of failure which occurs thematically so frequently in his fiction.

What is strange is that there is nothing eccentric about

William Troy's assessment. The great majority of critics continue to share his view. Fitzgerald's successes are in critical terms extraordinarily limited. He is the Leaning Tower of Pisa of American literature, his reputation sustained by the one unqualified success of *The Great Gatsby* (1925). Remove that support, and Fitzgerald would be down there in the valley of ashes. On the rest of his fictional output, the conventional critical judgement is surprisingly uniform. *The Last Tycoon* (1941)—a promising fragment, but where was it going? *Tender is the Night* (1934)—structurally flawed, its themes inadequately understood by its author. *This Side of Paradise* (1920) and *The Beautiful and Damned* (1922), to which this essay gives its attention, two immature pieces of writing, scarcely worthy of regard as serious novels. What else did Scott Fitzgerald produce? Large numbers of short stories—the great majority of which even he regarded as second-rate, written only for the purpose of a quick financial return—and one failed play.

Such a record leaves one asking whether there is any other major author who has written so little that has achieved general critical acclaim. Remember too that there are even those who are ready to question the status of *Gatsby*: is not the author ultimately complicit with the glittering surface he evokes . . . ? But even if we accept *Gatsby* as a major achievement, such a one-off success is hardly enough to justify any kind of claim to literary greatness. So is it the case that Fitzgerald is not a major author? The point is not a tedious debate over the precise meaning of 'major'. Rather it is the contrast between the evaluation of Fitzgerald's individual works and the widely held sense of his importance as a writer. Everywhere Fitzgerald is read and attended to. He seems to matter. For most of us Jazz Age America is what Fitzgerald said it was. His books are kept in print—in fact in recent years every scrap he wrote seems to be regarded as well able to command an enthusiastic audience. How can this be? How can a writer, so consistently seen by the critics as failing to produce satisfactory work, not merely survive, but seem to flourish? Let me offer two tentative answers, both of which suggest that the problem lies with the critics rather than the writer.

The first is that Fitzgerald's other work has been victimized critically by the success of *The Great Gatsby*. Because his other

18

novels are not *Gatsby*, they are failures. Before *Gatsby*, Fitzgerald was still learning how to write a novel; after *Gatsby*, he never managed to find a way of doing it again. The single jewel shadows the crown. In fact, Fitzgerald was perfectly aware that *Gatsby* did not provide a model for all of his fiction. He knew that he had chosen to write at least two different kinds of novel—even if from time to time he used slightly different terms to distinguish between them. In a letter to John Peale Bishop, in 1933, he called *Gatsby* a 'dramatic' novel while *Tender is the Night* was a 'philosophical, now called psychological' one. To compare the two would be like 'comparing a sonnet sequence with an epic'.[2] The difference is further explicated in a letter of 1937. *This Side of Paradise* and *The Great Gatsby* were 'selective'; *The Beautiful and Damned* and *Tender is the Night* were 'full and comprehensive'. 'In *This Side of Paradise* (in a crude way) and in *Gatsby* I selected the stuff to fit a given mood or "hauntedness" or whatever you might call it. . . .'[3] *The Beautiful and Damned* and *Tender is the Night*, that is, attempt to provide the fullness and depth of detail that the other two omit. In any event, the point is that *Gatsby* was not seen by Fitzgerald as providing a single model for the writing of a novel. Just as some critics were disappointed because *The Beautiful and Damned* did not try to follow up the popular success of *This Side of Paradise*, so others were disappointed that *Tender is the Night* was so unlike *Gatsby*. On both occasions Fitzgerald was determined to do something different; his critics' taste was less catholic than his own.

Of course, there is always the possibility that his critics were right: perhaps the dramatic novel was in fact Fitzgerald's strength. He should have recognized this, and stayed with it. Perhaps. But there is another case to be put. The 'selectiveness' of *Gatsby* does help to explain its jewel-like brilliance and perfection; but the fullness and comprehensiveness of *Tender is the Night* unquestionably add to its power to engage and move. At the time when *The Beautiful and Damned* was being published, Fitzgerald characteristically blamed himself for having 'devoted so much more care . . . to the *detail* of the book' than to 'thinking out the *general* scheme', but he was clearly wrong to do so; the strength of *The Beautiful and Damned* lies precisely in its dense accumulation and weight of detail, not at all in any profundity of philosophical or interpretative scheme.[4]

19

The second explanation I would offer to the paradox of Fitzgerald's apparently simultaneous existence as a successful and failed writer involves an answer to the following question. Has there ever been an author more patronized, more put down, more condescended to, by an established critical orthodoxy than Scott Fitzgerald? The answer of course is no. And this is the bottom line that those of us who love Fitzgerald—and find it possible to sympathize with the struggles of his life both as a writer and a man—are reluctant to accept or even tolerate. Yet one has to try to understand how that critical tradition originated.

Right from the start Fitzgerald had all the wrong credentials for being accepted as a great artist and writer. Attending Princeton, he had gone to the wrong—too glamorous— university; he was strikingly handsome; he was married to a beautiful woman; he insisted on leading an expensive way of life which involved pleasure and the pursuit of happiness; he took up no fashionable political cause; above all, he achieved fame and success when he was still remarkably young. Youth, beauty, success—how many critics are prepared to tolerate such a combination? (Just imagine—if you dare—what Fitzgerald's fate would have been had he been a woman writer.) The answer was the creation—whether entirely consciously or not does not matter—of a view of Fitzgerald as writer which has never ceased to dominate critical thinking about him. The lineaments of that view were as follows. First, Fitzgerald was not to be taken seriously as conscious artist; such success as he achieved was to be attributed solely to his 'natural' talent as a writer. His gift for writing was somehow virtually independent of the man; some freak of fate had endowed him with it, and on occasion it would emerge in work of the highest quality. In other words, just as the Edinburgh *literati* decided that Robert Burns was a 'heaven-taught ploughman', so America's intellectuals decided that Fitzgerald was a 'heaven-taught Freshman' of a writer. Secondly, and quite logically, the same intellectual critics announced that Fitzgerald was an unintelligent writer; his critics were all a great deal cleverer than he was. Where there should have been intellectual grasp and understanding, there was at best a capacity to gesture towards concepts which poor old Scott barely understood anyway. He had read a few books at Princeton, and listened to other people's ideas, but where was the intellectual sharpness or philosophical grasp? So Fitzgerald wrote by instinct and had no ideas. Thirdly, Fitzgerald was said to be a writer who never grew up. His work was *immature*. (*Gatsby* of course was 'more mature' than *This Side of Paradise* and *The Beautiful and Damned*, but the process of maturation was not sustained.) So there it was: Fitzgerald conveniently packaged by his early critics as a natural but immature writer of limited intellectual understanding. Once established, this critical tradition has to a substantial degree persisted down to the present.

How did such a view establish itself? Well, I have already indicated how Fitzgerald's entire personality and way of life struck his serious-minded contemporaries as incompatible with a literary achievement that demanded to be taken seriously. Fitzgerald belonged to the 'smart set' of Jazz Age society and chose frequently to write about precisely that kind of world. The majority of critics seem to have found it impossible to believe that such a world could provide material appropriate to the needs of serious fiction. The assumption was that superficial characters in a superficial society meant superficial art. In 1934, in the Introduction to the Modern Library edition of *The Great Gatsby*, Fitzgerald at last allowed himself to protest at such an assumption:

> . . . I had recently been kidded half haywire by critics who felt that my material was such as to preclude all dealing with mature persons in a mature world. But, my God! it was my material, and it was all I had to deal with.

(I would argue that nothing contributed more to Fitzgerald's problems as a writer than the excessive respect he constantly showed for the patronizing opinions of his critics. If he had been prepared to answer back, in the way he is doing here, ten years earlier, his career might have developed quite differently.) But in fact the problem went deeper than Fitzgerald allows here. It was not just that he was dealing with the wrong kind of material; he was not seen to be taking a sufficiently critical attitude towards it. Too involved in the Jazz Age way of life he wrote about, how could he ever hope to be taken seriously?

Perhaps there was another factor, however, that ensured the

21

creation of the critical tradition I have been describing. Fitzgerald suffered from what in Glasgow would be described as the 'Aye, I knew his feyther' syndrome. His early critics, that is, knew him too well on a personal level ever to be able to assess his work objectively. They remembered him as an under-graduate at Princeton—the Fitzgerald they knew remained just that. The idea that he—and not the Edmund Wilsons or John Peale Bishops—should be the major writer of their generation was never going to be acceptable to them; their Fitzgerald remained just the not very clever Scott they had known. Hence the inevitable tone of superiority they adopted in writing about him.

Let me dwell on one dimension of this tradition of critical disparagement for a moment or two longer. The charge of 'immaturity' has probably done most permanent damage to Fitzgerald's standing as a writer. I have no idea when the term 'mature' emerged in the critical vocabulary as a form of critical praise. Nor, I suspect, are we all entirely clear about what precisely is meant when an artist is described as 'mature': except presumably that more is involved than being over 40. However we are confident that to be mature is a good thing, whereas to be labelled 'immature' is very bad news indeed. Given that Fitzgerald was 23 when *This Side of Paradise* was published, it was more or less inevitable that it should immedi-ately have been dubbed immature.

However, hindsight allows us to see that Fitzgerald's literary precociousness was not at all uncharacteristic of the 1920s in general. Dos Passos was no more than a year older than Fitzgerald when he published his first novel—and he had published another three before he was 30. Both Hemingway and Faulkner were still in their twenties when their first novels appeared. Even more significant, perhaps, is the fact that Edmund Wilson, when he wrote the *Bookman* essay that did more than any other single piece to establish the orthodox critical view of Fitzgerald as a natural, but immature and intellectually defective writer, was himself still under 30. Now it may well be true that different people mature at different speeds; indeed that some of us never mature at all. The point remains that we should not accept the notion of 'maturity', in critical discourse, in a wholly uncritical manner. At the very least we should be particularly alert to the possible limitations of the term when it is bandied about by young men in their twenties about their contemporaries.

What I have been trying to do is to explain how the conventional critical wisdom about Fitzgerald's work came into being. What have been its consequences? For the purpose of this essay, the important consequence is the patent neglect of the early novels. *The Great Gatsby* is a novel which miraculously manages to stay afloat in the ocean of words which has been created around it; by comparison, *This Side of Paradise*, and still more so, *The Beautiful and Damned*, are texts which remain as dry as a bone. Given both the fineness and the busyness of the mills of American literary scholarship in recent times, this degree of neglect is extraordinary. It can mean only one thing: the still more extraordinary power of the received critical orthodoxy that the early novels are no more than immature, apprentice, works. The early novels have been neglected because the myth has prevailed that they are not worthy of serious, grown-up, critical attention. In fact, of course, they are entirely worthy.

2

Not, however, that I am about to argue that *This Side of Paradise* and *The Beautiful and Damned* are great novels. What they are, though, are good novels, eminently readable, written with verve, and containing substantial amounts of often self-contradictory emotional honesty and power. The flaws that the conventional critical tradition have concentrated on are there: the excesses, the romantic extravagance, the sometimes failed lyricism, the name-dropping and intellectual pretentiousness. But these faults are in no way sufficient to deprive the novels of their freshness and appeal. The early readers of *This Side of Paradise* who were electrified by the book, who insisted that their lives were changed by it—John O'Hara's 15,000,000 men and women readers between the ages of 15 and 30 who fell in love with it[5]—all those who were sure that they were reading a serious novel by a serious novelist: these readers had it right. They at least were responding to the book as it was, their reactions unsullied by the Fitzgerald myth. Likewise those who found in *The Beautiful and Damned* a development in Fitzgerald's ability to unify and focus his material were also correct. Infinitely more correct certainly than those critics who tried to insist that the second novel, in its portrayal of individual disintegration and defeat, reflected only Fitzgerald's recent reading of Dreiser and Norris: as though a sense of failure was something alien to Fitzgerald's own experience.

And yet one cannot help noting how inevitable it was that such an obvious misinterpretation of *The Beautiful and Damned* should have quickly established itself. The novel needed to be explained away. It had been agreed by 1922, on the basis of *This Side of Paradise* and the early collection of short stories, *Flappers and Philosophers* (1920), that Fitzgerald's only subject was the rich and the glamorous. And there was already, as I have said, a question over how far the author was taken in by the superficial charm of the world his fiction evoked so brilliantly; did he clearly recognize the moral corruption of the Jazz Age society he continually wrote about? But here was *The Beautiful and Damned*, a long novel portraying, not the glamour and glitter of the lives of the young, the beautiful and privileged, but rather the slow draining away of youthful charm and hope into bleakness and despair. Clearly something has gone wrong. This is not Fitzgerald's kind of book. Never mind, the answer is to hand. He has been reading the American naturalists, and in his usual impressionable way has decided that they hold the key to the meaning—or non-meaning—of life. Not of course that *The Beautiful and Damned* could be seen as a successful exercise in the naturalistic mode. The reasons for the decline of Gloria and Anthony Patch are never made clear; are they to be seen as victims of fate, of external social circumstances, the corrupt world they live in, or are they themselves responsible for what happens to their lives? Fitzgerald is unable to make up his mind, and the novel therefore lacks any firmness of moral point-of-view.

In fact, one of the most appealing aspects of Fitzgerald's early novels is precisely a question of his uncertainty, or lack of conviction, about what is right and what is wrong. The texts refuse judgement because the author is concerned to delineate experience without any absolute confidence about which aspects matter more than others. Hence the moral ambiguities, even the moral absences, that traditional critics have seen as damaging flaws. The position is complicated by the obvious contradictions within Fitzgerald himself. Clearly his temperament included quite a powerful impulse towards judgement. He once explained his refusal to become simply a popular entertainer because of his desire to 'preach at people in some acceptable form'.[6] In *The Great Gatsby*, where he may seem to worry us by inviting admiration for a man who is clearly corrupt and criminal, he reassures us of his moral soundness by having Nick Carraway tell us at the end that Tom and Daisy Buchanan were 'careless people' who 'smashed up things and creatures and then retreated back into their money or their vast carelessness. . . .'

Similarly, it is easy to find in *This Side of Paradise* and *The Beautiful and Damned* passages or episodes that uphold wholly conventional moral judgements. On the other hand, as an artist creating and peopling a fictional world, Fitzgerald allowed other dimensions of his own responsive openness to life and experience to emerge in what he wrote. The moral censoriousness of which both Amory Blaine and Anthony Patch are capable is never the whole story. And often it is the absence of simple judgements, the uncertainties and confusions, the sense of being bewildered by things—not quite in the Jamesian sense, but in a way that James would have understood—that give life and appeal to the early novels. It may well be the case that in these fictions Fitzgerald was trying to work out his own problems in coping with experience; that he is not able to come up with hard and fast answers is not necessarily a weakness. Indeed, as a long-term admirer of Keats, it is hardly surprising that Fitzgerald came to subscribe to something akin to the doctrine of negative capability. In *The Crack-Up*, for example, he observed that 'the test of a first-rate intelligence is the ability to hold two opposed ideas in the mind at the same time, and still retain the ability to function.'[7] In a general sense that kind of capacity had always been present in his fiction, working against the strain of moral puritanism in his make-up.

Let me cite a simple example of the kind of moral openness which I see as important in contributing to the success of the early novels. At the point in *This Side of Paradise* when the beautiful Rosalind is trying to explain why she cannot marry a penniless Amory, she is asked whether she intends to marry the wealthy Dawson Ryder. 'Oh, don't ask me', replies Rosalind,

> You know I'm old in some ways—in others—well, I'm just a little girl. I like sunshine and pretty things and cheerfulness—and I dread responsibility. I don't want to think about pots and kitchens and brooms. I want to worry whether my legs will get slick and brown when I swim in the summer.[8]

Such an admission is of course from one point of view overwhelming evidence of Rosalind's utter selfishness and moral irresponsibility. And indeed this passage has been adduced as a prime example of how Rosalind comes across to the reader as a much more essentially superficial character than Fitzgerald realizes. In my view, though, the passage resists such a simple judgement. What it conveys is a sense of Rosalind's youth and beauty and desires—'I like sunshine and pretty things and cheerfulness.' For her, whether or not her legs are tanned in summer is something that matters, and she wants it to go on mattering. Fitzgerald is not in the business of condemning her for that. Like Amory, he understands Rosalind's need and thus cannot condemn it. This is the kind of understanding that helps to explain the novel's vast appeal to its youthful audience.

3

This Side of Paradise was published in March 1920. Fitzgerald had worked hard to get it into print. Two earlier versions of the novel—when its title was 'The Romantic Egoist'—had been turned down by Scribner's. However, encouraged by H. L. Mencken's acceptance of two short stories for his magazine *The Smart Set*, Fitzgerald undertook a third rewriting in the summer of 1919, and this time Scribner's decided to publish. The novel's success was immediate. Fitzgerald became a celebrity overnight. If there were aspects of the novel that the President of Princeton found objectionable, that only helps to explain the book's instant appeal to a new generation of post-war Americans, no longer able to accept without question the conservative values of the past. Such critical attention as the novel has subsequently received has of course been much concerned with trying to explain—or explain away—its popular appeal. Many of the points that have been made no doubt are true. Everyone agrees that the novel did somehow succeed in articulating something of the sense of doubt and uncertainty characteristic of at least some areas of American society in the immediate post-World War I period. All readers may not have identified with Amory Blaine, but the novel's hero's sense that the world in which he was living was a new and changing one does seem to have touched a sensitive contemporary nerve. The fact that the novel was about college men, and described college life, also contributed to its appeal. Like the old Victorian 'silver fork' novels, with their putative accounts of the lives of the English aristocracy, the book offered its enthusiastic readers vicarious insight into the way of life of one kind of American élite. Then the novel's form, with its variety of modes—prose, poetry, dramatized scenes—its headings and sub-headings, which Fitzgerald said later he borrowed from Shaw's Prefaces, must have struck at least some readers as new and radical and modern.

Fitzgerald was inevitably dizzied by the success of *This Side of Paradise*. Indeed the expectations it created in terms of sales and money were never met by any of his subsequent novels. On the question of how good it was, however, he came to share in later years the views of most of his sterner critics. And it has to be said that not even a Fitzgerald enthusiast can deny that the novel is uneven, often naïve and uncertain in tone, structurally weak, and on occasion sentimental and self-indulgent. Its debts to Fitzgerald's reading have always been recognized: Compton Mackenzie and Booth Tarkington mix oddly as influences with H. G. Wells and Henry Adams. Fitzgerald himself once called the book 'A Romance and a Reading List', and it is true that the undergraduate characters are much given to literary name-dropping. (Altogether the text mentions sixty-four titles and ninety-eight writers.)[9] Yet Fitzgerald was never ready to dismiss the book entirely. In 1925, he wrote in his own copy: 'I like this book for the enormous emotion, mostly immature and bogus, that gives every incident a sort of silly "life".'[10] What was most bogus he decided—correctly in my view—was the fourth and final of Amory Blaine's adventures with women. Of the Eleanor episode Fitzgerald wrote: 'This is so funny I can't even bear to read it.'[11] Even as late as 1938, his general view of

27

the book had not changed significantly. In a letter of that year, he wrote:

> Looking it over, I think it is now one of the funniest books since *Dorian Grey* in its utter spuriousness—and then, here and there, I find a page that is very real and living.[12]

Perhaps these are the pages he had in mind when he said, later in the same year, that he had written in the novel of 'a love affair that was still bleeding as fresh as the skin wound on a haemophile.'[13]

On the whole, then, Fitzgerald was a push-over for his critics. He lacked the intellectual and literary self-confidence to answer back. How significant it is that when Gertrude Stein praised *This Side of Paradise* in 1925, Fitzgerald was impelled to respond almost wholly negatively: 'it honestly makes me shiver to know that such a writer as you attributes such a significance to my factitious, meretricious *This Side of Paradise*.'[14] Yet presumably it was qualities other than its factitiousness and meretriciousness that made John O'Hara's 15,000,000 youthful readers fall in love with the book. Alfred Kazin has written that Fitzgerald 'is easier to appreciate than to explain' and that is very much the case with his first novel.[15] In any event, critical appreciation rather than condescension is what *This Side of Paradise* merits.

There is another reason why *This Side of Paradise* matters. When it is read less as a self-contained, autonomous work than as an opening statement in Fitzgerald's career as a writer, then it reveals further levels of meaning. When he was writing *This Side of Paradise*, Fitzgerald was struggling to discover what kind of writer he wanted to be; simultaneously, though, he was trying to establish the kind of man he was. To find a satisfactory and satisfying definition of himself as man and as writer was to remain a central problem for the rest of his life. All too often it seemed that the two rôles pulled in opposite directions: as a writer, Fitzgerald felt he needed to be detached and objective, an observer of life and experience; as a man, however, he was committed, engaged, given himself up to life, using and being used by it.

Ultimately, this is why in *The Crack-Up*, the autobiographical essays written in 1936 trying to explain the disintegration he feels has overtaken his life, he comes to the extremely bitter conclusion that he has failed as a writer by being too much a man. The solution, he decides, is 'to continue to be a writer', but 'cease any attempts to be a person—to be kind, just, or generous'. As a man, he has exhausted himself, used himself up physically and spiritually, by too much giving of himself. Now he will become the detached, uninvolved artist only, no longer 'identified with the objects of [his] horror or compassion'. So at last he tells us he has 'become a writer only. The man I had persistently tried to be became such a burden that I have "cut him loose". . . .'[16] The tone of all of this is, of course, as I have said, deeply bitter and disillusioned. Fitzgerald knows full well that it is late in the day to be thinking of turning himself into a James or a Joyce; in truth, he could never be that kind of artist figure. But *The Crack-Up* is no more than a tough-minded and clear-sighted articulation and summing-up of a problem that had haunted Fitzgerald from the beginning of his career; hence it is hardly surprising to find aspects of the same problem constantly recurring in the text and sub-text of his fiction.

It is in the closing pages of *This Side of Paradise* that the issue emerges most directly. The context is Amory Blaine's car ride towards Princeton during which he argues the case for socialism with a wealthy industrialist and his secretary. Traditional criticism has tended to disparage the episode, arguing that there has been no preparation for Amory's sudden espousal of socialist principles. But the strength of the episode is exactly its unexpectedness and open-endedness: Amory—like Fitzgerald— is in the process of working something out for himself, and the answers are no more than tentative. In the course of the argument, Amory, attempting to discriminate between the social attitudes of different categories of people, comes up with the notion of the 'spiritually married man'. Marriage here, significantly, becomes a metaphor for entrapment in the social status quo; the spiritually married person has lost his independence, can no longer afford to be neutral or dispassionate— 'Life's got him', as the text beautifully puts it. To remain free, to be in a position to work for change, to be any kind of radical— and writers fall into this category—it is essential to remain 'unmarried'. But the point is that Amory Blaine's ambitions throughout most of *This Side of Paradise* drive him in precisely the opposite direction: success at school and college, and the fulfilment of his romantic, emotional yearnings, all involve a commitment to things, a surrender of the self to others. After attending the funeral of Monsignor Darcy, his spiritual mentor, Amory had decided that more even than to be loved, what he wanted was 'to be necessary to people, to be indispensable'.[17] Clearly neither position is compatible with detachment. Again, having recognized a link between beauty and evil, he decides that he can never be the kind of dedicated artist for whom beauty alone is what matters: 'it seemed so much more important to be a certain sort of man.'[18] The unresolved question for Fitzgerald was whether being that sort of man was compatible with remaining the spiritually unmarried artist.

4

The Beautiful and Damned, Fitzgerald's second novel, published in March 1922, remains easily his most neglected book. Writing the Fitzgerald chapter in the 1978 *American Literary Scholarship* volume, Jackson R. Bryer refers to it as 'this strangely sprawling and bitter novel which has been, for the most part, ignored by critics'.[19] Such neglect powerfully underlines one of the central points I have been trying to make: the enduring strength of the critical tradition that dismisses Fitzgerald's early novels as immature works of little artistic value. Even more so than in the case of *This Side of Paradise*, such a judgement is inappropriate to *The Beautiful and Damned*. Fitzgerald's second novel is an extraordinary piece of work, an advance on *This Side of Paradise* in terms of structural unity, characterization and control of tone. Yet something of its power undoubtedly derives from the existence of *This Side of Paradise*. It is a book very much about the loss of paradise. In *Le Grand Meaulnes* Alain Fournier wrote: '*les seuls paradis sont les paradis qu'on a perdus.*'[20] When he was writing *The Beautiful and Damned*, Fitzgerald clearly had already recognized that whatever paradise Amory Blaine had yearned for was already beyond recall: Anthony Patch's experience in the second novel is the experience only of paradise lost.

Given the interest that has always been taken in the doomed lives of the Fitzgeralds, the neglect of *The Beautiful and Damned*, with its extraordinary prophetic quality, is all the more surprising.

Fitzgerald himself was in no doubt about the relevance of the novel to his own life with Zelda. In 1930 he wrote to his wife, 'I wish the Beautiful and Damned had been a maturely written book because it was all true. We ruined ourselves—I have never honestly thought that we ruined each other.'[21] (Note the typical acceptance of the maturity criticism.) Ten years later, writing to his daughter, he qualifies the autobiographical dimension of the book, but does not repudiate it:

> Gloria was a much more trivial and vulgar person than your mother. I can't really say there was any resemblance except in the beauty and certain terms of expression she used, and also I naturally used many circumstantial events of our early married life. However the emphases were entirely different. We had a much better time than Anthony and Gloria had.[22]

That at least is good to know.

Perhaps it is only with the benefit of hindsight that the source of the sense of pain and bitterness, present in *The Beautiful and Damned*, can be so readily identified in Fitzgerald's own life with Zelda. And if at the time Scott and Zelda seemed only like beautiful people, perhaps that helps to explain why the early critics were so eager to see the novel as no more than Fitzgerald's response to his reading of Norris, Dreiser, Harold Frederic, and the rest. On the other hand, to explain the novel in such terms is only possible on the assumption that Fitzgerald was a kind of *tabula rasa* of a writer, responding almost automatically to what he had been reading—not an artist in his own right. I do not mean that Fitzgerald's portrayal of Anthony Patch's slow decline owes nothing to literary sources. Only that it is absurd to see the entire portrayal of the lives of Anthony and Gloria, from the early brilliance to the despairing end, as no more than a kind of pastiche of American literary naturalism. Robert Roulston's more recent conclusion seems to me to be altogether more convincing:

> . . . surely the bitterness, the unrelenting misogyny, the want of *joie de vivre*, and the almost equal contempt for those who strive and those who repine owe more to Fitzgerald's own state of mind than to literary or philosophical models.[23]

The Beautiful and Damned has obvious thematic links with *Tender is the Night*. Both novels are concerned with the disintegration of a man's life; both let us see how early promise is slowly overtaken by failure and defeat. The commonest critical charge made against both books is that Fitzgerald fails to clarify the causes of decline—as though the explanation of failure is more significant than the experience of it. Certainly in *The Beautiful and Damned*, Fitzgerald offers no single explanation for Anthony Patch's collapse; a variety of factors, some of them perhaps contradictory, seem to be involved. At some stages Anthony is portrayed as temperamentally weak, morally irresponsible, retreating from an unpleasant reality into a life of non-stop partying and drinking. At others, Anthony appears to be the victim of a corrupt and money-dominated world which has rejected the values of the past but found nothing with which to replace them. Sometimes it seems to be his addiction to Gloria, even more than his addiction to alcohol, that is the problem. Or is it ultimately the nature of reality itself that is in question— the slow but inevitable process of life's running down or wearing away?

The point is that Fitzgerald may well not have known how precisely to explain the failure he was portraying—what he could do was to imagine its movement, its successive stages, with such impressive power that a comparison with Dreiser's portrayal of the fall of Hurstwood in *Sister Carrie* is in no way inappropriate. Particularly from the brilliant theatrical moment when Anthony's rich and puritanical grandfather arrives in the midst of the novel's wildest party in Marietta, to its uncertain ending, the novel offers a series of episodes and scenes which dramatize Anthony's disintegration with compelling conviction. The vivid account of the South, and Anthony's involvement with Dorothy Raycroft during his army training, his attempt at becoming a salesman in New York, his drinking at Sammy's, the drunken and violent confrontation with Bloeckman—all of these scenes are effectively and dramatically portrayed.

In 1922, in a letter to Edmund Wilson, Fitzgerald insisted that he did intend Anthony and Gloria to be representative figures: 'They are two of the great army of the rootless who float around New York.'[24] To read the novel in the light of that remark is to approach it as a novel of manners or social comment: *The Beautiful and Damned* then becomes a work meant to expose the careless and useless lives of the essentially hollow characters who make up Jazz Age society. Here is the reality that lies beneath the superficial glamour and charm. Such a reading is possible. *The Beautiful and Damned* is Fitzgerald's 'Waste Land' novel, evoking the sterility and loss of values of the post-war world. In the essay called 'Early Success', written in 1937, Fitzgerald describes how, even before he began writing *The Beautiful and Damned*, he had developed a sense of the under-current of violence and danger in the booming America of the 1920s: 'All the stories that came into my head had a touch of disaster in them . . .', and he goes on to say that he was 'pretty sure living wasn't the reckless, careless business these people thought—this generation just younger than me'.[25] *The Beautiful and Damned* gives considerable substance to these comments; its text and sub-text articulate a general sense of a society lacking direction or purpose, morally confused, potentially violent. Nevertheless, in my view it is the novel's personal dimension that gives it its true force. As always in Fitzgerald, wider social observation and comment derive from a deeply felt individual context; the consciousness that is responding to and recording experience remains not that of his characters but Fitzgerald's own. Inevitably, then, his own concerns and preoccupations constantly emerge into the text he creates.

In 1920, writing about the new novel he was then at work on (provisionally entitled *The Flight of the Rocket*), Fitzgerald said of his protagonist Anthony Patch: 'He is one of those many with the tastes and weaknesses of an artist but with no actual creative inspiration.'[26] From the first, that is, Fitzgerald had conceived of Anthony as a version of the inadequate or failed artist; and of course throughout *The Beautiful and Damned* Anthony Patch does make several attempts to rescue his position by succeeding as a writer. But Amory Blaine's hopes of helping to create 'the living consciousness of the race' find no kind of fulfilment in the work of Anthony Patch. At first Anthony believes he can become a gentlemanly historian with a history of the Renaissance popes as his subject—he even succeeds in publishing a single essay on the topic. Later he thinks he will be able to raise cash by turning out short stories for the popular magazine market; this attempt is a dismal failure. But for most of the novel, Anthony's writing exists only as an unrealizable dream—it is something he is always about to do . . . In a crucial scene, Gloria attacks him for promising much but achieving nothing:

> 'Work!' she scoffed. 'Oh, you sad bird! You bluffer! Work—that means a great arranging of the desk and the lights, a great sharpening of pencils, and 'Gloria, don't sing!' and 'Please keep that damn Tana away from me,' and 'Let me read you my opening sentence,' and 'I won't be through for a long time, Gloria, so don't stay up for me,' and a tremendous consumption of tea or coffee. And that's all. In just about an hour I hear the old pencil stop scratching and look over. You've got out a book and you're 'looking up' something. Then you're reading. Then yawns—then bed and a great tossing about because you're all full of caffeine and can't sleep. Two weeks later the whole performance over again.'

The scorn and derision present here are more than enough to discomfort Anthony; he can find little to say in reply. Inevitably, however, one suspects that the power of the scene derives from its origins in Fitzgerald's own experience—just as elsewhere in *The Beautiful and Damned* he gives expression to other aspects of his own problems as a writer. Clearly in the figure of Richard Caramel, who writes a good best-seller and then allows financial considerations to destroy his artistic integrity, Fitzgerald delineates a possible future for himself. But it is through the picture of Anthony Patch—as the passage I have just quoted makes clear—that Fitzgerald gives fullest expression to his own doubts and uncertainties. Anthony is endowed with beauty, charm and wealth; his life initially seems full of promise—paradise seems eminently attainable. With his marriage to Gloria he seems to have made it. However, just as Gatsby senses after his reunion with Daisy that the famous green light ceases to be an enchanted object, so Anthony discovers that paradise and reality are incompatible.

However, for Anthony as for Dick Diver in *Tender is the Night*, 'the manner remains intact for some time after the morale cracks.' Indeed Anthony can usefully be seen as an early version of Dick Diver. Only in the later novel Fitzgerald has got the sub-text problem into clearer focus—almost as clear as in the direct personal analysis of *The Crack-Up*. Diver is the doctor-scientist who breaks the cardinal rule of his profession: instead of remaining the detached observer, treating his 'cases', he becomes identified with the objects of his compassion. Endowed with a 'fatal pleasingness', he cannot resist total involvement with those around him. His marriage to Nicole is his inevitable final commitment to 'life' rather than to the science or medicine which Fitzgerald intends to be analogous to art. Diver is too much a man to be a successful artist. In *The Beautiful and Damned* the picture is less clear, but the outline is already present. Anthony Patch, the artist manqué, finds himself so committed to a style of living that he can never extricate himself from it. The vague philosophising in which he intermittently indulges provides him with no firm, alternative resource. With Gloria he gives himself up to living—a commitment which is not compatible with his survival as a writer. This, I would suggest, is the fear that haunts Fitzgerald and provides the sub-text of the novel.

The Beautiful and Damned made the *Publishers Weekly* monthly bestsellers' lists for March, April and May 1922—*This Side of Paradise* had made the same list only twice. The initial sales of the two novels were very much the same—around 50,000 copies. But *The Beautiful and Damned* did little to enhance Fitzgerald's contemporary reputation. Most critics had presumably antici-pated a more straightforward follow-up to *This Side of Paradise*. H. L. Mencken and George Jean Nathan praised the novel, but Fitzgerald's Princeton friends John Peale Bishop and Edmund Wilson mingled praise with blame and decisively established by their comments the disparaging critical tradition that Fitzgerald has suffered from ever since. Not that he has ever been entirely lacking in enthusiastic admirers and defenders. It is Henry Dan Piper who reminds us that in 1944, when Fitzgerald's reputa-tion was at its lowest, Charles Jackson, author of *The Lost Weekend*, wrote:

> People will be going back to Fitzgerald one day as they now go back to Henry James. . . . His writing is the finest, purest, the most entertaining and most readable that we have in America today.[28]

Perhaps now is the time to go back to the early novels.

NOTES

1. William Troy, 'Scott Fitzgerald—the Authority of Failure' in Alfred Kazin (ed.), *F. Scott Fitzgerald: The Man and his Work* (New York, 1951), p. 188. Troy's article was originally published in *Accent*, 1945.
2. Andrew Turnbull (ed.), *The Letters of F. Scott Fitzgerald* (Harmondsworth: Penguin Books, 1968), p. 383.
3. Ibid., p. 571.
4. Ibid., p. 373.
5. See Matthew J. Bruccoli, *Some Sort of Epic Grandeur: The Life of F. Scott Fitzgerald* (London, 1981), p. 127.
6. Ibid., p. 135.
7. F. Scott Fitzgerald, *The Crack-Up with Other Pieces and Stories* (Harmondsworth: Penguin Books, 1965), p. 39.
8. F. Scott Fitzgerald, *This Side of Paradise* in the Bodley Head Scott Fitzgerald, Vol. III (London, 1960), p. 189.
9. See Dorothy Ballweg Good, ' "A Romance and a Reading List": The Literary References in *This Side of Paradise*', *Fitzgerald-Hemingway Annual* (1976), 35–64.
10. Quoted by Bruccoli, op. cit., p. 122.
11. Ibid., p. 125.
12. *Letters*, p. 297.
13. Ibid., p. 598.
14. Ibid., p. 504.
15. Kazin, op. cit., p. 17.
16. *The Crack-Up*, op. cit., pp. 52–3, 55.
17. *This Side of Paradise*, op. cit., p. 255.
18. Ibid., p. 269.
19. See J. Albert Robbins (ed.), *American Literary Scholarship 1978* (Durham, North Carolina, 1980), p. 170.
20. I am indebted for this reference to a forthcoming article on Fitzgerald and Fournier by John Coyle.
21. See Bruccoli, p. 155.
22. Ibid.
23. See Robert Roulston, '*The Beautiful and Damned*: The Alcoholic's Revenge', *Literature and Psychology*, 27 (1977), 162.
24. *Letters*, p. 351–52.
25. *The Crack-Up*, op. cit., pp. 59–60.
26. *Letters*, p. 163.
27. *The Beautiful and Damned* in the Bodley Head Scott Fitzgerald, Vol. IV (London, 1961), p. 189.
28. See Henry Dan Piper, *F. Scott Fitzgerald: A Critical Portrait* (London, 1965), p. 94.

2

'A quality of distortion': Imagining *The Great Gatsby*

by A. ROBERT LEE

> As he sat there talking so sincerely I seemed to see him at night in his study. I looked at him in wonder, the author of *The Great Gatsby*, pouring over some dumb unsympathetic review, hoping for one little flash of insight that might touch his imagination, make him aware of some flaw in his work, make him a better artist.
>
> —Morley Callaghan, *That Summer in Paris*[1]

1

Few accounts of American literature would be considered complete, or indeed wholly serious, which did not give Scott Fitzgerald's *The Great Gatsby* (1925) full acknowledgement, a triumph at once critical and popular and by the widest of margins. If it shines as a classic of period, the Jazz Age caught at full tilt and in all its show of glamour and violence, it also invites an exploration of certain perennials within the human condition—the interplay between 'dream' and 'foul dust',[2] or, to use a newer idiom, between desire and its consequences. However otherwise read, too, as a reworking and critique of the American Dream, a tale of doomed errantry, a peculiarly American comedy of manners, a sexual pathology of sorts, or even a tacit Marxian onslaught on capitalism and the fetish of commodity, by consensus *Gatsby* stands out just as forcefully as a first among literary equals. That judgement has been altogether deserved.

Nor does *Gatsby* have a claim to pride of place simply by its evident fascinations of theme. It also represents a miracle of story-telling. Fitzgerald's style rarely shows itself more nuanced while remaining spare and economic. Despite its novella length, it offers a round of memorably particular characters with Gatsby at their centre, a narrator as interesting as the tale he tells, a framing image of Grail and Wasteland which is picked up at every turn, and an overall flair to its management of scene and action which Fitzgerald rarely again quite matched. In virtually every aspect, *Gatsby* reflects its begetter's sureness both of subject and form.

Furthermore, to speak of the imagination which went into the making of *Gatsby* is to link together still other implications. It helps make emphatic Fitzgerald's own sense of the specialness for him of this more than any of his novels, an effort he would look back to both with pride and the bitterest regret that he had not held himself to a continuing seriousness of vocation. It directs us to the bravura with which he monitored his own progress in giving expression to his essential themes, the novelist watching his art work through him. It even functions as a theme important in its own right, not least in regard to Gatsby's astonishing self-invention and subsequent pursuit of Daisy Fay. The issue, then, of the imagination both behind and within *Gatsby*—in the latter respect imagination as a series of purposive and brilliant 'distortions' to use Fitzgerald's own phrase in the story—has everything to do with its singularity.

2

None too surprisingly, perhaps, much of the discussion of *The Great Gatsby* has taken its point of departure from Fitzgerald's letter of July 1922 to Max Perkins, his exemplary and long-serving editor at Charles Scribner's Sons. There, with just a whiff of the rising star's grandiloquence, Fitzgerald offered his memorable declaration of intent: 'I want to write something *new*—something extraordinary and simple + intricately patterned.'[3] The upshot, at least as it came to him in a first draft two years later, Perkins immediately and intelligently recognized

as indeed 'extraordinary'—'an extraordinary book' is the literal
echoing phrase in his own reply, and one also 'to be proud of'
and 'suggestive of all sorts of thoughts and moods'.[4] He clearly
saw it, in addition, as a quite major advance for all their
popularity on both *This Side of Paradise* (1920) and *The Beautiful
and Damned* (1922).

Perkins may have expressed a worry about the 'somewhat
vague' contour of Gatsby himself and about the largely un-
specified sources of his wealth. He may also have felt that in
having Gatsby speak with unusual volubility about his Army
and Oxford past Fitzgerald seemingly had departed from 'the
method of the narrative', namely Nick Carraway as the book's
presiding voice of disclosure. But his essential, and prophetic,
emphasis falls upon 'the general brilliance of the book', its
'unequaled' characters and its imparting of a sense of 'eternity'
to the main workings of the story. He speaks, too, of 'the
amount of meaning you get into a sentence', a manuscript 'full
of phrases which make a scene blaze with life', in all an
achievement infinitely more than mere 'craftsmanship'.[5] For
Perkins, Fitzgerald had drawn upon powers of imagination
deeper and simply more startling than ever previously. It is,
too, exactly those same powers of imagination, so lavishly
endowed yet about which Fitzgerald rarely felt other than
vulnerable, to which Morley Callaghan recurs some four distant
decades later in *That Summer in Paris*, his Canadian memoir of
Left Bank life and expatriation in the 1920s.

The rise of *Gatsby* from Perkins's first estimate to its present
'canonical' status has become the stuff of scholarly legend.
Especially so if one recalls the novel's sales during Fitzgerald's
own lifetime, obviously no disaster but nothing more than
modest as he himself pointed out frequently and with great
ruefulness. Scribner's in fact published it in an initial printing of
just over 20,000 in April 1925. A second printing of 3,000
followed in August of the same year. Chatto & Windus then did
an English edition in 1926, and the novel's last incarnation
while Fitzgerald was still alive was its reissue as a Modern
Library edition in 1934.[6] The real acclaim was to arrive posthumously, a dramatic, indeed stupendous, ascent in esteem
throughout the postwar years.

Maxwell Perkins, however, was not alone in foreshadowing

this eventual impact. He had company in an admiring inner circle of Fitzgerald's fellow writers. Much to present purposes, the shared grounds for their admiration can be seen to have centred upon the virtuosity of imagination in *Gatsby*, its persuasiveness of invention. This shows through in the early, supporting letters of recognition—from Gertrude Stein ('You are creating the contemporary world much as Thackeray did in *Pendennis* and *Vanity Fair* and this isn't a bad compliment'); from Edith Wharton ('let me say at once how much I liked Gatsby, or rather His Book, & how great a leap I think you have taken this time—an advance upon your previous work'); and most celebratedly of all, from T. S. Eliot ('it has interested and excited me more than any new novel I have seen, English or American, for a number of years. . . . In fact it seems to me the first step American fiction has taken since Henry James'). Nor can the letters from Fitzgerald's still more immediate mentors be overlooked, those of Edmund Wilson ('Your book came yesterday and I read it last night. It is undoubtedly in some ways the best thing you have done—the best planned, the best sustained, the best written') and of H. L. Mencken (' "The Great Gatsby" fills me with pleasant sentiments. Evidences of careful workmanship are on every page. The thing is well managed, and has a fine surface').[7] Neither Wilson nor Mencken held back on reservations they had about *Gatsby*; Wilson felt that the characters were 'mostly so unpleasant in themselves' and Mencken that 'the basic story is somewhat trivial'. But like Fitzgerald's other correspondents they spoke up unhesitatingly for the novel's strength of imagination, the qualities Wilson in a subsequent letter of May 1929 to Hamilton Basso would call its 'vividness and excitement'.[8]

Fitzgerald himself supplies a number of relevant other pointers. Following on his vital exchange of letters with Perkins during 1924–26 about each meticulous change and redrafting of *Gatsby*—long the object of investigation[9]—there stand out two crucially illuminating pieces of retrospect. First we have his Introduction to the Modern Library edition of 1934, easily and too often misunderstood as no more than a bad-tempered slap at reviewers who had not understood either his own work or that of his best contemporaries. But greatly of more importance, and again of immediate purpose, has to be the Introduction's expression of Fitzgerald's imaginative debt to the example of Conrad.

For in invoking Conrad's Preface to *The Nigger of the Narcissus* he clearly saw it as a credo, a set of necessary standards by which to measure his own performance in *Gatsby*. With an implicit reference back to Conrad's famous paragraphs on the need to achieve 'the perfect blending of form and substance' and on the writer's obligation 'to make you *see*', he moves on to the issue of fiction-writing (and writing in general) done in the imaginative all; or, as Conrad puts it, with a 'clear' conscience. His predecessor's words press tellingly from behind his own:

> Now that the book is being reissued, the author would like to say that never before did one try to keep his artistic conscience as pure as during the ten months put into doing it. Reading it over one can see how it could have been improved—yet without feeling guilty of any discrepancy from the truth, as far as I saw it; truth or rather the *equivalent* of truth, the attempt at honesty of imagination.[10]

Yet however conscious of Conrad, Fitzgerald speaks finally only for himself or at least for the regimen he recalls having followed in the writing of *Gatsby*. The '*equivalent* of truth' nicely underscores how distinctive Fitzgerald himself thought the imagining of *Gatsby*, its unusualness not only of vision but utterance. And as to 'honesty of imagination', a keynote Fitzgerald phrase for the considerations of this essay, which of his longer fiction can be said to have aspired more fiercely or dedicatedly to that end?

Gatsby as the upshot of an artistic conscience kept 'pure' he similarly recalls in a letter to his daughter, Scottie, written in June 1940, a scant six months before his death.[11] Thinking back on how as in none of his fiction either before or subsequently *Gatsby* had affirmed his literary calling, he again seems to have had Conrad somewhere in mind—especially Conrad's exacting desideratum that the true 'worker in prose' pursue his course 'undeterred by faltering, weariness, or reproach'.[12] But as exempt from reproach as Fitzgerald may have believed *The Great Gatsby* in particular, his words about himself generally in the aftermath of the novel read laden with reproach, and of that bitterest kind, self-reproach. For in his own mind's eye, as subsequently in the eyes of many others, he had too readily

41

gone on to do less than justice to his unique imagination, the promptings of his special gift of talent. The Jazz Age legend, the partying and 'restlessness', the psychic wars of love and attrition with Zelda, the recurrent descents into booze and Hollywood hack-work and the eventual 'crack-up': all of these, as he rightly came to see, amounted to steerings off-course. In consequence, despite the continuing if intermittent stories, despite *Tender is the Night* (1934) and *The Last Tycoon* (1941), his rare last novel still in process of being composed at the time of his letter to Scottie, he finds himself looking back on *The Great Gatsby* as a vital turning-point, evidence of imaginative 'duty' done in honest (and now accusatory) good conscience:

> What little I've accomplished has been by the most laborious and uphill work, and I wish now that I'd *never* relaxed or looked back—but said at the end of *The Great Gatsby*: 'I've found my line—and from now on this comes first. This is my duty—without this I am nothing.'[13]

The publication of *The Crack-Up* in 1945 did service on a number of fronts. It expressed Edmund Wilson's personal homage to his lifelong Princeton friend (*'that gleam of intellect/ That spilled into the spectrum of tune, taste,/ Scent, color, living speech, is gone, is lost . . .'*),[14] and it gave even greater impetus to the dizzying upward spiral of Fitzgerald's posthumous reputation. The assembled essays, letters, notebook entries and jottings underscored the writerly, serious Fitzgerald—which is anything but to say he lacked playfulness, a due antidote to the Fitzgerald all too easily celebrated as the stylish high priest of 1920s glamour. Not only did Wilson call upon Stein, Wharton and T. S. Eliot, but upon immediates like Thomas Wolfe, Glenway Wescott, John Dos Passos and John Peale Bishop. Each, assuredly, spoke from intimate friendship, but as much also from having been stirred, and often inspired, by the freshness of Fitzgerald's story-telling imagination. For all of them *Gatsby* recurs as a touchstone.

Once launched this augmentation of Fitzgerald's place in American literary ranks has known almost no check. Comparisons with stylists like Flaubert and Keats, Turgenev and James, have become almost commonplace. The editions, the criticism, the biographies, and the different film and T.V.

adaptations of his fiction have proliferated—the Mia Farrow/
Robert Redford 1974 version of *Gatsby* simply being among the
most recent. It makes for a considerable far cry from the
exploratory early essays of Malcolm Cowley (the first of which
appeared in 1926 no less), Lionel Trilling (1945) and Marius
Bewley (1954), from Arthur Mizener's ground-breaking critical
biography of 1951 and Alfred Kazin's essay-anthology of the same
year, from James E. Miller's first full-length critical study of 1957
(rev. 1964) and even from *The Letters* of 1963.[15] What persists is the
focal place given *Gatsby*, the one agreed peak in Fitzgerald's
fiction even acknowledging occasional expressions of dissent as in
Scrutiny and elsewhere.[16] Intimidatingly, *Gatsby* in its own right on
a recent count has been the occasion of nearly 200 articles and
several full-length books, a stimulus to interest which might have
amazed Max Perkins not to say Fitzgerald himself.[17]

By comparison, *This Side of Paradise* and *The Beautiful and
Damned* regularly come under fire for shallowness or their too
'literary' styling. *Tender is the Night*, too, though more encom-
passing in canvas and in exploring human behaviour under
stress has never wholly persuaded as to being the clear sum of
its parts. In turn, *The Last Tycoon*, for all that it joins with Orson
Welles's *Citizen Kane* as a landmark portrait of mogulship in the
media, can never step round the fact of its uncompletedness.
The Great Gatsby alone would seem to win through on all, or
nearly all, counts, tale and telling definitively merged into an
imaginative whole. Which is not to avoid taking into account
the fuss about Nick Carraway as 'reliable' narrator or otherwise
(in a special sense Nick's 'unreliability' needs to be seen as
utterly intrinsic to Fitzgerald's imagining of the story). In his
notable recent essay, and without doubt speaking as much from
the vantage-point of practising novelist as critic, George Garrett
offers the representative judgement when he calls Gatsby un-
ashamedly 'marvellous', a novel so strikingly well-imagined
that it 'shines with authentic inner light'.[18]

3

All of the foregoing speaks to the imagination which went
into the making of *Gatsby*, its confirmation for Fitzgerald as
much as for admirers of a creativity put under Conradian

discipline. But what of the imagining within the text itself, the brilliant, linked 'distortions' by which in the guise of Nick Carraway Fitzgerald weaves his fable of Gatsby's Great Expectations? For from start to close one cannot but recognize that 'Gatsby, His Book', in Edith Wharton's neat formulation, depends upon a peculiarly magnified form of telling, as if only a mode daring enough to meet the story's intrinsic extravagance yet itself kept just the right side of extravagance, would do. That is, a mode as colourful and even lavish as need be, but never given over to mere luxuriance or too intruding a display.

Involved here is something more than an attention to 'style' in any narrow or workaday sense, much as Fitzgerald has justly had his acclaim for his different turns of phrase and aphorism. It means, too, doing more with Nick Carraway merely than as a point of view, dutifully as he has been pursued in this respect and tracked back to figures in stories like 'Absolution' and 'Winter Dreams' and to Conrad's Marlow. It means attempting to elicit why—from Nick's opening declaration of not wanting 'more riotous excursions with privileged glimpses into the human heart' through to his final vision of a Lost America as the 'fresh green breast of the new world'—*Gatsby* so especially seems marked out by its imagining, Fitzgerald's almost page for page meticulousness or daring of invention. For as Nick affects at the story's outset to draw breath, to position himself as observer where once he was participant, so we find ourselves, too, called upon to enter the spirit of his telling, to show a willingness to 'imagine' the story in precisely the magnified terms that he does himself. Only that way, if Fitzgerald is to be understood aright, can Jay Gatsby, Jimmy Gatz as was, truly loom before us as 'The Great Gatsby'.

A number of other clues as to the kind of imagining at work in *Gatsby* suggest themselves. Did Fitzgerald vacillate as much as he did about a right title because he was looking for one which would carry to perfection his novel's overall mode? Those he considered include *Trimalchio, Trimalchio at West Egg, Gold-Hatted Gatsby, The High-Bouncing Lover, On the Road to West Egg* and *Under the Red, White, and Blue*, the latter which he urged upon Max Perkins even after *The Great Gatsby* had been printed up on the title-page. In each case, whether an allusion to Petronius's infamous party-giver in the *Satyricon*, or to some fantasy-style lover, or to the American flag as an emblem of the nation's moral and emotional health, Fitzgerald appears to have sought a title gesturally at one with the imaginative spirit of his novel.

A connecting note is struck in the quatrain he placed under the eventual title (*'Then wear the gold hat, if that will move her;/ If you can bounce high, bounce for her, too,/ Till she cry "Lover, gold-hatted, high-bouncing lover, I must have you!" '*). 'Gold-hatted' and 'high-bouncing' take up the discarded titles directly, but the lines point to a wider kind of reference in ballad or popular song or even nursery-rhyme. They have the sprightliness, the exaggeration, of some refrain grown familiar by repetition and engaging both to ear and eye. Even the supposed author, 'THOMAS PARKE D'INVILLIERS', looks suitably factitious, a well-born Keatsian or Hardyian balladeer perhaps. The fact that a writer of the same name appears in *This Side of Paradise*, based upon John Peale Bishop, merely adds point.

Then there is to hand F. Cugat's original dust-jacket for *Gatsby* (donated by Charles Scribner, Jnr. to the Princeton Club of New York and lately again pressed into service for Scribner's paperbacks), a painting which shows the fatal last car crash as a fireball, a vivid impressionistic blur of colour. Overhead hovers the line-drawing of a flapper's face, eyes bloodshot and lips puckered and rouged to required Clara Bow style. A speeding automobile, Daisy at the wheel if we have resort to the text, heads out of the conflagration—one final, murderous 'care-lessness' in the line of many. The dust-jacket, too, thereby, gives another kind of notice of the book's spirit, Gatsby's saga as plausibly actual or historic but better still comprehended as though magnified, fascinatingly distorted.

4

As he tries to get the experiences of his Summer 'down East' into some kind of imaginative order, Nick Carraway offers a backward glance as vivid as any in *The Great Gatsby*:

> Even when the East excited me most, even when I was most keenly aware of its superiority to the bored, sprawling towns beyond the Ohio, with their interminable inquisitions which spared only the children and the very old—even then it had for me a quality of distortion. West Egg, especially, still figures in

my more fantastic dreams. I see it as a night scene by El Greco: a hundred houses, at once conventional and grotesque, crouching under a sullen, overhanging sky and a lusterless moon. In the foreground four solemn men in dress suits are walking along the sidewalk with a stretcher on which lies a drunken woman in a white evening dress. Her hand, which dangles over the side, sparkles cold with jewels. Gravely the men turn in at the house—the wrong house. But no one knows the woman's name, and no one cares.

Nick's musings serve not only as his own call to memory but as a species of surreal checklist for all that has passed in the novel: 'the East' as a locus for what in connection with his part of Long Island he calls 'spectroscopic gaiety'; Gatsby's pursuit of Daisy as for all its mix of the demented and the ludicrous a truly 'magnificent obsession'; the drunken woman in her gown of white and her jewels and with her attendants to hand as a fallen Daisy Fay, a besotted Fairy Queen as somehow the Spirit of the Age; 'carelessness' as one of the great *mots clef* in the novel— from the 'riotous' partying at Gatsby's 'World's Fair' of a mansion to the brute insouciance of the Buchanans to Nick's affair with Jordan as a form of 'bad driving' to the literal bad driving in which Daisy runs down Myrtle Wilson and Tom encourages her husband to think Gatsby the killer; and the beguiling double-standard of dress-suit and evening-gown formality with an anything-goes licence. Under Nick's remembering, from 'beyond the Ohio', only an El Greco canvas or its like will serve to explain this dazzle of wealth, extravagance, corruption and exhaustion.

And how Nick remembers signifies equally with what he remembers. The Gatsby saga as indeed belonging to 'my more fantastic dreams', to 'a night scene by El Greco', directs us to the manner in which the novel at large is imagined. As, most of all, do the words 'a quality of distortion', the story so the speak unravelled from Nick's reeling senses. Writing from a year or so on and from the surer ground of his heartlands Middle West, Nick finds he can only look back with any degree of equanimity if indeed he pictures Gatsby and 'the East' as belonging to a dream, to some apparent dumbshow ritual etched upon a baroque Spanish canvas. Only 'distortion', careful, writerly 'distortion', will on Nick's envisioning do justice to the distortions of the story itself.

Fitzgerald understandably took pride in how he had surrogated out the telling of *Gatsby* to Nick. If this Yale-educated, gentrified son of small-town America can speak at the outset of the book as a giver or withholder of moral approval, he will also confess by the end to his 'provincial squeamishness' in the face of events which have entangled him for ever in the doings of Gatsby, Tom, Daisy and Jordan. Not unlike Hawthorne's Miles Coverdale in *The Blithedale Romance*, Nick frequently finds himself barely able to catch up with his own story, or to convey its intrinsic strangeness and magic.[19] He will, quite confessedly, edit scenes, imagine conversations he could not have witnessed, fill in background and biography, and above all seek a language to do full justice to his own wonderments and shock. A 'night scene' from El Greco offers but a single, yet utterly symptomatic, instance of all the 'distortion' which must enter his own telling if he is truly to play chronicler, an accurate custodian of the parade gone by. Rarely can anyone quite have sought out the consolations afforded by narrative, 'distortion' as a way of making order from disorder.

This same use of 'distortion', Nick's style of often fantastical and certainly amazed remembering, also links back to how Fitzgerald has him open his account. The coolness with which he speaks of the 'fundamental decencies' being 'parceled out unequally at birth' belongs less to the would-be moral soothsayer than to a man who has been violently knocked off his high moral perch. Is not his the voice of wryness, self-mockery, the witness to things which have obliged him to flee in disarray back to his once-scorned origins (a Middle West of the Carraway 'wholesale hardware business' whose provincialism is typified in the family boast of a connection to the Dukes of Buccleuth)? Hardly now the student 'politician', the figure famed for his reserve and for being the beneficiary of unsought 'confidences' and 'the secret griefs of wild, unknown men', he has come to require of the world only that it 'be in uniform and at a sort of moral attention for ever'. '*My* Middle West' so serves as a restorative to 'the East', a refuge after so many 'riotous excursions with privileged glimpses into the human heart'. Like a witness pressed to get his competing energies of memory into sequence, Nick reaches for a whole imagery and language of displacement as if the survivor of precisely a night-time dream.

47

Another major clue to Nick as story-teller lies in his opening observation on the novel's title figure: 'Only Gatsby, the man who gave his name to this book, was exempt from my reaction.' Would-be moral arbiter or not, in making this observation Nick also sets out his own stall as author, his literary self-in-waiting as it were. Having guyed his one-time sureness of moral judgement (not out of keeping in someone who has failed to report a murder), he also mocks his own earlier attempts to play the author. 'I was rather literary in college', he confides self-deprecatingly, the begetter of 'a series of very solemn and obvious editorials for the *Yale News*'. But this time he takes to the pen as no brash editorialist, rather as a man compelled to utterance. He even throws in a bit of hard-won wisdom which has keen literary implications. 'Life', he avers, 'is much more successfully looked at from a single window after all', a nice if veiled contribution to the whole 'point of view' debate, especially coming from the aphorist who refers back to his hopes of combining the bondsman with 'that most limited of specialists, the "well-rounded man"'.

The rest of the chapter acts on these cues and stylings to perfection. Nick teasingly connects the West Egg/East Egg promontories which jut out into 'the great wet barnyard of Long Island Sound' with the Columbus story, the deftest of inlaid historical references. He sets himself up, too, as a latter-day Leatherstocking, bivouaced in his 'weather-beaten cardboard bungalow', the self-named 'guide', 'pathfinder' and 'original settler' on the strength of being able to direct a stranger to West Egg village, the neophyte money-maker drawn to 'the shining secrets' of the dollar who seeks entry into the fantastical realms of 'Midas and Morgan and Maecenas'. Nick personifies a figure in pursuit of the 'story' of his life, the returnee who still earlier has come back 'restless' from the Great War. Everything about him points to the incipient story-teller.

Turning to the immediate landscape of 'the East', he delineates Gatsby's house in all its gorgeous fake antiquity, not perhaps Hearst's San Simeon but the 'factual imitation of some *hôtel de ville* in Normandy', an edifice 'spanking new under a thin beard of ivy'. Like one of the baronial confections in Raymond Chandler's Los Angeles, Gatsby's house belongs to a near historical fantasy-world, a 'present' as Nick sees it fashioned—

distorted—from a European past. The Buchanan home, equally, one of 'the white palaces of fashionable East Egg', looms for Nick like further historical pastiche. Bought at unconscionable price from 'Demaine, the oil man', with its hint of Texas wild-catting and liquid gold, it gives itself forth as a 'cheerful red-and-white Georgian Colonial Mansion'. If Gatsby's house represents new money, Tom's means old money, parvenu wealth as against socially laundered wealth. These two 'houses', each styled to be what it is not and with Gatsby and Tom as cus-todians and Daisy caught like jewelled royalty in between, take us far beyond scene-setting. The 'landscape' of *The Great Gatsby*, not only West and East Egg but the Valley of Ashes, Wilson's garage, Wall Street, Myrtle's apartment and even the road where she will be run down by Daisy—in all 'the East' as Nick teases it out from his memory—amounts indeed to a 'distortion', places of re-imagined feeling as much as any actual geography.

Similarly our first view of the Buchanans: Tom, 'enormously wealthy', a Yale football legend, Nick depicts with a Hogarthian instinct for the placing detail. His body of 'enormous power', his arrogance of eye and gesture, his 'cruel', 'restless' temperament give the outward show of the man within, a man believably contemptible. Once he gets launched on 'this man Godard's' *The Rise of the Colored Empires*, preposterous, comic, crypto-fascism, he assumes a larger-than-life status but in no sense one imaginatively out of control. Nick gets him just right, each detail a part of the whole, the 'enormous leverage' of the body matched to 'something pathetic in his concentration'.

All Nick's 'authorial' resources are brought to bear, too, with Daisy and Jordan. He conjures them into being like fantasy creatures, buoyed up on a balloon-like couch, clad in 'rippling and fluttering white', Daisy for her part 'p-paralyzed with happiness' and Jordan 'slender' and 'erect' like a sculpture in metal. Both these icons of wealth talk with 'bantering incon-sequence', a 'tense gaiety'. Nick even 'invents' himself for Daisy, the courtier reporting Chicago's 'desolation' at her absence and through the tribute of each car's 'left wheel painted black as a mourning wreath'. He casts the overall scene as a remembered but fractured present: Tom's bluster, Myrtle's 'phone call, the notion of the impending 'longest night of the year', the room's 'groan of a picture', Daisy's insistence on the candles, the recollections of Daisy's Louisville 'white girlhood' and his own slight disgust at this brittle ostentation. He alludes, too, to the evening as 'broken fragments', 'a trick of some sort', as if to acknowledge that he is seeking to re-imagine this particular occasion as refracted through time and an eventual larger sense of the whole. He acknowledges, so to speak, that his is a 'distorted' account.

The transition to Gatsby follows in kind. 'The silhouette of a moving cat' presages his appearance, a figure who emerges from 'shadow' and looks in isolation out and upward to 'the silver pepper of the stars'. He appears 'content to be alone', his arms 'stretched towards the dark water in a curious way'. Nick speculates as to whether Gatsby trembles as he gazes towards the 'single green light' which means Daisy. He 'vanishes' as promptly as he has appeared, self into shadow as he has transformed shadow into self. Nick re-imagines him to perfection, the Gatsby who lives inside and shapes whatever Gatsby the world deceives itself it has so far known, a man who has willed his own distortion re-imagined 'distortedly'.

5

This same 'distortion' plays across the entire span of the novel, a story which in Nick's telling amounts to a consummate parody of 'authoritative' first-person narration. As the ensuing chapters fill out the drama for which Gatsby acts as the human centre, they do so through an idiom which subtly shows itself to have absorbed Nick's every past shock of feeling, his every tilt and bias of memory ('Memory, of course, is never true' Hemingway would write in *Death in the Afternoon*). Nick's account might indeed best be thought 'distortion', the plausible but dramatic lie of autobiography. He can tell his story only as he feels and remembers it, or even recovers from it, in this sense paradoxically a 'truer' account than a supposed objective re-telling of the facts in the case.

A number of selective highlightings will give this emphasis still further weight. In Chapter 2, Nick invokes for the first time the Valley of Ashes, the 'fantastic farm' which again suggests painterly impressionism, a parodic, hellish image of America as an inverted 'wheatfield' peopled by 'ash-grey men' about their 'obscure operations'. Presided over by the 'blue and gigantic' retinas of Dr. T. J. Eckleburg, 'eternal blindness' rather than images of sight, this Wasteland makes for a species of phantasma, Nick's perfect correlative metaphor for all the 'bleak dust' which will hover ruinously over Gatsby and his dream of possessing Daisy. Nick so blends the distortion of fact into his own story-telling 'distortion'.

The rest of the chapter, too, follows in kind. Wilson's garage, indeed Wilson himself ('a blond, spiritless man, anemic, and faintly handsome'), Nick invokes as though belonging to an American Gothic or Edward Hopper painting. The move to Myrtle's apartment and the 'artificial laughter' of her im-promptu party could not more be like a transition in dream or excited, vexed memory. Myrtle herself, fleshly, stimulated by Tom and her own play-acting, looms up in Nick's memory as precisely one of the mongrel 'bitches' Tom so sullenly buys for her outside the station. The party, a prelude of sorts to one of Gatsby's, becomes a carefully composed blur of place, time and people ('People disappeared, re-appeared, made plans to go somewhere, and then lost each other, searched for each other, found each other a few feet away').

The very décor of the room takes on the properties of a memory-chamber, a place as much imagined as actual. Nick recalls a picture comically akin to 'a hen sitting on a blurred rock' which resolves itself into 'the countenance of an old lady' (Melville's Spouter Inn 'Cape-Horner' in *Moby-Dick* makes for an instructive parallel). A surreal, or at least half-displaced, run of other 'distortions' build up. He reads, fitfully, a chapter from a volume entitled *Simon Called Peter*. He admits to his own spiralling drunkenness. The 'white spot of lather' on McKee's cheekbone agitates him immeasurably. He hears passing men-tion of Gatsby as 'a nephew or a cousin of Kaiser Wilhelm's'; endures the shock of Tom's breaking Myrtle's nose and the sight of her blood; and serves as the barely sober but captive audience for McKee's photographic 'studies' as the latter shows them clad only in his underwear and in bed (a scene which hints, too, of Nick's sexual 'distortion'—is he, for instance, attracted to Jordan because both have something of the andro-gyne about them?). Nick's final memory is of being 'half-asleep in the cold lower level of Pennsylvania Station' waiting for the 'four o'clock train'. These truly do make for pictures of a broken world, fragments from past time and place. Each, too, is imagining as much as fact, one 'distortion' linked to another more by the intensity of feeling aroused in Nick than by any simple narrative logic.

So, in like manner, Nick discloses what follows of Gatsby's story. The first of the great parties (Chapter 3), he invokes through a concourse of lights and colours: the 'blue gardens'; the welcoming station-wagon which resembles 'a brisk yellow bug'; the chauffeur in his 'uniform of robin's-egg blue', and more. The music, too, together with the banter, the myths which circulate about Gatsby—each a 'distortion' in itself faithfully recorded by Nick, the bar-flies and partygoers who 'dissolve and form in the same breath', the crashed cars and Nick's celebrated conversation with Jordan about 'bad driving' . . . . all weave into yet more 'distortion', a sustained cycle of remembrance which blends light with colour, sound with sensation. Fitzgerald even adds a nice touch of self-reflexivity in the startlement of the owl-eyed man that Gatsby's books are real, a well-inserted reminder that despite everything this is also actuality and not a page from a formula romance or love-story.

In Chapter 4, the blend of pastiche into fact takes the form of the listing of the guests who descend on Gatsby's parties throughout the summer. Like all well-turned lampoon, P. G. Wodehouse's from an earlier age or more consequentially that of Nabokov or Borges in our own, this tour-de-force veers brilliantly close to any actual social register but offers at the same time yet another of Nick's 'distortions', one both funny and deflationary. The list also makes an apt prologue for Gatsby's July morning appearance in his hydroplane, the would-be society figure replete with his 'Old Sport' upper-class lingo and the like. His car, too, 'monstrous in length', loaded down with its 'triumphant hatboxes and supper boxes and toolboxes' and its 'labyrinth of windshields', might well suggest some ultimate fantasy car, a baroquely comic modern stagecoach. Yet just as Nick begins to assign Gatsby to a world elsewhere, he finds himself obliged to recognize a stratum of fact beneath all the hoopla and ostentation.

For despite Gatsby's talk of living 'like a young rajah' and, oddly, of originating in San Francisco as 'the Middle West', there will in truth be grounds for his reference to 'something sad that . . . . happened to me long ago'. His war experiences, too, where he alleges he lived 'an enchanted life', yield the unexpected evidence of his Montenegro medal, 'For Valour Extraordinary'. Equally his 'Oxford days' are attested to in the form of the photograph of Trinity Quad, Gatsby with of all things 'a cricket bat in his hand'. As Gatsby builds towards asking Nick's help in bringing Daisy to within his reach, Nick senses the imminence of yet more from the conjuror's hat. 'I was sure the request would be something utterly fantastic', he recalls. Again, when Gatsby takes him to meet Meyer Wolfsheim and they cross the Queensboro Bridge, Nick's thoughts—the thoughts he remembers himself having—give off a swirl of excitement (' "Anything can happen now that we've slid over this bridge" '). 'Even Gatsby', he thinks, 'could happen', as if to underscore that in all his self-invention, Gatsby, still, is real, a fantasy self-actualized into reality.

The meeting at 'roaring noon' with Wolfsheim, legendary fixer of the World Series, relies in its every aspect upon a similar 'distortion'. The three meet in a Wall Street cellar under a ceiling of 'Presbyterian nymphs', a locale close to 'The Old Metropole' with its Capone-style criminal glamour in the death of 'Rosy Rosenthal'. Wolfsheim's offer of 'a business gonnegtion', like his certification of Gatsby as 'an Oggsford man', suggests a Dickensian command of pastiche, an infinitely interesting modern Fagin. Even the tracking-back to Gatsby's Louisville courtship of Daisy and the account Jordan gives of her despairing resort to the bottle on her wedding-day mixes truth with embellishment, events remembered and editorialized over first by Jordan and then by Nick. 'Fact' in Gatsby's story exists only at the behest of memory, and that memory as the words finally go on to the page is Nick's. His 'distortions' cannot be other than both inevitable and necessary if he is to meet in story-telling kind that which in 'life' has set itself before him. They are also, one wants to add, exhilarating.

If Chapter 5 has a single point of gravity it has to be Gatsby's show of his shirts to Daisy, the strange, ritualized first reunion for which all his parties and extravagance have been conceived. At a 'pitch of intensity' he puts them before her like fetishized commodities, a scene remembered by Nick as a blaze of colour, eroticism, movement and Daisy's wonderfully apt descent into the seeming commonplace (' "It makes me sad because I've never seen such—such beautiful shirts before" '). The 'soft rich heap' and the different shades and styles of monogram serve as the very metaphors of wealth which Gatsby has everywhere brought to bear. Nick even distortedly has Gatsby think of his possessions 'in a dazed way, as though in [Daisy's] actual and astounding presence none of it was any longer real'. Which, exactly, is also how he seeks to recreate the scene.

His recall, too, of Gatsby's allusion to Dan Cody, the mentor preserved in a photograph and later to be described as the 'pioneer debauchee', adds just the right touch of further mystery—one eventually unravelled as Nick recreates the onward march of Jimmy Gatz into Jay Gatsby, the farmboy from South Dakota who wills himself into a Playboy of the Western World. In Cody lies the fantastical patriarch, the human model in whose image Gatsby starts to amass the loot with which to ensnare Daisy. Nick's recall also goes back to the tune played by the 'boarder', Ewing Klipspringer, as Gatsby seeks to give a Jazz Age musical setting for himself and Daisy as they dance themselves back into the past. Klipspringer takes to the piano with 'The Love Nest', a choice of song whose zany appropriateness Nick underlines by quoting three of its best-known lines (' "In the morning,/ In the evening,/ Aint we got fun—" '). He leaves the pair caught up in their own stage-set, would-be young lovers again 'repeating the past' if only for a moment and as though figures in a dream sequence or ghost sonata. Nick might well describe them as looking at him 'remotely', as having 'forgotten' him; they offer yet another 'distortion' which in his telling becomes also ours.

6

The following three chapters (6, 7 and 8) take us through to Gatsby's death and Nick's retreat to 'my Middle West'. The lens of 'distortion' persists and deepens the pattern so far established. Nick conjures up Jimmy Gatz's initial self-transformation into Jay Gatsby, the 'heart' which once met up with Dan Cody, his *Tuolumee*, Ella Kaye and the prospects of unthought-of wealth, gives way to 'grotesque and fantastic conceits', 'ineffable gaudiness', the 'unreality of reality'. Nick almost defies himself to imagine the course of Gatsby's 'Platonic conception', the identity 'spun' into being and 'educated' by the 'savage violence of the frontier brothel and saloon' whose harbinger is Cody. 'All the beauty and glamour in the world' takes form for Gatsby in Cody's yacht, at once a literal and a dream boat, a craft which might ferry him into his own projected destiny. The same energies, too, which feed his invention of himself, he will redirect to Daisy, his Grail, his Green Light, his Jazz Age geisha made over into a Fairy Queen. In bidding to 'repeat the past', to stop time (at Nick's house in the first meeting with Daisy he just about prevents 'a defunct mantelpiece clock' from falling), he distorts Daisy Fay into 'flower' and 'incarnation', truly his Day's Eye. Hardly to his own surprise, Nick can barely keep pace.

He recognizes that as Daisy has progressed for Gatsby from pampered Southern belle to Dream, this all most likely amounts to 'appalling sentimentality', sheer preposterousness. Yet he is reminded, too, of 'an elusive rhythm, a fragment of lost words', as if Gatsby's compulsion, his vow indeed to re-enact the past, carries in it an indispensable human hope. Even when (in Chapter 7) Gatsby acknowledges that Daisy's voice is 'full of money' or (in Chapter 8) that her undoubted early married passion for Tom was 'just personal', his dream whether distorted or not persists. Little wonder that when Tom reveals that he has discovered Gatsby's bootlegging, Nick finds himself looking upon Gatsby's face as that of a man who might in all truth have 'killed', a face which 'could be described in just that fantastic way'.

Nick looks back also to the time when, Daisy regained, Gatsby lets go of 'his career as Trimalchio', his 'whole caravansary'. The hotel scene in New York which follows, another episode subject to Nick's 'distortion', sets up an afternoon which points on to 'death' and 'the cooling twilight'. The music on this occasion as Tom and Gatsby compete for who most has Daisy's love is grotesquely 'the portentous chords of Mendelssohn's Wedding March from the ballroom below'. The dénouement, similarly, offers a run of high-speed distortions: the running down of Myrtle on the journey home ('her left breast ... swinging loose like a flap'); Wilson's pursuit at Tom's instigation of Gatsby (his voice distorted into a near animal moan—

' "Oh, my Ga-od! Oh, my Ga-od! . . ." '); and the closing pistol shots and double-killing which leave Gatsby dead on his dream-like mattress. In the uneasy calm after all this trauma, Nick feels a mixture of disgust, guilt and above all fatigue ('I'd had enough of them all for one day'). Yet the revelation that Gatsby, cavalier to the end, has pretended to be at the wheel of the 'yellow car' which ran down Myrtle arouses what reserves of surprise he still has left.

The world of Gatsby, nonetheless, has become for him a 'twilight universe', marked out by 'dark spots', 'dust' and seemingly as of always headed for 'holocaust'. These are his own terms, of a kind with the 'frightening dreams' (Chapter 8) he endures the night following Myrtle's death. It is a night he spends 'half sick', pulled between 'grotesque reality' and 'dream' and unsure which is which. Gatsby's life appears to him as at once substance and shadow, a hybrid of the real and unreal. In this mood of troubled contemplation, he thinks back, too, to how Daisy ditched the penniless Gatsby in Louisville and 'vanished into her rich house, into her rich, full life'. He thinks, too, of Gatsby and the power of his desire, Daisy as everything for him despite her 'careless', 'artificial' world with its rhythms set by 'snobbery' and 'orchestras'. In so overwhelming a dream, Nick realizes, Gatsby has set in train the disasters to follow, Myrtle's death, his own, and finally Wilson's. In having seen, also, that the Buchanans will escape blame and certainly persecution, one more triumph of established wealth over morality, Nick is left only with his riot of impressions and his 'provincial squeamishness'. Almost the only resort he has is to the written word. Having presided over the funeral arrangements for Gatsby's death, so he finds himself compelled to become the literary memorialist of all the 'distortions' which have made up Gatsby's life.

For a man so largely unsure of his own identity, sexually as much as in terms of a career or purpose, Nick in fact has managed to come most into his own in the face of Gatsby's 'colossal vitality'. He finds his authenticity in the contemplation of Gatsby's masquerade or self-impersonation. Thus in giving Gatsby a last plaudit ('You're worth the whole damn bunch put together'), he arrogates to himself a right of judgement, his own self-confirming arbitration of things (as he will again, if weakly, on meeting Tom on Fifth Avenue, where he judges things 'all very careless and confused'). Is not the real truth that only in making a formal narrative of all his 'confusions', all the 'distortions' in play throughout Gatsby's story, can he regain his *own* possession, a way through to his own identity?

7

In rounding out his account to its close (Chapter 9) Nick begins by contracting time, the 'past' of Gatsby's death as irresistibly and hauntingly a time present. 'After two years', he confesses, 'I remember the rest of that day and that night and the next day. . . .' Meyer Wolfsheim's letter seizes him as from another world. As do, in turn, the 'phone calls from Chicago about 'Young Parke' and the under-the-counter bonds and from Klipspringer about his pair of shoes and inability to be present at the funeral. 'Fantastic dreams' and 'nightmare', as Nick terms the events which have led to Gatsby's death, they take on even greater magnification when set against the arrival and pride in his son of Mr. Gatz. His homely, threadbare presence and affecting comparison of Gatsby with a robber-baron ('If he'd of lived, he'd of been a great man. A man like James J. Hill') offer a keen ironic counterpoint to the 'gaudiness' of Gatsby's eventual life. His presentation to Nick of the 'old copy' of *Hopalong Cassidy*, equally, with its Franklinesque 'SCHEDULE' on the back page indicates where Gatsby's dreams began, the self-distortion into Jay Gatsby whose ambiguous Boswell it is Nick's fate to become. Just as Gatsby has, however, gone well beyond anything Benjamin Franklin might have postulated as the self-made man, so in moving 'down East', as Mr. Gatz refers to it, he has moved into a realm well beyond mere place. Fact has yielded also to fantasy, his mansion the site of his 'web' to catch Daisy as much as any simple place of residence.

This same 'down East'—Gatsby's, but also that of the 'vast carelessness' of the Buchanans, Jordan's in the form of her bad driving, Nick's own—becomes on his own admission 'haunted'. Or, in a striking repetition of the expression he has used in likening West Egg to the El Greco painting, 'distorted beyond my eyes' power of correction'. And it is with two different but connecting last 'distortions' that the novel comes to rest. The first is personal, Nick's sense of Gatsby's parties and world as exactly a haunting, an inner memory, a set of happenings from beyond any actual history. He thinks back as follows:

> I spent my Saturday nights in New York, because those gleaming, dazzling parties of his were with me so vividly that I could still hear the music and the laughter, faint and incessant, from his garden, and the cars going up and down his drive. One night I did hear a material car there, and saw its lights stop at his front steps. But I didn't investigate. Probably it was some final guest who had been away at the ends of the earth and didn't know the party was over.

This belongs very much on a par with the El Greco painting. A 'material car' there may be, but it belongs with 'the music and laughter' of Gatsby's parties—things and events transformed by imagination, reshaped into the components of a quite fantastical past. Each and all, like Gatsby himself, they have come to exist most for him in the realms of his imagining, part fact, part memory, part invention.

Nick's other distortion carries more general implications, and points less to the surreal or grotesque than to the sublime. It refers us to the larger mythic frame of the story, Gatsby's rise and fall as emblematic drama. With the 'dust' of the obscene word erased from the 'white steps' of Gatsby's mansion, Nick allows his imagination explicitly again to take hold. Long Island dissolves before him from its present befouled condition into the 'fresh green breast of the new world', that which 'flowered once for Dutch sailors' eyes'. He so offers a final and more embracing act of remembrance, that of a pristine, 'dream' America, a new found land as yet still clear of carelessness and money and even glamour. This vision, out of fable as much as fact, belongs in kind with all that has gone before in Nick's account of Gatsby, one last imagining to give the story its overall context, one last supreme and lyric 'distortion'.

'A quality of distortion'

NOTES

1. Morley Callaghan, *That Summer in Paris: Memories of Tangled Friendships with Hemingway, Fitzgerald and Some Others* (New York: Coward-McCann, 1983), pp. 206–7. I would like to acknowledge the encouragement and suggestions of Professors Rex Burns and Joel Salzberg of the University of Colorado in the writing of this essay.
2. *The Great Gatsby* (New York: Charles Scribner's Sons, 1925), Ch. 1. The full quotation reads: 'No—Gatsby turned out all right in the end; it is what preyed on Gatsby, what foul dust floated in the wake of his dreams that temporarily closed out my interest in the abortive sorrows and short-winded elations of men.'
3. F. Scott Fitzgerald to Maxwell Perkins, July 1922, in Andrew Turnbull (ed.), *The Letters of F. Scott Fitzgerald* (New York: Charles Scribner's Sons, 1962). Also John Kuehl and Jackson Bryer (eds.), *Dear Scott/Dear Max: The Fitzgerald-Perkins Correspondence* (New York: Charles Scribner's Sons, 1971).
4. Max Perkins to F. Scott Fitzgerald, 20 November 1924 (*Letters*, op. cit.).
5. Ibid.
6. These publication figures are taken from Matthew J. Bruccoli, *Apparatus for F. Scott Fitzgerald's 'The Great Gatsby' (Under the Red, White, and Blue)* (Columbia, South Carolina: University of South Carolina Press, 1974), p. 6. The full reference to the 1934 reissue is: F. Scott Fitzgerald, *The Great Gatsby*, Modern Library Edition (New York: Random House, Inc., 1934).
7. All of this correspondence is to be found in Edmund Wilson (ed.), *The Crack-Up* (New York: New Directions, 1945).
8. Edmund Wilson to Hamilton Basso, 9 May 1925. Reprinted in Scott Donaldson (ed.), *Critical Essays on F. Scott Fitzgerald's 'The Great Gatsby'* (Boston, Massachusetts: G. K. Hall & Co., 1984), p. 268.
9. See, for instance, Kenneth E. Eble, 'The Craft of Revision: *The Great Gatsby*', *American Literature*, Vol. 36, November 1964, 315–26.
10. Introduction to *The Great Gatsby*, Modern Library Edition (op. cit.).
11. F. Scott Fitzgerald to Frances Scott Fitzgerald, 12 June 1940 (*Letters*, op. cit.).
12. The appropriate passage in Conrad's Preface to *The Nigger of the Narcissus* reads: 'The sincere endeavour to accomplish that creative task, to go as far on that road as his strength will carry him, to go undeterred by faltering, weariness, or reproach, is the only valid justification for the worker in prose. And if his conscience is clear, his answer to those who, in the fullness of a wisdom which looks for immediate profit, demand specifically to be edified, consoled, amused; who demand to be promptly improved, or encouraged, or frightened, or shocked, or charmed, must run thus: My task which I am trying to achieve is, by the power of the written word to make you hear, to make you feel—it is, above all, to make you *see*. That—and no more, and it is everything.'
13. F. Scott Fitzgerald to Frances Scott Fitzgerald, 12 June 1940 (*Letters*, op. cit.).

14. Edmund Wilson (ed.), 'Dedication', *The Crack-Up*, op. cit.

15. The Cowley, Trilling and Bewley essays have been frequently reprinted and appear in most collections of materials on *The Great Gatsby*. For a complete bibliographical reference, however, see: Jackson R. Bryer, *The Critical Reputation of F. Scott Fitzgerald* (New Haven, Connecticut: Archon, 1967) and *The Critical Reputation of F. Scott Fitzgerald, Supplement One through 1981* (New Haven, Connecticut: Archon, 1984); Jackson R. Bryer, 'F. Scott Fitzgerald', in *Fifteen Modern American Authors: A Survey of Research and Criticism* (Durham, North Carolina: Duke University Press, 1969); Matthew J. Bruccoli, *Checklist of F. Scott Fitzgerald* (Columbus, Ohio: Charles E. Merrill, 1970); Matthew J. Bruccoli, *F. Scott Fitzgerald: A Descriptive Bibliography* (Pittsburgh: University of Pittsburgh Press, 1972); and Linda C. Stanley, *The Foreign Reputation of F. Scott Fitzgerald: An Analysis and Annotated Bibliography* (Westport, Connecticut, 1980). The other references are as follows: Arthur Mizener, *The Far Side of Paradise* (Boston: Houghton Mifflin Co., 1951); Alfred Kazin (ed.), *F. Scott Fitzgerald: The Man and his Work* (New York: World, 1951); James E. Miller, *The Fictional Technique of Scott Fitzgerald* (The Hague: Martinus Nijhoff, 1957), rev. edn., *F. Scott Fitzgerald: His Art and his Technique* (New York: New York University Press, 1964); and Andrew Turnbull (ed.), *Letters*, op. cit.

16. See, for instance, D. W. Harding, 'Scott Fitzgerald', *Scrutiny*, Winter 1951–52, and John Farrelly: 'Fitzgerald: Another View', *Scrutiny*, June 1952. For a still later dissent, see Ron Neuhaus, 'Gatsby and the Failure of the Omniscient "I" ', *Denver Quarterly*, 12, No. 1, Spring 1977.

17. Among the available essay collections are: Frederick J. Hoffman (ed.), *'The Great Gatsby': A Study* (New York: Charles Scribner's Sons, 1962); Ernest Lockbridge (ed.), *Twentieth-century Interpretations of 'The Great Gatsby'* (Englewood Cliffs, New Jersey: Prentice-Hall, 1968); Scott Donaldson, *Critical Essays on F. Scott Fitzgerald's 'The Great Gatsby'* (Boston, Massachusetts: G. K. Hall & Co., 1984); Matthew J. Bruccoli (ed.), *New Essays on 'The Great Gatsby'* (Cambridge University Press, 1985); and Harold Bloom (ed.), *F. Scott Fitzgerald's 'The Great Gatsby'* (New York, Philadelphia, New Haven: Chelsea House publishers, 1986). I particularly want to acknowledge the full-length studies: John S. Whitley, *F. Scott Fitzgerald: 'The Great Gatsby'* (London: Arnold, 1976); and Robert Emmet Long, *The Achieving of 'The Great Gatsby': F. Scott Fitzgerald, 1920–1925* (Lewisburg: Bucknell University Press, 1979); also, for their particular relevance to the present essay, Chapters 10–12 in André LeVot, *F. Scott Fitzgerald: A Biography* (New York: Doubleday & Company, 1983).

18. George Garrett, 'Fire and Freshness: A Matter of Style in *The Great Gatsby*', in Matthew Bruccoli (ed.), *New Essays on 'The Great Gatsby'* op. cit.

19. Another comparable narrator would be Emily Bronte's Lockwood in *Wuthering Heights*.

3

Tender is the Night: Fitzgerald's Portrait of a Gentleman

by HAROLD BEAVER

> I wonder what the hell the first actor who played Hamlet thought of the part? I can hear him say, 'The guy's a nut, isn't he?'
> —Fitzgerald to Mrs. Edwin Jarrett, 7 February 1938

Tender is the Night is F. Scott Fitzgerald's most thoroughly Jamesian fiction. All its settings (bar glimpses of Virginia and New York State) are European. All its characters are 'overwhelmingly American and sometimes scarcely American at all', as they flit unceremoniously from Cannes to Paris, to Zurich, Munich, Innsbruck, Monte Carlo, Rome. Its very theme seems a cross between *The Sacred Fount* and *The Wings of the Dove*: with Nicole Warren as another 'angel with a thumping bank account', mortally ill when she comes to Europe, though desperate to live; another vampire battening on to and draining the energy out of her husband. Even the initial point of view is Jamesian. For it is through the eyes of a 17-year-old voyeur that we gaze at the Divers's beach, sensing the discrepancy between their social charade and the 'things unspoken and untouched, unspeakable and untouchable' (in James's phrase) that lie behind it. The whole aim of that chronologically displaced opening (of which Fitzgerald later despaired) had been to signal

61

those semantic games, those silent signs, to which only the flashback of Book II would supply the clue.[1]

The intricate organization, then, in its vast unfolding, is Jamesian. Those sixty-one chapters, divided into three books, were arranged as dramatic moments whose scenic design was to suggest a philosophy of history, 'a cultural clue to the meaning, the moral development, of an era'.[2] That is what Fitzgerald meant by a 'philosophical novel' as opposed to a 'dramatic novel' (like *The Great Gatsby*). The two books had nothing in common, he was at pains to explain:

> The dramatic novel has canons quite different from the philo-sophical, now called psychological, novel. One is a kind of *tour de force* and the other a confession of faith. It would be like comparing a sonnet sequence with an epic.
>
> The point . . . is that there were moments all through the book where I could have pointed up dramatic scenes, and I *deliberately* refrained from doing so because the material itself was so harrowing and highly charged that I did not want to subject the reader to a series of nervous shocks in a novel that was inevitably close to whoever read it in my generation.[3]

This may seem excessive pleading for a book that figures a punch-up, an assassination and a corpse planted on a hotel bed. Yet such scenes are all tangential to the main action. Harrowing accounts of schizophrenic breakdown are reduced to two: Nicole's hysteria in the bathroom, that concludes Book I, and her riot at the fair (Bk II, Ch. 15). Fitzgerald's aim was clearly not to write a 'psychological' novel in any clinical or Freudian sense. His model, rather, was *Vanity Fair*, with a narrator constantly obtruding his own epigrammatic commentary.[4]

The composite effect, then, was hardly Jamesian at all. It was more like one of those loose, baggy monsters that James ritually deplored. At least the first reviewers thought so. Most con-temporary readers thought so. Fitzgerald himself must have thought so while fiddling with yet another chronological draft in his notebook (still uncompleted at the time of his death). To no avail! His 'romance', naturally enough, was altogether post-Jamesian, post-Victorian, post-World War. It was nothing if not up-to-date with its salute to 'Miss Television', its casual mention of 'Sturmtruppen' and 'aeroplane bombs'.[5] Its restless, jumpy movement, cutting from 'take' to 'take', obviously owed a good deal to the new techniques of Hollywood (where Fitzgerald had worked on film scripts in 1927). What was news was no longer the rapacity of the rich, but its accompaniment to the pop banality of ragtime and the movies. *Tender is the Night* is syncopated throughout by the lyrics of popular songs and the meretricious glamour, the 'fun', the 'high excitement' of the movies.

That was Rosemary Hoyt's rôle, which even Fitzgerald seems to have forgotten, in introducing the Divers to us on their beach. They constitute, so we are to believe, the first (and last) calm and voluptuous oasis on the Riviera soon to be deluged by a restless horde of celebrities, starlets, Associated Press photographers and 200,000 annual American tourists 'spending ten million a summer'.[6] The Russian princes had long departed. A few British nannies remained 'knitting the slow pattern of Victorian England'. But a Gaumont film lot was already up at Monte Carlo; 'Franco-American Films' were already operating projection rooms and screen tests in Paris.

The Divers, too, had long ago been corrupted. Nicole wooed her handsome doctor to the sound of phonograph records, singing:

> Lay a silver dollar
>   On the ground
> And watch it roll
>   Because it's round—

Jazz constituted the universal code and semiotics of their love. Nor can Dick disentangle 'Tea for Two' from his obsession with Rosemary. But by the end of the 'romance' it is movies that are triumphant. When Nicole woos Tommy Barban aboard the *Margin*, she begins: 'You look just like all the adventurers in the movies. . . .' To which, after a brief exchange:

> 'I only know what I see in the cinema,' he said.
> 'Is it all like the movies?'
> 'The movies aren't so bad—now this Ronald Colman—have you seen his pictures about the Corps d'Afrique du Nord? They're not bad at all.'
> 'Very well, whenever I go to the movies I'll know you're going through just that sort of thing at that moment.'
>
> (Bk III, Ch. 5)

Between 1919 and 1929 Nicole Diver (née Warren) shifts her allegiance from man to man to the lyrics of dance music and the images of Hollywood.

This take-over by pop culture is one major break with the age of Edith Wharton and Henry James. Another, of course, is the Great War. The millions dead haunt this book. Everyone— combatant and non-combatant alike—is a casualty; especially Dick Diver who, like Fitzgerald himself, was notably a non-combatant. 'All my beautiful lovely safe world blew itself up here . . .', he sighs. All the duels and fist fights and drunken brawls are seen as aspects of the shell-shocked trauma of a post-war generation. Even their parties are consistently described in terms of war, engaged in 'a series of semi-military turns, shifts, and marches' (Bk I, Ch. 17), 'dependent on supplies of attention as an infantry battalion is dependent on rations' (Bk I, Ch. 18). A visit to the battle fields of the Somme ends with Dick making 'a quick study of the whole affair, simplifying it always until it bore a faint resemblance to one of his own parties', just as his parties bear more than a faint resemblance to war.

Neutral Switzerland is exposed as the very nerve-centre of this disaster, where 'the long trains of blinded or one-legged men, or dying trunks . . . crossed each other between the bright lakes of Constance and Neuchâtel' (Bk II, Ch. 1). 'Routes cross here', the narrator later remarks, '—people bound for private sanitoriums or tuberculosis resorts in the mountains, people who are no longer persona grata in France or Italy' (Bk III, Ch. 2). So combatants are substituted for non-combatant victims of revolution, tuberculosis, drugs, drink, or sex. 'Non-combatant shell-shock', Dick Diver ironically notes in his diary after a nightmare; then sets off on his clinical round to a painter, blinded with the puffed sores of nervous eczema:

> . . . her voice came up through her bandaged face afflicted with subterranean melodies:
> 'I'm sharing the fate of the women of my time who challenged men to battle.'
> 'To your vast surprise it was just like all battles,' he answered, adopting her formal diction.
> 'Just like all battles.' She thought this over. 'You pick a set-up, or else win a Pyrrhic victory, or you're wrecked and ruined— you're a ghostly echo from a broken wall.' (Bk II, Ch. 14)

That painter is Dick Diver's *alter ego*, as he all but recognizes. He too will be left a ghostly echo. He too will become a victim of sexual war. 'So many smart men go to pieces nowadays', as Nicole casually remarks early on.

For he is not merely doomed by his wealthy marriage. He is the perennial victim of females who challenge him to battle, especially 18-year-olds such as Nicole in 1919 (when he was 28) or Rosemary in 1925 (when he was 34). He is persistently shown as wooed, not wooing. He is propositioned in person and by letter. 'And if I don't know you're the most attractive man I ever met you must think I'm still crazy', Nicole tells him. Hardly has he met Rosemary but he is told: 'I fell in love with you the first time I saw you.' Naïvely susceptible to such hero-worshipping girls, he had early developed 'a habit to be loved'. That is the third theme reverberating through this 'romance': such women are dangerous. Their cropped and shingled hair poses an indefinite sexual threat. Rosemary's is described as 'an armorial shield'; a girl seen at the Gare Saint-Lazare wears her 'straw hair like a helmet'. Nicole, in Rosemary's eyes, becomes 'a viking Madonna'; in her own, she is 'Pallas Athene'. Such women are made of steel. They are survivors. It is Dick Diver, the sensitive male, who takes a long, faltering dive.

At some point it certainly occurred to Fitzgerald that Dick was a kind of Hamlet who 'had made his choice, chosen Ophelia, chosen the sweet poison and drunk it' (Bk III, Ch. 10). Except that it was mad Ophelia who had really chosen him. For Dick, too, is pictured as all charm, all courtesy, all tact; who can flatter newcomers with riveting attention; who holds court on the beach; who alone generates excitement and laughter; who is the cynosure of all eyes; who brings to the ordinary events of every day a touch of style and grace. Yet 'the excitement that swept everyone up into it . . . was inevitably followed by his own form of melancholy' (Bk I, Ch. 6). He is also the scholar-prince for whom study 'is the nearest of all things to heavenly peace'; who can contemplate madness and the causes of madness; whose mockery constantly recoils (like Hamlet's) in 'interior laughter'; who is acutely aware of himself as actor and rôle-player putting on 'a small show' (in the bank), for example, or 'a quiet little performance' (on the beach), or the gorgeous set-piece of a candle-lit dinner party at the Villa Diana[7]; who is for ever calculating and interpreting and qualifying; and who finally cracks (unlike Fortinbras victorious in war) in the domestic trenches. As he slips away into deeper and deeper obscurity, Ophelia's words can surely be heard:

> O, what a noble mind is here o'erthrown!
> The courtier's, soldier's, scholar's eye, tongue, sword;
> Th' expectancy and rose of the fair state,
> The glass of fashion and the mould of form,
> Th' observ'd of all observers,—quite, quite down![8]

For Dick Diver is Fitzgerald's portrait of an American gentleman. Far from being contemporary, he was already faintly old-fashioned by 1925 and by the end of that decade distinctly passé.[9] His father, by all accounts, was 'very much the gentleman' and bequeathed to his son 'the somewhat conscious good manners of the young Southerner coming north after the Civil War': what he called ' "good instincts", honor, courtesy, and courage'. To which Dick added his own spontaneous gift of imagination, of intuition, of social flair and charm: 'there was a pleasingness about him that simply had to be used.' In this he is much like the young homosexual whom he questions in Lausanne:

> It was as close as Dick had ever come to comprehending such a character from any but the pathological angle—he gathered that this very charm made it possible for Francisco to perpetrate his outrages, and, for Dick, charm always had an independent existence, whether it was the mad gallantry of the wretch who had died in the clinic this morning, or the courageous grace which this lost young man brought to a drab old story.
>
> (Bk III, Ch. 2)

In Francisco Dick Diver confronts another mirror image. Both exercised a charm 'that simply had to be used—those who possessed that pleasingness had to keep their hands in, and go along attaching people that they had no use to make of' (Bk I, Ch. 20).

There is, Fitzgerald suggests, something ambivalent about so much indiscriminate charm. The 18-year-old Nicole, in her first 'pathological' letter, is exactly right. He is like a cat. A cat, a white cat, she repeats: 'you seem quieter than the others, all soft like a big cat.' Dick is a purring, feline gentleman, not a vicious tomcat on the prowl like Tommy Barban (or Tom Buchanan of *The Great Gatsby*). He is Felix the cat, rather, master of ceremonies and illusion. He is 'Lucky Dick', producer of 'private gaiety', stage manager of pranks, impresario of 'richly incrusted happiness'. Part Hollywood mogul, part generalissimo, he 'sometimes looked back with awe at the carnivals of affection he had given as a general might gaze upon a massacre he had ordered to satisfy an impersonal blood lust' (Bk I, Ch. 6).

Such grace was to be effortlessly worn—as effortlessly as surf-riding. It was what Nicole called 'his awful faculty of being right'. The trick was to be graceful even in repose: as 'Dick said no American men had any repose, except himself'. But, of course, as Castiglione knew, there was effort involved. To courtesy, in *The Book of the Courtier*, he ascribed 'a certain nonchalance which conceals all artistry and makes whatever one says or does seem uncontrived and effortless'. The effort, paradoxically, is to seem effortless. 'So we can truthfully say', Castiglione continues,

> that true art is what does not seem to be art; and the most important thing is to conceal it, because if it is revealed this discredits a man completely and ruins his reputation.[10]

Sportsman, courtier, scholar, Dick Diver lives up to the whole gamut of Castiglione's expectations. A dandy, with cane and pince-nez, he seems the very 'model of correctness'. Yet the paradoxical effort finally broke him. It broke him partly because he ignored the implicit violence that made it possible, partly because he ignored the explicit violence of the world he served, the crude American source of Warren wealth (in Chicago) as much as Mussolini's blackshirts (in Italy) and the rise of the Nazis (in Austria and Germany). Dr. Diver's psychiatry was not so much a moral as an aesthetic education; and 'aesthetic education', as Paul de Man shrewdly observed, 'by no means fails; it succeeds all too well, to the point of hiding the violence that makes it possible'.[11]

Something of all this Dick Diver knew. He recognized 'that the price of his intactness was incompleteness'. He confronted the Jazz Age, that is, with all the hollow, if gentlemanly, virtues of the Gilded Age, being—in his own eyes, at least—'the last hope of a decaying clan'. So, instead of turning priest, like his father, he joined the new priesthood of the 1920s, psychiatry. He played 'father' to a whole community. As Fitzgerald had outlined in his General Plan:

> Show a man who is a natural idealist, a spoiled priest, giving in for various causes to the ideas of the haute bourgeoisie, and in his rise to the top of the social world losing his idealism, his talent and turning to drink and dissipation. . . .[12]

That spoiled priest was Dick.

For Rosemary ('Daddy's Girl') he was more than priest-like; he was 'Godlike'. She feels the smooth cloth of his coat 'like a chasuble', before dropping to her knees. She declares her love as to a father confessor. At the police station in Antibes (helping two lesbian friends out of custody) he even looks 'like a priest in the confessional'. That, in a godless world, is his rôle. It is a self-conscious, self-sacrificial rôle. He sacrifices his life for Nicole. Her final 'transference' to Tommy Barban is his. This makes his 'apostolic' gestures and final papal benediction doubly ambiguous. For he is both ironic jester and moral touchstone. He is the dandy as victim. That 'bright tan prayer rug of a beach' (of the second paragraph) seems quite properly blessed 'with a papal cross' (in the penultimate chapter).

Perhaps he is best summed up by his first appearance as the man with the rake, or Bunyan's 'Man with the Rake', or muckraker (in Theodore Roosevelt's phrase) so intent on his muck that he cannot see the celestial crown held over him. For he rakes and rakes the public beach, transforming its pebble piles to golden sand. *Tender is the Night* is so rich in symbolism that even this complex political image may have been in Fitzgerald's mind. Certainly he despaired of his readers. A 'whole lot of people just skimmed through the book for the story', he complained, 'and it simply cannot be read that way.'[13] *The Drunkard's Holiday* or *Dr. Diver's Holiday* (two discarded titles) accompanied him for nine years. He stuffed into it a vast range of observations from the Roman film sets for *Ben Hur* to the Murphys' Villa America at Antibes to Zelda's sanitorium in Montreux. But the final articulation of those sixty-one chapters is plotted by a point-counter-point of imagery as cunning as anything in Hawthorne or James. More than a racy story (of decline and fall) this is symbolist fiction based on a conscious range of paradigms, which might be codified as follows:

Riviera	Switzerland
beach	mountains
black	white
sun	moon
war	peace
experience	dreams
acting	imagination
male	female
sanity	lunacy
present	past
commerce	romance
cash	culture
sex	love

Mountain and shore, sun and moon, dark skin and pale govern these antitheses. Yet the novel frenetically zigzags between them in search of some synthesis—some intermediate, sun-tanned, golden brown or androgynous mean. All, in fact, it can offer is a pell-mell confusion of social, sexual and racial rôles. 'Well, what nationality are these people?' asks Tommy Barban, to be answered, pages later:

> Europeanized Americans who had reached a position where they could scarcely have been said to belong to any nation at all, at least not to any great power though perhaps to a Balkan-like state composed of similar citizens. . . .[14]

But they are not *all* Americans. There are hybrid Americans and hybrid Europeans like Tommy Barban (himself half French, half American, and educated in England). There are Afro-Europeans and Afro-Americans pursuing their Indian wars through the Paris streets. There is the ultimate amalgam of Mary North (once married to Abe North, or 'Mr. Afghan North'), now the Contessa di Minghetti, the papal title of her Kabyle-Berber-Sabaean-Hindu husband. Its sexual miscellany includes incest, paedophilia, transvestite lesbianism and a couple of simpering males. Nicole Diver is a diagnosed schizophrenic. But further split identities abound. A girl-boy (like

Baby who administers the Warren fortune) is matched by a boy-girl (like Francisco, 'the Queen of Chile'), whose fathers occupy matching suites in the same Swiss hotel. The star of 'Daddy's Girl', who is actually a mummy's girl, is assured by her mother that she too is economically 'a boy, not a girl'. Such symbolic chaos reaches into every crevice of the text. Even Dick Diver, the showman of this charade, sets the beach agog by exposing himself 'in transparent black lace drawers'. 'Well, if that isn't a pansy's trick!', exclaims an onlooker. ('Close inspection revealed that actually they were lined with flesh-colored cloth.')

The whole rootless set, to which Dick has dedicated himself, is marginal. That is the point of the *Margin*, the yacht owned by the (emblematically named) T. F. Golding. Their lives on the Riviera are as meaningless as their lives in Swiss nursing homes. Their wealth merely spawns confusion. Their fantasies mirror Hollywood and are mirrored by Hollywood's junk, dumped down near Monte Carlo in the form of 'a decayed street scene in India, a great cardboard whale, a monstrous tree bearing cherries large as basketballs'. What is a Rhodes Scholar and writer doing here? How can he hope to 'simplify' this mess? How can he hope to survive these Negro and Indian and Amazon wars? Mere politeness, a 'trick of the heart', could never be enough.

For ultimately it is not just the wealth, it is the wealth in the hands of the women, that unmans him. It was women like Baby Warren who had 'made a nursery out of a continent'. To them a young romantic like Dick was easy prey. Just a gulp, 'swallowed up like a gigolo . . . locked up in the Warren safety-deposit vaults' (Bk II, Ch. 18). For a while he tried to maintain his financial independence. But glutted with wealth, travelling like a latterday Lord Byron, he could hardly hope to teach 'the rich the ABC's of human decency'. Baby Warren, for one, could comfortably ignore his feelings. She could afford to bide her time. Only money, she knew, offered gilt-edged 'moral superiority'.

Her sister Nicole proves just as gutsy. She can snort 'Bull!' in the crudest Chicago style. Those predatory raids, called shopping, reflect her sense of fun:

> 'Good-by,' said Nicole. 'We had fun, didn't we?'
> 'Loads of fun,' said Rosemary. (Bk I, Ch. 12)

Together Dick and Nicole form the inseparable 'Dicole'. Oddly enough, they are hardly ever seen alone, except when probing each other for signs of strain. Theirs is a dual rôle. Just as Dick Diver combines the dual rôle of husband and nurse. So when his rôle as home nurse is finished, so is his marital rôle. The couple simply fall apart; and Dick Diver falls apart. His professional status had by that time been too thoroughly undermined. Even that exquisite house at Tarmes was a milestone along the way:

> The inception of the idea of the cliff villa which they had elaborated as a fantasy one day was a typical example of the forces divorcing them from the first simple arrangements in Zurich.
> 'Wouldn't it be fun if—' it had been; and then, 'Won't it be fun when—'
> It was not so much fun. His work became confused with Nicole's problems; in addition, her income had increased so fast of late that it seemed to belittle his work. (Bk II, Ch. 12)

He was hemmed in by flowers—Nicole's sinister 'black and brown tulips'—as intransigently as the most dangerous patients of the Swiss sanitorium had been housed behind her iron flowers. No wonder he wanted to smash it all up. 'Maybe we'll have more fun this summer', he tells Rosemary, 'but this particular fun is over. I want it to die violently . . .' (Bk I, Ch. 8). It is the first sign of his impending crack-up. And once the crack widened (what with too much drink and his affair with Rosemary) there was no holding it back. Certainly Nicole could not hold it back. In any case she was too busy reverting to type, which was the Chicago type, the Warren type that simply discarded an object once it was soiled. In that momentous slippage no one in his set could help him. Though acknowledging his style, no one (now Abe North was dead) could conceive the discipline needed to maintain it.

So Dick Diver retreated home, to upstate New York, while the Warren/Barban connection remained in occupation of the beach. It is a haunting close. The man with the rake had gone to rejoin the community of his father; he had returned to the hinterland of his dream republic. But that, too, was doomed. Its decent, provincial values had long since failed. No wonder his murdered friend, like Lincoln, was called Abe. No wonder he himself had twice been compared to Grant.[15] For Diver, like the general, was a god that failed. (Grant 'just invented mass butchery', in Dick's own words.) Like Diver, General Grant surrendered to the corrupt and powerful, presiding over the social anarchy of the Gilded Age.

That anarchy represented the triumph of commerce and sex. While Nicole surrendered to the 'anarchy' of her lover, a whore's pink knickers fluttered against the sky. 'Oh, say you can see the tender color of remembered flesh?' asks the namesake and descendent of Francis Scott Key, '—while at the stern of the battleship arose in rivalry the Star-Spangled Banner'.[16]

NOTES

1. Even in Book I the point of view occasionally shifts from the young Hollywood star (Rosemary Hoyt) to Dick and Nicole Diver. This is deliberately underlined: 'To resume Rosemary's point of view it should be said that . . .' (Ch. 6).

   I follow the first edition (1934: reprinted with emendations by Penguin Books, 1982), it can be seen, *not* the revised version (edited by Malcolm Cowley, 1951). Because of a shift in pagination between Penguin reprints since 1982, I annotate quotations by book and chapter only.

   That there are *two* versions of *Tender is the Night* has long been vexatious. Fitzgerald began reorganizing the novel soon after publication, but he clearly never completed the revision and may even have abandoned it. The idea was to restructure the chronological sequence, placing the 'flashback' of Book II, Chapters 1–10, at the beginning of the novel. His working copy contains a number of further alterations which Fitzgerald thought the new sequence required. So Cowley made hundreds more, entitling the new opening 'Case History: 1917–19' and dividing Fitzgerald's three books into five, each with a title and dates. But there is no evidence that Fitzgerald had more than toyed with this so-called 'new arrangement'. Far from editing the novel, Cowley rewrote it; and his version is now generally viewed with disfavour.

2. Milton R. Stern, *The Golden Moment: The Novels of F. Scott Fitzgerald* (Urbana: University of Illinois Press, 1970), Ch. 4, p. 291.

3. In a letter to John Peale Bishop, 7 April 1934.

4. What sometimes seems an echo of interior monologue is just as often authorial, i.e. 'In their rooms as they dressed for dinner, Dick and Nicole grimaced at each other in an awed way: such rich as want to be thought democratic pretend in private to be swept off their feet by swank' (Bk III, Ch. 4).

5. Even a casual name, like Maria Wallis, may be meant to evoke that contemporary *femme fatale*, Wallis Simpson.

6. Cf. 'So the well-to-do Americans poured through the station onto the platforms with frank new faces, intelligent, considerate, thoughtless, thought-for. An occasional English face among them seemed sharp and emergent. When there were enough Americans on the platform the first impression of their immaculacy and their money began to fade into a vague racial dusk that hindered and blinded both them and their observers' (Bk I, Ch. 19).

7. As Rosemary tells him, 'Oh, we're such *actors*—you and I' (Bk I, Ch. 24). Cf. also his thoughts on acting addressed to Rosemary (Bk III, Ch. 7) and Hamlet's address to the players (Act III, Scene 2).

8. *Hamlet*, Act III, Scene 1.

9. Note that he is five years older than Fitzgerald (born 1896), thus tied far more securely to Victorian values.

10. Spoken by Count Lodovico da Canossa in the First Book of *The Book of the Courtier* (Penguin edition, trans. George Bull, 1967), p. 67.

11. Paul de Man, *The Rhetoric of Romanticism* (New York: Columbia University Press, 1984), p. 289.

12. Fitzgerald, *Notebook* (1932). The 'General Plan' is given in full as 'Appendix B' of Arthur Mizener, *The Far Side of Paradise: A Biography of F. Scott Fitzgerald* (Boston: Houghton Mifflin, 1951; revised edition, 1965).

13. Letter to Gilbert Seldes, 31 May 1934.

14. *Tender is the Night*, Bk I, Ch. 4 and Bk III, Ch. 7.

15. At the opening of his career (Bk II, Ch. 1) and again in the final sentence. 'Abe North' had originally been called 'Abe Grant'.

   Though the episodes of Book III seem to predate the Wall Street Crash, internal chronology would indicate a date more like 1930 or even 1931. But those final, ever receding echoes seem to come from a country— as well as a man—in deep Depression.

16. *Tender is the Night*, Bk III, Ch. 8. *The Great Gatsby* was originally entitled *Under the Red, White, and Blue*. Francis Scott Key Fitzgerald was obsessed with 'The Star-Spangled Banner' (1814), which had become the United States national anthem, by Act of Congress, in 1931.

4

The Last Tycoon:
Fitzgerald as Projectionist

by ROBERT GIDDINGS

> Please do not turn on the clouds until the show starts. Be sure
> the stars are turned off when leaving.
> —Notice on the backstage switchboard of the Paradise Theatre,
> Farubault, Minnesota. Quoted in Ben M. Hall, *The Golden Age
> of the Movie Palace: The Best Remaining Seats* (1961)

> Irving Thalberg carried with him the accoutrements of an
> artist; hence he was unique in the Hollywood of the period. I
> don't know of anyone else who has occupied the position. He was
> like a young pope.
> —Budd Schulberg

1

It has become widely accepted that Fitzgerald was at his best
when writing about experiences known and observed first-
hand. In no respect has this been more alleged than in the
matter of the Jazz Age, Fitzgerald as its celebrant and victim
and in whose 'Jazz Age' fiction and essays (especially as
collected in *The Crack-Up*) the very essence of American history,
the decades of the 1920s and 1930s at least, apparently had
been caught on the wing. This may have started out as a way of
praising Fitzgerald, but it has produced its problems. Was
Fitzgerald the master or the servant of his materials? Other
than in *The Great Gatsby* (1925), by common agreement his one

sure masterpiece, did he in truth write as more than the chronicler, the historical painter of his period? And more to immediate purposes, when the issue is *The Last Tycoon*— admittedly unfinished at his death in 1940—which so conspicuously takes for its central figure of Monroe Starr a model literally as large (if not more so) as life, the studio mogul Irving Thalberg (1899–1936), can it be said that Fitzgerald not only kept but mastered his imaginative distance?

Arthur Mizener usefully sets out Fitzgerald's own exhilaration at the prospect of writing *The Last Tycoon*:

> Less than a year before his death, when he began the actual writing of *The Last Tycoon*, he was filled once more with the old, irrepressible excitement; you can hear it in the letter he wrote his daughter: 'Scottina: . . . Look! I have begun to write something that is maybe *great*. . . . It may not *make* us a cent but it will pay expenses and it is the first labor of love I've undertaken since the first part of "Infidelity!" '[1]

Mizener goes on to speak of *The Last Tycoon* as indeed fulfilling Fitzgerald's hopes, and essentially because, as always with Fitzgerald at his best, it offers not 'social history or even nostalgically evocative social history' but 'the history of a consciousness'. Fitzgerald, in other words, whatever the temptation to see this last novel as overwhelmingly tied only to its time and place and Hollywood materials, manages infinitely more. A torso only *The Last Tycoon* may be, but on my estimate at least, it truly ranks among Fitzgerald's most glittering prizes, and precisely in how it takes the 'life' figure of Thalberg, whose mogulship Fitzgerald had every occasion to observe in his Hollywood script-writing days, and transforms aspects of him into Monroe Stahr. So that one immediately says yes, Monroe Stahr *is* Irving Thalberg, but yes, also, and mercifully, he is so much more, a portrait—a fiction—indeed as 'maybe great' as Fitzgerald so fervently hoped he had it within him to create. And one also says that *The Last Tycoon* goes beyond even that, beyond any one figure or phase of American history, into a vision of how Art, as Fitzgerald conceived it, might 'project' History itself.

But to return first to Thalberg: his life has not wanted for documentation. Witness, for example, Samuel Marx, *Mayer and*

Thalberg: The Make-Believe Saints (1975), Bosley Crowther, *Hollywood Rajah: The Life and Times of Louis B. Mayer* (1960) and Bob Thomas, *Thalberg: Life and Legend* (1969). It all makes for fabulous reading. It is openly acknowledged that although Thalberg's name was technically not part of the company's title, he was the real driving force and elemental genius which made Metro-Goldwyn-Mayer the prosperous empire which it had become by the opening years of the 1930s.

And what an empire it was! It was the largest of the 124 subsidiaries owned by the huge conglomerate founded by Marcus Loew, the Australian-American tycoon, Loews Incorporated. Its plant in Culver City, California, covered fifty-three acres and was valued at $2,000,000. Its stars were paid $6,000 a week. It boasted the highest paid writing staff in the business with a payroll of $40,000 a week. Its parkland could be turned into anything required from battlefields to palace gardens. It had twenty-two sound stages and twenty-two projection rooms. Its films made the most money in the trade, each movie costing on average about $500,000. A billion people annually paid some $100,000,000 worldwide to go and see the products turned out by Metro-Goldwyn-Mayer. It could boast it had more stars than there were in Heaven—including Greta Garbo, Clark Gable, John Gilbert, Spencer Tracy, Lewis Stone, Laurel and Hardy, the Barrymores, Lon Chaney, Wallace Beery, Joan Crawford, William Powell, the Marx Brothers, Francot Tone and Norma Shearer—and among its most famous productions were *The Big Parade*, *Anna Christie*, *Grand Hotel*, *Ben Hur*, *The Thin Man* and *Mutiny on the Bounty*. These were not all produced during Irving Thalberg's period with Metro-Goldwyn-Mayer. He died in 1936, before the making of such money-spinning commodities as *Goodbye Mr. Chips* and *The Wizard of Oz*, which are such typical products of Culver City's active imperialism.

The company originated from Loew's which was initially an exhibiting company which bought into Metro Pictures in 1920. Immediately afterwards it produced two extremely successful films—*The Four Horsemen of the Apocalypse* in 1921, directed by Rex Ingram, which introduced Rudolph Valentino as a star, and *The Prisoner of Zenda* in the following year, again directed by Rex Ingram, with Lewis Stone and Ramon Navarro. By 1925 it had merged with the Goldwyn production company and been joined by Louis B. Mayer Pictures. Mayer epitomized the American dream. He was a Jewish refugee from Russian persecution who had crawled from the very bottom of the pile to the very top of executive power. Early in his career he had sold junk and this was a reputation he was to carry with him forever, whether deserved or not. He said himself, 'Look out for yourself or they'll pee on your grave', but he probably would accept Bob Hope's famous comment as his most fitting epitaph: 'Louis B. Mayer came west in the early days with twenty-eight dollars, a box camera, and an old lion. He built a monument to himself— the Bank of America.' Herman Mankiewicz, the scriptwriter immortally associated with *Citizen Kane*, was less generous: 'There but for the grace of God, goes God.' Nevertheless with Mayer as its production head the company thrived, though stories of his tyranny are infamous, including his physical violence upon the persons of Charlie Chaplin, Robert Taylor and John Gilbert, and his emotional violence upon the likes of Myrna Loy, for whom he faked a heart attack in order to blackmail her into playing a particular rôle. He lay on the floor murmuring: 'No . . . no. . . . Don't play the part, Myrna. . . . I understand. Please don't play the part. . . . I understand. . . . People will only say you played it so as to please a sick man.' She went on her knees to him and begged to be allowed the rôle she had originally refused. He reluctantly gave in as a doctor was called to his side. When she had left his office, Mayer leaped up from the floor and yelled 'Well, who's next?' and continued to keep his business appointments. Mayer dominated Metro-Goldwyn-Mayer for a quarter of a century. But this was the strange business world into which the frail but determined Irving Thalberg, original of Scott Fitzgerald's Monroe Stahr, entered as a young man. He was to provide the artistic flair, the cultivated and sophisticated tone, to counterbalance Mayer's shrewd understanding of mass public appetites.

3

During the early years of the decade following the Wall Street crash it has been estimated that Irving Thalberg was paid $500,000 a year, partly the result of a generous bonus system on Metro-Goldwyn-Mayer's productions. He worked very hard for it. His business methods and habits were strange, but they earned huge dividends. The Metro-Goldwyn-Mayer executive offices were a white wooden building, and Thalberg's office was on the second floor. He had a private projection room which had three desks, a couple of pianos and about thirty armchairs. He was seldom there before 10 a.m. But once there he devoted all his energies into ensuring that the company produced the best films in the world. His life story is another version of the American myth of the ordinary guy who makes it to the top of the tree. After leaving high school in Brooklyn, he worked as an office boy in Universal Pictures, where he had been 'discovered' by Carl Laemle, Snr., who was an executive producer, associated particularly with the success of *All Quiet on the Western Front* in 1930.

Thalberg's major business activity seemed to be talk and he used words quietly, sacredly and preciously, almost like a poet. He was fragile in appearance and less than 5' 2" in height. He used his hands to great effect when he spoke and was given to pacing up and down his office with his hands clasped behind his back when deep in thought. His voice was always calm and contained, as if he was determined to be sparing in its use. The items noticeable on his desk were his dictaphone, a large box of cigarettes which he never opened, plates of apples and dates which he frequently dipped into and many bottles of medicine. He did not give out the impression of massively good and robust health.

All those who have written about the professional qualities possessed and employed by Irving Thalberg agree that two particular qualities were outstanding: his ability to deal thoroughly with all aspects of motion picture production, and his ability to come up with ideas. To an outsider the activities of a typical day in Thalberg's working life might seem to lack cohesion and purpose. But he knew what he was doing, and the industry knew that he knew. Mae D. Huettig gives a reasonable account of what he actually seemed to do for a living:

> There is naturally no chance that Mr. Thalberg's activities will fall into routine. His efforts follow no pattern whatsoever, except that they consist almost exclusively of talk. He deals with actors, whose simple wants of avarice or vanity he finds it easy to appease. He deals with writers, with whom he seldom commits

the unpardonable blunder of saying: 'I don't like it, but I don't know why.' He is ceaselessly aware of Delores Del Rio's gifted husband, Cedric Gibbons, who designs MGM scenery, and of the tall, twittering hunchback Adrain, who drapes MGM's loveliest bodies. He deals with M. E. Greenwood, the gaunt studio manager, who used to be an Arizona faro dealer and now tells MGM's New York office how much the company has spent every week and how much to place on deposit for MGM's account at the Culver City branch of Bank of America. Through Mr. Greenwood, and sometimes more directly, Irving Thalberg observes the two thousand of the skilled but unsung: 'grips', assistant cameramen, 'mixers', cutters, projectionists, carpenters, unit managers, artisans, seamstresses, scene painters. Often he calls a group of these underlings into the projection room to consider pictures with him.[2]

But none of this Thalberg-supervised activity would have existed had it not been for the ideas which were the genesis of all movies. Here Thalberg's genius was even more apparent, his mind a seeming fount of good basic scripting ideas as well as brilliant ideas about points of detail.

Thalberg could sense the basic need at the very core and centre of a movie; it was his idea to borrow Tallulah Bankhead from Paramount to give much needed zest to *Tinfoil. Rasputin and the Empress* (1932) gave Lionel Barrymore one of his biggest and best rôles, but it was Thalberg's idea to have the movie directed by Richard Boleslavsky, the Polish stage director who came to Hollywood in 1930 from the Moscow Arts Theatre (he went on to direct *The Painted Veil*, *Clive of India* and *Les Misérables*). It was Thalberg who recognized and exploited the particular gifts of Howard Hawks, who had been in the industry since 1918 and who had become a household name certainly from *Scarface* 1932 on; Hawks had a penchant for grainy realism and action-packed drama as well as very polished and professional comedies. (He made *The Criminal Code* for Thalberg in 1931.) He encouraged the very cosmopolitan talents of Sidney Franklin, who directed *Beverly of Graustark* (1926), *The Last of Mrs. Cheyney* (1929), *Private Lives* (1931), *Smiling Through* (1932), *The Guardsman* (1932) and *The Barretts of Wimpole Street* (1933) and went on to produce the immortal *Mrs. Miniver* in 1942. The many-sided W. S. Van Dyke was another director in Thalberg's stable, whose films included *White Shadows in the South Seas* (1928), *Trader Horn* (1931), shot on safari in Africa, *Tarzan the Ape Man* (1932), which introduced the greatest of all ape-men, the former Olympic athlete Johnny Weissmuller, *Manhattan Melodrama* (1934) and the still very impressive disaster movie prototype, *San Francisco* (1936). Sam Wood, director of *A Night at the Opera* and *A Day at the Races*, who had a gift for football and college pictures and left his mark on *Goodbye Mr. Chips* (1939) and directed the future president of the United States in *Kings Row* in 1942, was another of Thalberg's favourites. Edgar Selwyn, master of soggy melodrama, who directed such films as *Night Life of New York, The Girl in the Show, War Nurse, The Sin of Madelon Claudet, Turn Back the Clock* and *The Mystery of Mr. X*, is additional evidence of Thalberg's range of interests, as was Tod Browning, who made his name directing early masterpieces of the cinema's gothic horrors: *The Unholy Three, London After Midnight, Dracula* and *Freaks*.[3] A director whose talents and inclinations might have seemed the most suited to Thalberg's taste was Clarence Brown, who specialized in rather fussy period subjects—*The Last of the Mohicans, Anna Christie, Anna Karenina*—but who showed a very sure touch in such dramas as *Goosewoman* (1925), which is still considered a picture of immense stature and authority and contains a brilliant performance by Marie Dressler as a retired opera singer who unwittingly implicates her own son in a murder case. Irving Thalberg seemed able to work harmoniously with these versatile creative talents.

But as well as exercising his diplomacy in dealing with these lofty persons, he could also deal with minute details of finance, committee work, casting, preparing and supervising scripts, conferring with his team of writers and resolving the numerous minor and not so minor industrial disputes between personnel during day-to-day production activities. All this was done with little external sign of anxiety or neurosis. He briefly developed one irritating habit which was soon cured. His therapeutic rolling of a twenty-dollar gold coin on his desk top during discussions was immediately cured by ridiculous satirical imitation by his colleagues.

Notoriously, Thalberg's day did not end at 5 p.m. The day's toiling over, the bargains all struck (J. B. Priestley wanted

$50,000 for *The Good Companions*—Thalberg got it off him for half the price), Irving Thalberg drove back to his mansion at Santa Monica overlooking the Pacific Ocean where he pored over scripts and watched Metro-Goldwyn-Mayer movies in his sitting room. He lived and died for the movies and nothing else seemed to interest him very much. He was married to Norma Shearer, star of *The Barretts of Wimpole Street* and *Romeo and Juliet*. His dying words seem humdrum enough: 'Don't let the children forget me.' But we shall not look on his like again. As Gene Fowler remarked: 'On the way down, I saw Thalberg's shoes in the hall, and no one has filled them.'

The remarkable thing about his treatment at the hands of Scott Fitzgerald in *The Last Tycoon* is the fact that very little of this is captured at all in the character of Monroe Stahr. What Fitzgerald preferred to do was to focus exclusively on just one or two aspects of Thalberg's character as far as it was revealed in his professional life and to work these facets up into very high definition. His identification of these particular aspects of Thalberg's personality, considering that he knew the Hollywood tycoon personally and professionally, tells us a great deal about Fitzgerald, even though the book may in fact do less than justice to Irving Thalberg.

4

The Last Tycoon is not a thinly disguised biography of Irving Thalberg. Although it deals with a leading figure in the motion picture industry, it is not even really about films. To read *The Last Tycoon* properly we must be careful not to mistake the evidence, impressive and convincing though much of it is, for the case Fitzgerald wanted to present. This fragment may only partially be described as 'his unfinished novel of Hollywood'.[4] For this mistaken emphasis, among several other things, we have Edmund Wilson to thank.[5] It is certainly the case that we are led into the novel's major themes by means of constant references to an omnipresent Hollywood right from the start:

> Though I haven't ever been on the screen I was brought up in pictures. Rudolph Valentino came to my fifth birthday party— or so I was told. I put this down only to indicate that even before

the age of reason I was in a position to watch the wheels go round.

I was going to write my memoirs once, *The Producer's Daughter*, but at eighteen you never quite get round to anything like that. It's just as well—it would have been as flat as an old column of Lolly Parsons'. My father was in the picture business as another man might be in cotton or steel... I accepted Hollywood with the resignation of a ghost assigned to a haunted house. I knew what you were supposed to think about it but I was obstinately unhorrified.[6]

Thus (and more) Cecilia Brady, college educated daughter of Monroe Stahr's partner in Hollywood. At the opening of the book we are given the traditional stereotypical view of the Hollywood producer. It is significantly embedded in an anecdote of Wylie White's:

Listen, Cecilia: I once had an affair with the wife of a producer. A very short affair. When it was over she said to me in no uncertain terms, she said: 'Don't you ever tell about this or I'll have you thrown out of Hollywood. My husband's a much more important man than you!'[7]

We cannot help but contrast this with the first impression of Monroe Stahr we are given only a few pages on. He is not presented as a money-mad mogul, crazy with his own power, but as a man with an almost magnetically spiritual quality about him. Cecilia falls over him accidentally, but there is a symbolic dimension here. She would easily fall for him. He was a man, she says, that any girl would go for with no encouragement at all. They would not be able to help it. They would be drawn to him. As his dark eyes look at her she wonders what they would look like if he was to fall in love:

They were kind, aloof and, though they often reasoned with you gently, somewhat superior. It was no fault of theirs if they saw so much. He darted in and out of the rôle of 'one of the boys' with dexterity—but on the whole I should say he wasn't one of them. But he knew how to shut up, how to draw into the background, how to listen. From where he stood (and though he was not a tall man, it always seemed high up) he watched the multitudinous practicalities of his world like a proud young shepherd to whom night and day had never mattered....[8]

Stahr is a mysterious figure. Initially he hides himself behind the mundane name 'Smith', but this only temporarily masks his star quality. Fitzgerald is at pains when introducing him to stress his superior attributes: he seems tall, even though he may not be; he has dark, mysterious eyes; qualities of gentle superiority are emphasized; he is in the world, yet not really part of it as he watches the multitudinous practicalities proudly like a shepherd. He has a god-like indifference to night and day as he seems removed from the passing of time which affects other mortals. As he twists the ring on his finger it seems to have a magical effect on Cecilia, who comes to believe that she has been rendered invisible. She can barely summon the power to address so charged a being: 'I never dared look quite away from him or quite *at* him . . . and I knew he affected many other people in the same manner.'[9]

His figure is a strange combination of the ethereal and the pugnacious. She reflects how the bulky ring on his finger contrasts with his delicate fingers and slender body. He has a slender face and arched eyebrows. His hair is dark and curly:

> He looked spiritual at times, but he was a fighter—somebody out of his past knew him when he was one of a gang of kids in the Bronx, and gave me a description of how he walked always at the head of his gang, this rather frail boy, occasionally throwing a command backward out of the corner of his mouth.[10]

Monroe Stahr is a Prince, an aristocrat among robber barons and warlords. He seems to stand for a particular set of values which include personal courage, skills and expertise, professionalism and ambition combined, but buffed and polished with sophistication, delicacy and refinement. He has all the American virtues, but they are refined to an almost aristocratic essence. But there is a very important element in this aristocratic personality as presented in Scott Fitzgerald's hero: he is not a patron of the arts, he is a creative person. This seems to interest Fitzgerald very much in his portrait of the last tycoon. Yes, it is undeniable that Stahr works for the motion picture industry, whose job it is to provide entertainment for the masses, but he is emphatically not presented to us merely as an executive of the industry. He is a man who expresses the essence of himself in what he does: he is an artist. Much of the essential Monroe Stahr is revealed in his relationship with the writer,

George Boxley. This is particularly true of the scene where Stahr explains to Boxley how films tell stories and indicates that film is not a narrative medium which apes printed literature; it is a language of its own, with its own vocabulary, grammar and syntax, *its own way of telling you things*.

Significantly, Boxley is British, with all the associations of history, tradition and an old-fashioned way of doing things which far too many Americans mistake automatically for 'class' and 'quality'. Typically, Boxley the novelist tends to despise the modern means of cultural production which feeds him and pays his mortgage and his other living expenses. Boxley feels that he is the victim of a conspiracy, that the 'hacks' who work with him on film scripting have a vocabulary of a mere few hundred words. Stahr tells him that the trouble with what he writes is that it is not appropriate to the medium he is writing for: 'it was just talk, back and forth . . . Interesting talk but nothing more.'

Boxley finds this insulting. How dare this American film executive, this example of the senior management whose concern is the proper control of finance and budgeting, tell him, the established British novelist, how to write?

> I don't think you people read things. The men are duelling when the conversation takes place. At the end one of them falls into a well and has to be hauled up in a bucket.[11]

Monroe Stahr rightly perceives that Boxley would consider writing for the movies cheap and vulgar, something beneath his real dignity as a *writer*. Part of the trouble is that Boxley himself does not even go to the movies. Why does he feel that about the movies? Because people are always duelling and falling down wells 'and wearing strange facial expressions and talking incredible and unnatural dialogue'. But Stahr has brought Boxley to Hollywood because he wants his films to be properly written. He is employing him as a professional writer, but he must not be so proud as to feel superior to the very matter he is expected to write:

> Slip the dialogue for a minute. . . . Granted your dialogue is more graceful than what these hacks can write—that's why we brought you out here. But let's imagine something that isn't either bad dialogue or jumping down a well. Has your office got a stove in it that lights with a match?

Boxley seems to think that it has, but he never uses it. Never mind, says Stahr, imagine that you are in your office:

> You've been fighting duels or writing all day and you're too tired to fight or write any more. You're sitting there staring—dull, like we all get sometimes. A pretty stenographer that you've seen before comes into the room and you watch her—idly. She doesn't see you, though you're very close to her. She takes off her gloves, opens her purse and dumps it out on a table—.[12]

Stahr stands up and tosses his key-ring on the desk. Boxley listens as he goes on:

> She has two dimes and a nickel—and a cardboard matchbox. She leaves the nickel on the desk, puts the two dimes back into her purse and takes her black gloves to the stove, opens it and puts them inside. There is one match in the matchbox and she starts to light it kneeling by the stove. You notice that there's a stiff wind blowing in the window—but just then your telephone rings. The girl picks it up, says hello—listens—and says deliberately into the phone, 'I've never owned a pair of black gloves in my life.' She hangs up, kneels by the stove again, and just as she lights the match, you glance around very suddenly and see that there's another man in the office, watching every move the girl makes—[13]

Here Monroe Stahr pauses again, and picks up his keys and puts them in his pocket. Boxley is really interested now and asks what happens next? Stahr replies: 'I don't know . . . I was just making pictures.' Boxley then attempts to indicate that he was not really interested, merely curious. It was just 'melodrama' he says. Stahr replies:

> Not necessarily . . . In any case, nobody has moved violently or talked cheap dialogue or had any facial expression at all. There was only one bad line, and a writer like you could improve it. But you were interested.[14]

This is a key moment in Fitzgerald's portrait of Stahr. It gives Stahr the artist, the creator, the man who makes things. It is of overriding importance to grasp this point as it is vital in the character construction of the leading figure in *The Last Tycoon*, and the novelist's investigation of the value system he has undertaken depends wholly on the use he makes of particular qualities selected from his observations of 'the boy wonder'—

Irving Thalberg. Monroe Stahr is a man who is clearly aware that in his daily work as a man who wants to make motion pictures of quality for the mass market which depends on the Hollywood studio system, he must negotiate the best relationship he can between the creative and the productive elements of the industry. Fitzgerald establishes this as a central problem for Monroe Stahr, as it was to him and as it was to Shakespeare, and Dickens and Trollope and D. H. Lawrence and the entire host of imaginative and sensitive and insightful storytellers before Scott Fitzgerald's time.

The writer—like the film maker—is immediately faced in modern times with a complex of relationships between himself and what he wants to tell the world (the stuff of literature) and the means of literary production—economic, technical, cultural and social—which have to be resolved as harmoniously as possible. No modern writer is able directly to address his audience. Monroe Stahr, the great film tycoon, stands emblematically for the figure of the storyteller in his relationship with the means of production and distribution on which the survival of literature depends. The strength and fascination of Fitzgerald's Monroe Stahr is the result not of his having based him on Irving Thalberg whom he knew in Hollywood, etc., etc. but in what Stahr stands for. This conversation with George Boxley brilliantly demonstrates Stahr's understanding of how man-made art works on the imagination. But he also understands, as a later discussion with Boxley shows, how important is the relationship between the artist and the means of production. These matters cannot be left to chance. The artist must understand them if he is fully to realize himself as an artist. It is no good feeling superior to them. The economics and the technology of artistic production are as important as the creative and imaginative aspects of art. In the greatest art, they become one and the same thing, and the greatest writers understand this— to the positive advantage of their development as artists in realizing the potential of the means to communicate what they have to say.[15]

Monroe Stahr puts this case to Boxley in the hope that the novelist will understand what motion pictures can do: suppose you were in a chemist's shop, buying medicine for a relative who was very ill, then whatever caught your attention through the window and distracted you would be material for pictures. Such as a murder outside the window, asks Boxley. Stahr implies that in motion pictures there is not always the necessity to pile into melodrama at the first possible opportunity. It might be a spider, working on the pane:

> 'Of course—I see.'
> 'I'm afraid you don't, Mr. Boxley. You see it for *your* medium, but not for ours. You keep the spiders for yourself and you try to pin the murders on us.'
> 'I might as well leave,' said Boxley. 'I'm no good to you. I've been here three weeks and I've accomplished nothing. I make suggestions, but no one writes them down.'
> 'I want you to stay. Something in you doesn't like pictures, doesn't like telling a story this way—'
> 'It's such a damn bother,' exploded Boxley. 'You can't let yourself go—'[16]

As he speaks, Boxley realizes that Stahr was a helmsman with many matters to take into account in steering a true course. He senses the stiff wind that must be sensibly battled against and the creaking of the rigging of a ship sailing in great awkward tacks along an open sea. Another analogy Fitzgerald uses is the feeling Boxley has that they are in a huge quarry where even the newly cut marble bears the tracery of old pediments and half-obliterated inscriptions from the past:

> 'I keep wishing you could start over,' Boxley said. 'It's this mass production.'
> 'That's the condition,' said Stahr. 'There's always some lousy condition. We're making a life of Rubens—suppose I asked you to do portraits of rich dopes like Billy Brady and me and Gary Cooper . . . when you wanted to paint Jesus Christ! Wouldn't you feel you had a condition? Our condition is that we have to take people's own favourite folklore and dress it up and give it back to them. Anything beyond that is sugar. So won't you give us some sugar, Mr. Boxley?'[17]

This seems to me a very good summing up of the assumptions Irving Thalberg had about the motion picture industry. He once said: 'The medium will eventually take its place as art because there is no other medium of interest to so many people.'[18] These are qualities of an ideal nature which Fitzgerald strongly indicates in his portrait of Monroe Stahr, and make him at once a powerful and vigorous figure, yet one prone to destruction. It is important to note the symbolic use Fitzgerald makes of leading figures taken from American history in this novel as well as in others—*Tender is the Night*, for example, with its echoes of Ulysses Grant.[19]

Fitzgerald was considerably influenced by his reading of the historical works of Henry Adams (1838–1918) whom the novelist knew personally. Adams was educated at Harvard and studied law in Germany. He taught history at Harvard for a time and published *The History of the United States During the Administration of Thomas Jefferson and James Madison* (1889–91). In much the same way as another major American writer—T. S. Eliot—Adams found modern times disturbing and believed civilization was about to disintegrate. Like Eliot he, too, looked to the Middle Ages for that harmony and permanence he found lacking in the twentieth century. This is the essential theme of Adams's *Mont-Saint-Michel and Chartres* (1904). General Grant was Adams's hope for maintaining liberalism, virtue and humanism in modern America. Grant was elected president, Adams believed, because he stood for moral order against the rising tide of greed, mammonism and anarchy. Adams came to see in Grant's two terms of office—1868–72 and 1872–76—a surrender of moral and political virtue to those very forces of materialism and corruption that he so feared would destroy the American nation. It is of considerable significance that Fitzgerald compares Dick Diver to Grant, and shows that he, like Adams's failed hero, succumbed to temptation when he found himself surrounded with the wealthy and socially distinguished. Like Grant, Diver is a dreamer destroyed by realities which he is too frail to combat.[20] In the character of Monroe Stahr Fitzgerald again draws on American history to provide symbolic texture to his themes.

5

Two other outstanding figures from the nation's history in this respect add conspicuous gravity to the thematic structure of *The Last Tycoon*: Andrew Jackson and Abraham Lincoln. Jackson is introduced quite early in the book as the group of ill-assorted characters stranded by transport problems go to visit the home of Old Hickory. In the zappy words of Wylie White:

> Just in time . . . The tour is just starting. Home of Old Hickory— America's tenth president. The victor of New Orleans, opponent of the National Bank, and inventor of the Spoils System.

Making allowances for the Hollywood scriptwriter's shorthand this does summarize the values and associations of Andrew Jackson (1767–1845). Jackson was, in fact, the seventh president, but in essence the career given here does embody the major features of his folkloric reputation. Andrew Jackson fought in the War of Independence and was captured by the British. He helped to frame the constitution of Tennessee and represented the state in Congress in 1796 and in the Senate in 1797. He was a judge of the supreme court of Tennessee.

He became a national hero during the 1812 war with the British after a series of brilliant victories against the Indians and defeating Sir Edward Michael Pakenham's army of 16,000 veterans at New Orleans. Jackson was governor of Florida and ran for the presidency in 1825 as a Democrat against John Quincy Adams, W. H. Crawford and Henry Clay. Jackson had the highest number of popular votes but not a majority. In 1828 he was elected with a majority of electoral votes. The strength of Jackson's image in popular history is to be located in the values he stood for: he was a genuine self-made man, a product of the socio-economic and political philosophy on which the United States was founded, he was courageous and he was a man of principle.

He was re-elected in 1832. To get things done he swept great numbers of officials from office and replaced them with his own partisans, coining the phrase, 'To the victor belong the spoils', to cover these actions. But it meant that he got things done. In spite of the censure of the Senate he broke the power of the Bank of the United States, asserting that it had too much power and was a corrupting element in American political life. During his second administration the national debt was fully paid and the surplus was distributed to the several states of the union. He retired at the end of his second term and died at his house, the Hermitage, Nashville, Tennessee. In *The Last Tycoon* the stranded party look at Jackson's house:

> It was still not quite dawn. The Hermitage looked like a nice big white box, but quite a little lonely and vacated after a hundred years. We walked back to the car. . . .[21]

One member of the party considers that even if people do not know much about Jackson or why he is important in American history, there must be something significant about him, if they have preserved his house all these years, and that Jackson must have been 'some one who was large and merciful, able to understand'. At both ends of life man needed nourishment: 'a breast— a shrine'. Significantly the visiting party are unable to gain access to the Hermitage, the house is locked. It is as if the values Jackson stood for are no longer available to these representatives of a more rapacious America in the twentieth century.

Monroe Stahr is directly associated with Abraham Lincoln. It is George Boxley who recognizes:

> that Stahr like Lincoln was a leader carrying on a long war on many fronts; almost single-handed he had moved pictures sharply forward through a decade, to a point where the content of the 'A productions' was wider and richer than that of the stage. Stahr was an artist only, as Mr. Lincoln was a general, perforce and as a layman.[22]

There is another important reference to Lincoln, seen through the eyes of a distinguished visitor to the studios, the Danish Prince Agge, who is described in Scott Fitzgerald's list of characters as an 'early Fascist'.[23] Agge obviously believes in the superiority of some races to others:

> He was hostile to Jews in a vague general way that he tried to cure himself of. As a turbulent man, serving his time in the Foreign Legion, he thought that Jews were too fond of their own skins. But he was willing to concede that they might be different in America under different circumstances. . . .[24]

But the panoramic view he gets of the crowded film studios is like the Melting Pot of Nations itself:

> Coming out of the private dining room, they passed through a corner of the commissary proper. Prince Agge drank it in— eagerly. It was gay with gipsies and with citizens and soldiers, with sideburns and braided coats of the First Empire. From a little distance they were men who lived and walked a hundred

years ago, and Agge wondered how he and the men of his time
would look as extras in some future costume picture.

Then he saw Abraham Lincoln, and his whole feeling suddenly
changed. He had been brought up in the dawn of Scandinavian
socialism when Nicolay's biography was much read. He had
been told Lincoln was a great man whom he should admire, and
he hated him instead, because he was forced upon him. . . .[25]

But now that he sees Lincoln before him he cannot help
staring at him. The actor sits there, with his legs crossed, his
kindly face fixed on his forty-cent dinner, 'including dessert',
with a shawl wrapped round his shoulders to protect himself
from the erratic air-conditioning: 'This then, was Lincoln. . . .'
Agge realizes that this is what they all meant to be. Much to his
surprise this glimpse into the inner meaning of things in this
new society, this man-made nation, is shattered as the living
presence from the past of American history, the great and good
Abraham Lincoln, father of the new nation state, unexpectedly
raises his hand and stuffs a triangle of pie into his mouth. In the
United States the extraordinary and the ordinary are all mixed
up together, and the best and the brightest can be seen rising
from humble origins and at the same time reasserting absolute
ordinariness; the historic and the humdrum are one and the
same. It is the dynamic of this society which has created
Monroe Stahr, and as Fitzgerald's plans for *The Last Tycoon*
survive to indicate, it was these same forces which would
threaten and destroy him.[26]

6

As Charles E. Shain opines, *The Last Tycoon* has the mark of the
'30s on it as surely as the early fictions had taken the American
boom as their theme: 'The subject was Hollywood as an industry
and as a society, but also as an American microcosm.'[27] But
there is mercifully more to it than that. *The Last Tycoon* is an
impressive and moving fragment, not just because it is a faithful
portrait of the motion picture industry at a particular period of
its development—to say that is to mistake the Hollywood for
the trees—but because Fitzgerald convincingly uses this material
to explore some of his driving interest in the creative processes
and their relationship with industry and mass society. As a

creative artist himself he could not fail to be interested in the compromise and negotiation which must take place between the various stages of the processes between ideas and conception, on the one hand, and production and consumption on the other. Had he lived to finish it, our impression of *The Last Tycoon* might well be gloomier. As it stands it remains a brilliant and dazzling achievement. The novel was filmed in 1976 with Robert de Niro as Monroe Stahr. It was not a very good movie, but its weaknesses are significant. It saw itself as part of a particularly strong tradition in film-making—the movie about movie-making, sardonically lifting the lid on the whole business. This line stretches back from *Sunset Boulevard* in 1950, through *The Star*, *The Barefoot Contessa*, *Hollywood Boulevard*, the various versions of *A Star is Born*, *The Day of the Locust* and *The Carpetbaggers*. Its period detail was excellent, and the recreation of the industry's technology and management was impressive. But its focus was awry. It was like a bad cake made with the best ingredients. *The Last Tycoon* is not about films. It is about art. Scott Fitzgerald wrote in his notebook: 'There never was a good biography of a good novelist. There couldn't be. He's too many people if he's any good.'[28] But *The Last Tycoon* is very nearly a great novel about a maker, unfinished as indeed it is.

NOTES

1. Arthur Mizener, *Introduction, F. Scott Fitzgerald: A Collection of Critical Essays* (New Jersey: Prentice-Hall, 1963), pp. 3–4.
2. Mai D. Hueling, 'Fortune-Metro-Goldwyn-Mayer', in Tino Balio (ed.), *The American Film Industry* (Madison, Wisconsin: University of Wisconsin Press, 1976), p. 259.
3. *Freaks* was completed in 1932 but was withheld from public showing by censorship for thirty years. It is a circus melodrama featuring genuine freaks. An odd movie to have been sponsored by the fastidious Irving Thalberg.
4. Marcus Cunliffe, *The Literature of the United States* (Harmondsworth: Penguin, 1968), p. 292.
5. For a discussion of *The Last Tycoon* as 'Hollywood novel' see Arthur Mizener, 'The Maturity of Scott Fitzgerald', in the *Sewanee Review*, LXVII (Autumn 1959), 658 ff.
6. F. Scott Fitzgerald, *The Last Tycoon*, in *The Bodley Head Scott Fitzgerald* (London: Bodley Head, 1966), Vol. 1, 167.

7. *The Last Tycoon*, ibid., p. 175.
8. Ibid., p. 180.
9. Ibid., p. 180.
10. Ibid., p. 181.
11. Ibid., pp. 197–98.
12. Ibid., p. 198.
13. Ibid., p. 198–99.
14. Ibid., p. 199. This is, in fact, an excellent account of how stories are told in pictures, and suggests that F. Scott Fitzgerald learned much from his days in Hollywood—cf James Monaco: *How to Read a Film: The Art, Technology, History and Theory of Film and Media* (New York: Oxford University Press, 1981), pp. 125 ff.; J. Dudley Andrew, *The Major Film Theories* (New York: Oxford University Press, 1976), pp. 220 ff.; Robert Scholes's essay 'Narration and Narrativity in Film' in Gerald Mast and Marshall Cohen (eds.), *Film Theory and Criticism: Introductory Readings* (New York: Oxford University Press, 1979), pp. 417–33, and Robert Richardson, *Literature and Film* (Bloomington, Indiana: University of Indiana Press, 1969), pp. 65 ff.
15. An obvious example would be Dickens, who seized the opportunities of reaching a growing readership by means of serial publication. *Bleak House, Great Expectations* and *Our Mutual Friend* are not masterpieces in spite of the mass production of literature in mid-Victorian Britain; they are masterpieces because of the means of production available to Dickens at that time.
16. F. Scott Fitzgerald, *The Last Tycoon*, op. cit., pp. 277–78.
17. Ibid., p. 278.
18. Quoted in John Robert Columbo (ed.), *Wit and Wisdom of the Moviemakers* (London: Hamlyn, 1979), p. 116.
19. C. W. E. Bigsby, 'The Two Identities of F. Scott Fitzgerald' in Malcolm Bradbury and David Palmer (eds.), *The American Novel and the Nineteen Twenties* (London: Edward Arnold, 1971), pp. 142 ff.
20. The case is persuasively argued by C. W. E. Bigsby, see 'The Two Identities of F. Scott Fitzgerald', ibid., pp. 14 ff.
21. *The Last Tycoon*, op. cit., p. 178.
22. *The Last Tycoon*, ibid., pp. 278–79.
23. Ibid., p. 211.
24. Ibid., p. 213.
25. Ibid., pp. 216–17.
26. Ibid., pp. 303–8.
27. Charles E. Shain, 'F. Scott Fitzgerald', in *Seven Modern American Novelists: An Introduction*, edited by William Van O'Connor (Minneapolis: University of Minnesota Press, 1964), p. 116.
28. Quoted in *The Bodley Head Scott Fitzgerald*, op. cit., p. 7.

5

'All Very Rich and Sad': A Decade of Fitzgerald Short Stories[1]

by HERBIE BUTTERFIELD

'The ten-year period that, as if reluctant to die outmoded in its bed, leaped to a spectacular death in October, 1929, began about the time of the May Day riot in 1919', wrote Fitzgerald, retrospectively, in November 1931.[2] He thought of that span of time as the Jazz Age, and more than any other writer, more than any other person perhaps, he is popularly identified with the period flavour (although it should be said that he had no ear for jazz and no respect for black culture generally). Literary celebrity in those years came to him chiefly through his novels, of course, but the larger readership must have been of his short stories, of which up till the end of 1930 he had published more than seventy,[3] in various magazines but especially and for a time exclusively in the *Saturday Evening Post*. Many of these are slight, hasty, or formulaic stuff,[4] but a few must rank with the finest of American short stories; and precisely ten I have found to stand out, to represent his best work in the genre from that decade,[5] and as a group to take their place alongside *The Great Gatsby* and *Tender is the Night* as the third peak of his literary achievement.

Like the two great novels, these stories together chart the course of that decade, as Fitzgerald, both a deeply involved participant and a highly judgemental observer, experienced it. Indeed, one of the earliest, 'May Day', is set on the very day that Fitzgerald singled out as the symbolic beginning of the era, 'when the police rode down the demobilized country boys gaping at the orators in Madison Square', which 'was the sort of measure bound to alienate the more intelligent young from the prevailing order'[6]; while the last to be written, 'Babylon Revisited', has as its imaginative fulcrum that financial crash in which the age so 'spectacularly' died. In kind they range from fantasies, reminiscent both of Poe's Arabesques and Hawthorne's allegories ('The Diamond as Big as the Ritz') to Joycean epiphanies ('Absolution') to Jamesian nouvelles ('The Rich Boy'); in verbal texture from an early tendency to decorative excess to the limpid economy of 'Babylon Revisited'; and in setting from the Middle West where he grew up, to the deep South where he did his army training and courted Zelda, to New York where he found fame, to Paris and fashionable Europe, where he spent and lost more than just his hard-earned money. As for the basic matter of the stories, it may all be discovered and contained in a brief biographical resumé: he was a lapsed Roman Catholic ('Absolution'), whose lineage on his Virginian father's side predisposed him to be youthfully entranced by the legend of the old sleepy time down South ('The Ice Palace', 'The Last of the Belles'); but whose entrepreneurial heritage on his McQuillan mother's side stirred him to be fascinated, albeit critically so, by the world of the rich ('May Day', 'The Diamond as Big as the Ritz', 'Winter Dreams', 'The Rich Boy'); and whose own professional success brought him at least a writer's measure of those riches, enough certainly for him to succumb to the characteristic ills, of conduct and spirit, that beset the rich ('The Rough Crossing', 'One Trip Abroad', 'Babylon Revisited'). But the ten stories are of course more than chronicles of a time or episodes from an auto-biography; they are, at their best, small masterpieces of art and imagination, and they make a critique, all the more searing for its being founded in sympathy, of a nation and its dominant assumptions, its yearnings and aspirations, its prevailing ideology.

'The Ice Palace', written when Fitzgerald was 23 and pub-lished in May 1920,[7] pivots upon the perception of extreme and ultimately irresolvable differences, of which the original and fundamental is that between the American South and the North. The idea for the story was apparently Zelda's,[8] but its power, remarkable despite the too artificial symmetry of its design, must derive from its enactment of the profound division within Fitzgerald himself, at once a child of the 'energetic' North and of the 'lazy' South, which imaginatively he favoured.[9] The Southern town here is Tarleton, Georgia—Zelda's Montgomery, Alabama, presumably, as much as anywhere else; the Northern city is coldly anonymous, but a version surely of St. Paul, Minnesota. The emblem of the South is the girl, 19-year-old Sally Carrol Happer, wholly identified with the South but attracted by 'a sort of energy' within her to the North, whose embodiment is her fiancé, Harry Bellamy. The South is all somnolence, elegance, memory, and melancholy. When we meet Sally Carrol she is gazing down 'sleepily . . . with a pleased and pleasant langour', in this town that is a 'languid paradise of dreamy skies and firefly evenings and noisy niggery street fairs', a place of 'drowsy picturesqueness', inhabited by 'gracious, soft-voiced girls, who were brought up on memories instead of money'. Facing backwards into the past, Sally Carrol has as 'one of her favourite haunts, the cemetry'; but her haunting there is not altogether morbid and Gothic, it being also to establish a temporal continuum, a flow of past into present, a bond between the dead and the living. 'Even when I cry I'm happy here, and I get a sort of strength from it.' For this is a world (idyllic, of course, not actual) of connections, of organic relationships, where 'over the trees and shacks and muddy rivers, flowed the heat, never hostile, only comforting, like a great warm nourishing bosom for the infant earth.'[10] 'Down from his Northern city', Harry enters abruptly, 'tall, broad, and brisk'. Not for him mellow reverie or musing retrospect. 'Are you mournful by nature, Harry?' 'Not I.'

If it's summer in the South, according to the story's pattern of oppositions it must be winter in the North, when Sally Carrol travels there in the Pullman, with the cold creeping in everywhere, and outside the prospect of 'a solitary farmhouse . . . ugly and bleak and lone in the white waste'. The differences are multiple and pervasive. For instance, the furnishings in the Bellamy household are mostly new and expensive, conjuring up in contrast for Sally Carrol 'an instantaneous vision of the battered old library at home'. Harry Bellamy explains: 'You Southerners put quite an emphasis on family, and all that . . . [Here] everybody has a father, and about half of us have grandfathers. Back of that we don't go.' Where the South is courtly, feminine, and, in Sally Carrol's word, 'feline', the North is bourgeois, 'a man's country', and 'canine'. The culmination of Sally Carrol's increasingly disenchanted Northern experience is the visit to the ice palace, an immense, fantastical construction out of blocks of ice, both a triumph of architectural engineering, whose proportions Harry tediously enumerates, and a symbol, in its very nature, of all that is ephemeral. When its blaze of electric lights goes out, Sally Carrol is left, confused, lost, likely to freeze to death, and terrified. Her terror, however, seems to be less of simply dying, than of dying here, 'frozen, heart, body, and soul', unable to be returned, earth to earth, in a place, such as her warm Southern cemetery, where flesh and soil more readily mingle.

Rescued, in her delirium she screams only: 'I want to get out of here! I'm going back home'; and we last see her in a brief tableau, again gazing sleepily at a Southern boy coming in his 'ancient Ford' to take her swimming in water 'warm as a kettla steam', under a sky whose 'wealth of golden sunlight poured a quite enervating yet oddly comforting heat'. She has recoiled from, rejected, the North; and, in addition to its climate and location, the North is, effectively and essentially, the culture of industrial capitalism, characterized by qualities cold rather than warm, by power rather than affection, efficiency rather than sentiment, severance rather than connectedness, ephemerality rather than continuity, the ice palace where 'all tears freeze' rather than the cemetery where 'even when I cry I'm happy.'

With its series of coincidentally overlapping stories, 'May Day', which was written soon after 'The Ice Palace',[11] seems to belong to an indeterminate genre; in its length and number of viewpoints it is more than a short story, yet not quite a short novel, nor formally James's 'beautiful and blessed nouvelle'. It is the most naturalistic of his shorter works, evidence of the fact that he had by this time read and admired Dreiser and Frank Norris. The events of the story begin exactly 'at nine o'clock on the morning of the first of May, 1919', to conclude barely twenty-four hours later, yet the story proper is preceded by an introduction that has the character and is in the generalized time of the folk-tale or parable: the contemporary events we are to witness are but the latest shapes of ancient injustice and recurrent wrong.

The principal elements that are drawn together in this neatly co-ordinated story are the recently demobilized soldiery, the socialist opposition, the unfortunate and impoverished, and of course the rich. The soldiers are typically illiterate, drunken, spasmodically violent, and mindlessly mobbish. They are portrayed, if not with sympathy, at least with pity for their poverty and hunger, despised and discarded as they are, 'finding the great city thoroughly fed up with soldiers unless they were nicely massed into pretty uniforms under the weight of a pack and rifle'.[12] And it must be on Fitzgerald's part in some sort of act of solidarity with their plight, as some expression of moral allegiance, that he gives to one of them his own family name of Key, 'a name hinting that in his veins, however thinly diluted by generations of degeneration, ran blood of some potentiality'. Key dies in a ludicrous accident, falling from a window while smashing up the offices of a socialist paper, which is edited by Henry Bradin, the idealist who seeks 'the latest cures for incurable evils', and whose legs are broken in the same fracas. We have come upon Bradin via his sister Edith, very much a socialite rather than a socialist, the former flame of Gordon Sterrett, a Yale graduate, full of artistic talent and promise, but down on his luck and now entangled in a relationship that is all unromantic reality, complicated, squalid, and touched by blackmail. Gordon needs money, desperately, and for a loan seeks out his college-friend, Philip Dean, who for this story represents the rich man, here un-redeemed by any splendour of imagination, merely complacent, hard-hearted, meanly calculating, grossly self-indulgent, and self-righteously reproving:

> 'You seem to be sort of bankrupt—morally as well as financially. . . . There's a regular aura about you that I don't understand. It's a sort of evil.'
> 'It's an air of worry and poverty and sleepless nights', said Gordon, rather defiantly.

But his is a small ration of defiance, and the story ends with this soft and sensitive man's suicide, while the boorish, overweening Philip cavorts in a drunken oblivion. The socialist, a marginal figure at best, is in hospital, broken by those he would strengthen; the cast-off warrior is dead, and the failed artist and foolish lover too. Only the rich survive intact, gambolling and gallivanting on May Day. In its connections, implicit and explicit, in its perception of a wholly interlocking society, 'May Day' is very much a political story, but also a very pessimistic one. 'The events of 1919', observed Fitzgerald many years later, 'left us cynical rather than revolutionary'.[13]

The rich in 'May Day', gathered at the Yale Club and Delmonico's are rich by inheritance; and their riches are simply what they have grown up accustomed to and have never been for them the fabulous stuff of dreams. There is no magic in 'May Day', as there will be magic in *The Great Gatsby*, for instance. Nor is there magic in the quintessentially entitled 'The Rich Boy', though its opening section contains the famous sentences, which Hemingway thought he lampooned: 'Let me tell you about the very rich. They are different from you and me.' Written and published some five years after 'May Day',[14] 'The Rich Boy', which traces Anson Hunter's early life until the age of 29, is more truly a nouvelle than the earlier work. It is also a study, not one of Fitzgerald's fables; but a singular study, not a sociology: 'There are no types, no plurals. There is a rich boy, and this is his and not his brother's story.' Even so, we know that this rich boy's is an exemplary tale.

And what is exemplified first is the supreme self-assurance and self-assumed superiority of one born not only to great wealth but also to an established and elevated social station. Anson's father 'was a man somewhat superior to his class, which composed New York society, and to his period which was the snobbish and formalized vulgarity of the Gilded Age'. He is evidently a figure out of the pages of Edith Wharton, who bequeaths to his son, living in Fitzgerald's pages, the comfortable knowledge that 'this was his city . . . where his name had flourished through five generations'. He has the extraordinary luxury of being rich as an American and *haut* as a European; he is a member of a small, very particular tribe: the old Eastern rich.

99

There is nothing especially vicious about Anson, and early on at least he is capable of love and tears. But gradually his wealth chills and hardens and shrinks him, until he is at best letting others do the living for him (taking 'a vicarious pleasure in happy marriages'), and at worst casually destroying trust ('Dolly Karger, lying awake and staring at the ceiling, never again believed in anything at all') and purposefully creating the circumstances that drive another man to suicide, for his part in which human disaster he 'never blamed himself'. He fends off any self-questioning, comes to let nothing touch him deeply, fully reach him. At 29 he is something of a beached shell, dry, deserted, around New York society displaced by arrivistes, indeed a hollow man in a waste land[15]; but, as he sails world-wearily for a summer in Europe he still has charm and desire enough for a mildly revivifying shipboard romance. Such affairs, the measured, ironic narrator observes,

> perhaps . . . promised that there would always be women in the world who would spend their brightest, freshest, rarest hours to nurse and protect that superiority he cherished in his heart.

'The Rich Boy' is less pathetic and less catastrophic than many of Fitzgerald's tales of life amongst the rich, but it is in many respects bleaker and morally more devastating, with its last glimpse of a superior young man, trying to shore up the walls within which he may continue to immure himself in a numbed and sterile solipsism.

According to Hawthorne's differentiation of the Novel from the Romance, 'May Day' and 'The Rich Boy' in their social and psychological realism belong, their lack of length apart, within the order of the Novel. In contrast, 'The Diamond as Big as the Ritz', which had been written in the Autumn of 1921, is entirely a Romance, or a Fantasy as Fitzgerald himself categorized it for its inclusion in *Tales of the Jazz Age*[16]; from which it should not be inferred that its principal intent is anything other than symbolically to uncover the hidden, dangerous, and altogether real power in the hands of the very rich, those who hold the world's purse-strings.

John T. Unger comes from 'a small town on the Mississippi', Hades, not to be 'confused with another place that was abolished long ago', Twain's world surely, of boosters and suckers and hoaxers and con-men and Tall-Tale-tellers. Sent back East to St. Midas's School to learn a knowledge of priorities, he befriends Percy Washington, whose father is simply 'by far the richest man in the world', and is invited to spend a holiday with him at his home 'in the West'. Out there in the Montana Rockies there is revealed to him what is indeed a religious vision for one who 'has the earnest worship of and respect for riches as the first article of [his] creed'. The Washington estate, an uncharted El Dorado in a mountain stronghold, is a paradise of infinite riches, and the home a fabulous castle 'in a sort of floating fairyland', a dream of oriental magnificence translated to the occident, which Fitzgerald delineates in a tour de force of exotic description and extravagant detail.

The source of this immeasurable wealth is the mountain itself, 'literally nothing else but solid diamond . . . bigger than the Ritz-Carlton hotel', which Percy's grandfather, FitzNorman Washington,[17] had stumbled upon by accident. The Washingtons and their experience are to be taken as archetypally American. They are descended from the first national hero and president, and also, so that catholics may not feel excluded from the heritage, from the Roman Catholic founder of Maryland, Lord Baltimore. The fortune stems from sheer chance, as in many a gold and oil strike. The smooth running of affairs requires an ignorant, complaisant, and uncritical work-force (here a line of black slaves who do not realize that the Civil War is over). And the place is the West, whither vast wealth progressively, boundlessly, moves. Bribery, general corruption, all manner of falsification, misapplication of science, and murder have been amongst the methods by which FitzNorman and his son Braddock have preserved their riches, the secret of the amount of those riches and their origins, and ultimately their control of the world economy. For Braddock Washington now is not just the richest man in the world but its absolute monarch, even if unknown to his subjects, the 'Emperor of Diamonds, king and priest of the age of gold'. When finally the world breaks through and threatens his kingdom, it is 'not in suppliance, but in pride' that, 'magnificently mad', he addresses God as an equal, offering Him a bribe to turn back time, unable to believe that anything in the Universe, even its creator, is beyond price. But

God, with 'a mutter of dull, menacing thunder, . . . refused to accept the bribe'. Whereupon, with dynamite, not yet nuclear weapons, Braddock Washington blows up his world, leaving John T. Unger (in the company of Braddock's two daughters, whose sentimental sideshow has rightly not detained us) to 'escape to tell thee', like Ishmael escaping from that other world-destroying megalomaniac. Fabulously opulent as William Randolph Hearst, fabulously secretive as Howard Hughes, Braddock Washington, with his wealth and his power, is no figure of fantasy.

The Great Gatsby partakes of both the romance of 'The Diamond as Big as the Ritz' and the realism of 'The Rich Boy', but its closest affinity is with 'Winter Dreams',[18] which is in important respects the seed-bed of the novel. For Jimmy Gatz, not yet Jay Gatsby, digging clams on the shore of Lake Superior, read Dexter Green, caddying on the golf-course in Black Bear; for Daisy Buchanan, read Judy Jones, whose voice (like Daisy's 'full of money'), whose smile, and not least whose tantrums, at the age of mere 11, enthrall Dexter, himself 'not yet fourteen', so that abruptly he changes the shape of his young life, 'unconsciously dictated to by his winter dreams'. The girl, with her style born of money, composes an image of another world, beyond present reach, beyond hope of immediate entry, but not beyond dream and aspiration. So over the next few years, Dexter acquires first a preliminary social undercoat at 'a famous university in the East', and then, almost effortlessly, 'he made money. It was amazing.'

Now he meets Judy again, if not as her equal, at least self-confident in the knowledge that he is 'the rough, strong stuff from which [the rich, her kind] eternally sprang'; poetical rough stuff, though, enchanted by 'the sound of a piano over a stretch of water', and of course enchanted by Judy, a spoiled child, playful and fanciful, 'entertained only by the gratification of her desires and by the direct exercise of her own charm'. In their intermittent involvement that follows, blown hot and cold at Judy's whim, they hurt others and they hurt themselves, twisting in 'webs of tangled emotions'. He comes to know 'deep happiness', and he comes to know 'deep pain', for their romance is as marvellous as their relationship is impossible. Then she ends it. Seven years later he hears of her again, a faded beauty now, by no means wretched, but married, as Daisy will be, to a man who 'drinks and runs around'. Her ordinary, slightly sad, slightly shabby fortune rings a death-knell for him; it signals the loss of a certain kind of vision, of a sense of possibility, of a glow around the edge of things. 'Even the grief he could have borne was left behind in the country of illusion, of youth, of the richness of life, where his winter dreams had flourished.' A tale eventually of disenchantment and dis-illusionment, 'Winter Dreams' is nevertheless as affecting as it is precisely because of the conviction with which Fitzgerald casts the earlier spell of enchantment and conducts the play of illusion, a hint of the triumph to come.

'Absolution' also has a connection with *The Great Gatsby*, being a reworking of a discarded opening to the novel.[19] Of all Fitzgerald's works, it is the one most concentrated upon Roman Catholicism, although it would seem to be less closely auto-biographical than many of his other stories. It is a tale of release, of escape from a markedly puritanical version of the faith, and of entry into the life of the world. To one side is the church, requiring denial of appetite and desire, and dominating through fear; to the other is the world, warm and natural and sensual by day, bright and artificial and glamorous by night. In the middle, as he feels it, is Rudolph Miller, 'a beautiful, intense little boy of eleven', who has already felt 'a strange, romantic excitement' on overhearing 'immodest things' spoken of between a boy and a girl, yet who, fumbling in the confessional and inadvertently telling a lie, is still gripped by a terror of God's supernatural power. The priest to whom he confesses, in this small town in the prairie heartlands, is Father Schwartz, who from 'cold, watery eyes' shed cold tears, 'because the afternoons were warm and long, and he was unable to attain a complete mystical union with our Lord'. And there is Rudolph's father, Carl, a dim, drab man, but a zealous all-American catholic, whose 'two bonds with the colourful life were his faith in the Roman Catholic Church and his mystical worship of the Empire Builder, James J. Hill', and who beats his son with 'savage ferocity' to force him to go to Communion, when the son, unbeknown to the father, is in a state of sin. But the heavens do not fall, God does not pitch him into hell-fire; and Rudolph, carrying his mortal sin quite lightly, returns to make one last confession to Father Schwartz. And there before his eyes, the old priest, cracking apart under the strain of years of repressed longings and 'unclean thoughts' and self-thwarting, goes frighteningly, blatheringly mad, chattering to the little boy of crowds and parties and amusement parks, full of 'the heat and the sweat and the life', and the 'glitter' and, many times, the 'glimmering' of things—all the light and movement of the world, of which his faith has deprived him. As he collapses, in nervous exhaustion and hysterical laughter, bringing down his faith with him, Rudolph runs from the priest's house, runs from the church, into the arms of the world, ready for its romance and sensuous magic, having discovered that 'there was something ineffably gorgeous that had nothing to do with God.' Heaven will be a different place from now on, more worldly, more American, though no less heavenly and no more tangible; and Rudolph may begin to dream of golden girls and fairy riches, and metamorphose into Jay Gatsby.[20]

If in 'Absolution' Fitzgerald, in the guise of Rudolph Miller, walks away from the Roman Catholic Church, of which his mother in particular was a devout member, so in 'The Last of the Belles' he bids farewell to the South, emptying his heart of the mystique that his father had inculcated in him. Written in November 1928,[21] by which time relations between Scott and Zelda were deteriorating, it may also reflect the fact that by now his own Southern Belle appeared very much as a real person rather than a romantic ideal. Apart from 'The Rich Boy', whose narrator is peripheral and spectatorial, it is the only one of these ten stories to be told in the first person by one who is very much a participant.

It is set, like 'The Ice Palace', in Tarleton, Georgia, at the time of the First World War, and features again, though here as a secondary character, Sally Carrol Happer. On centre stage is her friend, the last of the belles, Ailee Calhoun, her 'lovely name' an echoing symbol of the old ante-bellum South, as she in herself is symbolic, 'the Southern type in all its purity', with 'notes in her voice that ordered slaves around, that withered Yankee captains'.

But already she has one foot in the real, modern world, where she overdoes her make-up, putting 'too much fever-coloured rouge on her face'; she is transmogrifying herself into the contemporary form of the flirt, or more specifically the flapper. With the officers' training camp nearby, she is surrounded by suitors, though, properly, sentimentally dynastic, she will marry only a man who 'measures up' to 'her brother who had died in his senior year at Yale'. One suitor, to her barely disguised thrill, kills himself in unrequited love of her; another, a Harvard man who might well 'measure up', seems to be leading the field, until the arrival in camp of Lieutenant Earl Schoen from New Bedford. Schoen certainly does not 'measure up'; promoted from the ranks, he does not come 'out of any background at all', and Ailee immediately spots him as a street-car conductor. Yet he is 'as fine a physical specimen as I have ever seen', and in his uniform, 'high-tempered and commanding'. He is as sexually alluring as, for Ailee, he is socially, sportively tantalizing, and, taking him off another girl, she begins an affair with him that belongs to the genre of wartime, or holiday, romance. Inevitably, after the war, out of uniform, dressed now according to his vulgar individuality, he appears to Ailee quite impossible. ' "Well, that's the end of it", he said moodily'; and on the train back North turned his attention to another girl, another 'jane'. And there for the time being the story ends, with Ailee, having played the wrong cards, bereft of all her suitors. There is a sequel, six years later, when the narrator, Andy, returns nostalgically to Tarleton and, meeting Ailee, thinks he discovers he has always been 'deeply and incurably in love with her'. But she is pledged now to a fellow-Southerner, in whom, unlike in a Northerner, she can feel secure, about whom she cannot be mistaken. Making one last visit to the site of the training camp, of which not a vestige remains, Andy shakes off the Southern spell:

> All I could be sure of was this place that had once been so full of life and effort was gone, as if it had never existed, and that in another month Ailee would be gone, and the South would be empty for me for ever.

'The Last of the Belles' is Fitzgerald's latest improvization on his major theme of disenchantment, of awakening in sour dawns from sweet dreams.

After this story of loss, with its diminuendo closure, Fitzgerald a few months later wrote 'The Rough Crossing',[22] all tumult and crescendo, with a hesitant and pointedly unresolving coda. It is set on a transatlantic liner sailing from New York to Le Havre and meeting in mid-ocean with a hurricane, and it begins with a marvellous evocation of departure, the confusion, the excitement, the awe, 'when the past, the continent, is behind you; the future is that glowing mouth in the side of the ship'. Into that glowing mouth pass, with their children and their children's nurse, Adrian and Eva Smith, specifically a successful young playwright and his wife, but generally Adam and Eve Everyman we are surely invited to infer. The ship in which they sail will become a ship of fools, and the voyage, at the extremity of the storm's delirium, something of a dance of death. Personal emotion and the impersonal elements pace each other through the story, skilfully plotted on parallel courses. For Adrian Smith, somewhat jaded with wealth and fame, there will be, as the storm rises and exhilarates his blood, a hectic, restorative 'affaire' with a young girl whose 'youth seemed to flow into him, bearing him up into a delicate romantic ecstasy that transcended passion'. For Eva, untranscendently and comprehensively seasick, yet with enough awareness of things to be also comprehensively infuriated, there will be a different kind of ecstasy, a midnight drama of the self, as she ranges the ship in a fever of alcohol and jealousy. Eventually, climactically, at the height of the hurricane, she and Adrian, embodiments of nervous excess and emotional indulgence, are flung into one another's arms by wind and wave, and clinging together for the sake of their lives manage—this time—just—to survive. Meanwhile, as above deck the rich have disported themselves or plaintively suffered their bouts of seasickness, below the ship's doctor and nurse have all the time been trying and at length failing to save the life of a young steward. Coming upon him taken ill in her cabin, Eva, absorbed in her own mild biliousness, had groaned, ' "It made me sick to look at him. I wish he'd die" ', although she does have grace enough later to regret these words. His funeral, even in the midst of the hurricane, is conducted with due order and dignity. It is a British ship, and the funeral was all 'very British and sad'. 'The Rough Crossing' is a story in the best tradition of American self-criticism and self-admonition, as it extends back through James to Cooper: these rich making such a distasteful, disorderly and undignified show of themselves are also, exclusively, these Americans. It is in all a thoroughly ominous story, permeated by a sense of engulfing disasters, individual and communal, to come.

The two remaining stories of my group of ten were both written in 1930, after the Wall Street Crash of the preceding October and at a time when the Fitzgeralds' marriage, now of ten years' duration, was about as steady and as promising as the national economy. Over the past few years, which they had spent mainly in France—in Paris and on the Riviera—Scott's drinking had become increasingly uncontrolled, and Zelda's nervous health, also under alcoholic pressure, had finally collapsed in April 1930, when she entered a clinic in Switzerland with a severe breakdown. Together with the portentous 'The Rough Crossing', the stories of this time reflect, literally or symbolically, the experiences both of the Fitzgeralds personally and of the American nation, experiences which Fitzgerald felt to be significantly entwined.

If 'Winter Dreams' was a jotting for *The Great Gatsby*, 'One Trip Abroad'[23] is even more clearly a sketch for *Tender is the Night*. The story's Nelson Kelly will emerge, fully portrayed, as Dick Diver; his wife is already forenamed Nicole. A rich young American couple, they are making their way around the old world, North Africa first, where they 'survive a plague' of locusts, as they may not in their travels survive a less natural, more social plague. It is here that they first come across another young couple, Mr. and Mrs. Liddell Miles, personifications of blasé aloofness and posturing world-weariness, opining that 'every place is the same. The only thing that matters is who's there.' In Sorrento they dabble in the arts, drink too much, and offend the English. (Where Fitzgerald's Americans are subtly and importantly discriminated, his English are caricatures: the unlikely figure of a cockney airman, and a choleric general and his choleric wife.) By Monte Carlo Nicole is being lightly reproved by a well-wisher for wasting her time with 'that crowd of drunks you run with';

> 'Well, then, where are the amusing people', she asked impatiently.
> 'Off by themselves somewhere. . . .'

In Paris they descend further into pathos and ridicule when, as representative Americans, they are spectacularly bamboozled, publically taken for a ride, 'ripped off' as we would now say, by a sophisticated Europe, in the masquerading shape of a Count. And everywhere they go, mysteriously they catch a glimpse of the Mileses. At length, alcoholically and nervously deranged, they seek refuge in Switzerland, pitiably self-questioning: 'Why did we lose peace and love and health, one after the other?' So it seems have the Mileses, for they too are here, he looking 'weak and self-indulgent', she with 'eyes, intelligent enough, but with no peace in them'. One wild night, as the storm is lifting, Nelson and Nicole wander out into the garden of their hotel, where a late flash of lightning draws from Nicole 'a sharp, terrified cry'. For in that moment of illumination, of piercing insight, she sees in the garden the Mileses yet again and knows them, in all their spiritual sickness and vacancy, to be their döppelgangers: 'They're us! They're us! Don't you see?' It is a powerful and entirely convincing effect, and for Fitzgerald in the writing painfully and unflinchingly self-revealing.

In the last month of that year of breakdown and disintegration, Fitzgerald wrote 'Babylon Revisited',[24] an exceptionally, exquisitely poignant story, told with a fine simplicity of means, his best story I think. It is Fitzgerald's definitive review both of his and Zelda's expatriate years and of the American 1920s and their collapse. Charlie Wales, now working in Prague, returns to Paris after eighteen months' absence—long, long ago, it feels, in part because so much has changed, and in part because Fitzgerald's sense of past time is always long-focused and essentially nostalgic. The American era, the American occupation is over. Financially triumphant, 'we were a sort of royalty, almost infallible, with a sort of magic around us'; but now the court is deserted:

> The stillness in the Ritz bar was strange and portentous. It was not an American bar any more—he felt polite in it, and not as if he owned it. It had gone back into France.

Those royal days had been lavish and extravagant—and ephemeral:

> He thought, 'I spoiled this city for myself. I didn't realize it, but the days came along one after another, and then two years were gone, and everything was gone, and I was gone.'

Now he wishes to reassert something more austere and traditional; perhaps the true republican America: 'He believed in character;

he wanted to jump back a whole generation and trust in character again as the eternally valuable element.'

Charlie Wales is here back in Paris, hoping to be reunited
with his 9-year-old daughter Honoria. Her mother, Helen, has
died amidst the alcoholic delirium of the age of royalty, and
Honoria lives now under the legal guardianship of Helen's
sister, Marion Peters, who with a cold, level hatred blames
Charlie for Helen's death and for most other things too. But
Charlie has worked hard on himself, rigorously controlled his
drinking, and set his heart, for Helen's sake too and in her
memory, on making a home with and for Honoria. It begins to
seem that his quest will be successful and that even a reluctant
Marion may be agreeable, until Nemesis falls upon him from a
great height in the shape of two drunken friends from the past
who invade the Peters's house, sickening and shocking Marion,
and reconfirming her in her opinion of Charlie. Defeated by
these circumstances and now again rebuffed by Marion, he
must pay for and be seen to pay for the human damage of the
careless years. It is a moral matter, Fitzgerald knows, before
and after it is financial. It was not in the crash that Charlie
Wales had lost. No,

> 'I lost everything in the boom.'
> 'Selling short.'
> 'Something like that.'

Yet, for all the further sentence of loneliness, he is newly
resolute and by that resolve self-confident. 'He would come
back some day; they couldn't make him pay forever. . . . He
wanted his child, and nothing was much good now, beside that
fact.' It is a sad ending, of course, but a far less depressing
ending than those to all the other stories we have read about the
lives of the American rich, for it ends with an understanding of
and a commitment to, not romance, but love.

These stories that have opened, followed and closed a
peculiarly compact decade ensure Fitzgerald's place amongst the
foremost American practitioners of the genre of the short story.
At the same time, since they do not offer in their formal shapes
and characters the very highest level of aesthetic satisfaction,
they do not put him quite in the company of the outstanding
masters of the form amongst his immediate predecessors and

contemporaries, whom I take to be, in the English language, James, Kipling, Conrad, Joyce, Lawrence and Hemingway. Only 'Babylon Revisited', in its emotional concentration and in its rare fusion of intensity and reticence, is a story to rank with the very few and finest.

Nevertheless, not having read some of these stories before and not having read others for some time, I have been surprised to discover how good these ten are. The voice is at once awed (in the tradition of wonder and enthusiasm) and ironic (in the tradition of discrimination and judgement); and the style is at once sumptuous and melancholy, and always marvellously cadenced, as if his adored Keats had been translated through time and space and literary form to ode in story the American 1920s. And as for their substance, what a highly charged and well founded critique they provide of the world of the rich, or of the adventures of the capitalist economy, flourishing and floundering by turns, setting up and incidentally casting off its human elements. (It is a critique conducted, it seems to me, from midway between the wistfully patrician standpoint of John Peale Bishop and the panoramic Marxism, incipient in the late 1920s, of Fitzgerald's other closest literary friend at Princeton, Edmund Wilson.) The critique is all the more telling because it is regularly also a self-criticism, or stems from a self-criticism, oblique but severe; and in being of such a kind it is thereby able to demonstrate all the more effectively the attraction and allure of that money-making, money-mesmerized ethos.[25]

NOTES

1. The phrase is taken from the short story, 'The Last of the Belles', considered here.
2. 'Echoes of the Jazz Age'.
3. 72 is my rough count from Fitzgerald's ledger, included as Appendix 2 in Matthew J. Bruccoli, *Some Sort of Epic Grandeur: The Life of F. Scott Fitzgerald* (London: Hodder & Stoughton, 1981).
4. I have not read them all, but enough of those I have read, as they are collected in The Bodley Head (1963) and Penguin (1986) volumes, deserve to be characterized in such a way.
5. And not only from that decade; I find few, if any, that he was to write in the following years to set beside these ten.

6. 'Echoes of the Jazz Age'.
7. It was published in the *Saturday Evening Post* and later in the volume of short stories, *Flappers and Philosophers* (1920). It is not included in the Penguin *Collected Short Stories*, but may be found in The Bodley Head *Scott Fitzgerald*, Vol. V.
8. André Le Vot, *F. Scott Fitzgerald: a Biography* (London: Allen Lane, 1984), p. 65.
9. Brian Way, *F. Scott Fitzgerald and the Art of Social Fiction* (London: Edward Arnold, 1980), p. 7, comments on this 'lifelong preference for the defeated South in the Civil War, fed both by boyhood reading and family memories'.
10. It occurs to me how similar, in preliminary outline, are the basic assumptions of 'The Ice Palace' to those that John Crowe Ransom, Allen Tate, Donald Davidson and others would shortly be weaving into an elaborate tapestry of cultural values; and we may remember also that Fitzgerald's earliest literary friend and mentor at Princeton was John Peale Bishop.
11. In March 1920. It was published in *The Smart Set* in July of that year and later in the volume of short stories, *Tales of the Jazz Age*, 1922. See Bodley Head, Vol. V, and the Penguin collection.
12. They are surely the American cousins of Kipling's 'Tommy';

    'For it's Tommy this, an' Tommy that, an' "Chuck him out, the brute"!
    But it's "Saviour of 'is country" when the guns begin to shoot'.

13. 'Echoes of the Jazz Age'.
14. Written between February and July 1925, 'The Rich Boy' was published in *The Red Book* in early 1926 and later in the volume of stories, *All the Sad Young Men* (1926). See Bodley Head, Vol. V, and the Penguin collection.
15. The descriptive figure allows me to recall that Eliot was by some way Fitzgerald's favourite contemporary poet.
16. First published in *The Smart Set* in June 1922. See Bodley Head, Vol. V, and the Penguin collection.
17. Note the element of ironic, tangential self-association that led Fitzgerald to name the grandfather FitzNorman.
18. Written in September 1922, published in *Metropolitan* in December of that year and later in *All the Sad Young Men*. See Bodley Head, Vol. V, and the Penguin collection.
19. First published in the *American Mercury* in June 1924, then in *All the Sad Young Men*. See Bodley Head, Vol. V, and the Penguin collection.
20. Henry James's archetypal American boy is of course Randolph Miller, younger brother of Daisy. Did Fitzgerald intend a connection to be made with his Rudolph Miller?
21. Published in the *Saturday Evening Post* in March 1929 and later in the volume of stories, *Taps at Reveille*, 1935. See Bodley Head, Vol. V and the Penguin collection.
22. In March 1929, published in the *Saturday Evening Post* the following June. See Bodley Head, Vol. V, and the Penguin collection.
23. Written August 1930, and published in the *Saturday Evening Post* in October, not collected by Fitzgerald in book form. See Bodley Head, Vol. VI.

24. Published in February 1931, in the *Saturday Evening Post*, later in *Taps at Reveille*. See Bodley Head, Vol. VI, and the Penguin collection.
25. I am not widely familiar with Fitzgerald criticism, and for these purposes have made use mainly of biographical information. But one debt I would wish to acknowledge, that to a good friend, the late Brian Way, whose *F. Scott Fitzgerald and the Art of Social Fiction*, op. cit., strikes me as being an exemplary study of a writer.

6

'Made for—or against—the Trade': The Radicalism of Fitzgerald's *Saturday Evening Post* Love Stories

by BRIAN HARDING

In 1940, looking back over a twenty-year career as a producer of what he called high-priced commercial writing for the magazines, Fitzgerald claimed (in a letter to Zelda) that he had brought 'intelligence and . . . good writing and even . . . radicalism'[1] to his work for the *Saturday Evening Post*. Since no less than sixty-six of his stories appeared in the *Post* between 1920 and 1937, the quality of his work for that magazine is not uniform, but there is no reason to doubt Matthew Bruccoli's judgement that Fitzgerald's commercial writing was 'highly professional'[2] and not just hackwork.

Its 'radicalism', however, is problematic. What Fitzgerald meant by the term becomes clear from the rest of his letter to Zelda. In it he explained that Lorimer (the former editor of the *Post*) had appreciated this quality in his work, whereas the new man (Wesley Stout) was indifferent to literature and published 'almost nothing except escape stories about the brave frontiersmen, etc., or fishing, or football captains—nothing that would even faintly shock or disturb the reactionary bourgeois'. Evidently, then, Fitzgerald imagined that he had been able to

113

'*épater les bourgeois*' in some, at least, of his *Saturday Evening Post* stories, even though they were written to make him money and had, therefore, to confirm middle-class fantasies about the glamorous lifestyle of the very rich.

It may be, of course, that in 1940 Fitzgerald was merely looking for ways to explain his loss of popularity with the magazine-reading public in terms flattering to himself. His 'radicalism', then, would account for his diminished commercial value as a writer. After all, he had written of his own magazine writing in a far less flattering style in 1929, when he told Hemingway that 'the *Post* now pays the old whore $4,000 a screw'.[3] Less withering, but more damaging in its considered self-deprecation, was Fitzgerald's comment on his uncollected magazine stories when, in 1935, he drew up a balance-sheet for a projected posthumous volume of tales. Asking Max Perkins to choose from a list of twenty-four titles (another twenty-nine were listed as 'scrapped'), Fitzgerald said that he had not seen fit to reprint any of them because each had a fault, whether that was sentimentality, weakness of construction, confusing change of pace, or simply that it had been 'too obviously made for the trade'.[4]

Taking Fitzgerald's retrospective comment on his *Post* stories seriously, I shall argue that in some of those on the theme of love and marriage the gestures towards romance that were made 'for the trade' were undercut by ironies of characterization and plot. Matthew Bruccoli's statement that Fitzgerald managed to avoid some editorial proscriptions and frequently modify the obligatory happy ending into the ominously happy ending[5] seems to me accurate, but it does not go far enough. The disparity between what we are allowed to see of character and what is obviously dictated by the machinery of the plot makes for an obvious implausibility that subverts the norms on which the fiction depends. There is, I believe, a tendency towards self-parody in the commercial fiction that has radical implications.

My starting-point is Scott Donaldson's very useful survey of the stories on the theme that Fitzgerald considered his very own: that of 'the unfairness of a poor young man not being able to marry a girl with money'. In his 'Money and Marriage in Fitzgerald's Stories'[6] Donaldson examines the relevant tales

from 'May Day' (1920) to 'The Bridal Party' (1930). Starting
from the observation that love and money became inextricably
entangled in Fitzgerald's mind and in his writing, Donaldson
comes to the conclusion that the stories can be classified as
belonging either to the group that depicts the poor young man
as successful in wooing the rich girl or to the group in which he
is rejected in his quest or subsequently disappointed. The
former group contains the less effective tales, in Donaldson's
opinion, because the 'boy makes money, gets girl' stories lack
conviction; they tend to be overplotted and manipulated (to be
made for the trade, one might say).

While not wishing to dispute Donaldson's value judgements
on individual stories, I intend to challenge his classification of
the stories and, in so doing, to offer an alternative reading of
some of the tales he groups together as less 'effective'. My
contention is that the success or failure of the poor young man
(or woman) in winning the rich and glamorous partner in
marriage is less significant than the treatment of the dream and
the character of the dreamer in each of the tales of love and
marriage. In the 'commercial' stories, Fitzgerald's lack of
concern with authenticity of characterization enabled him to
express his stark recognition of the corruption of the dream at
its source.

'Winter Dreams' was not a *Post* entry; it was published in the
Metropolitan in December 1922. Since Fitzgerald thought
enough of this tale to collect it in *All the Sad Young Men*, he
presumably did not consider it written merely for money.
Consequently, it is a useful touchstone for the other stories that
deal with the dream of love and marriage with the rich,
glamorous partner. Since its author regarded it as 'a sort of first
draft of the Gatsby idea',[7] it is appropriate that the protagonist—
Dexter Green—is a romantic whose dreams can only be
fulfilled in his relationship with the beautiful rich girl with
whom he becomes infatuated. Dexter is not as poor as James
Gatz will be at the beginning of his life, for his father owns the
second-best grocery business in Black Bear, Minnesota. Nevertheless, Dexter's chance encounter with the 11-year-old daughter
of the immensely rich Mr. Mortimer Jones (while Dexter is a
caddy at the exclusive Sherry Island golf club) so exacerbates
his sense of class differences and so wounds his pride (Judy

Jones peremptorily demands his services as caddy) that he begins his rise to riches. The young boy resigns his job at the golf club, passes up a chance to take a business course at his State university, and attends an Ivy League college, even though that means being an outsider there because he is relatively poor. At the time of his next chance meeting with Judy Jones, when she is an irresistible beauty of 20 and he is a rising young businessman of 23, Dexter has an ecstatic experience in which his mood is one of

> intense appreciation, a sense that, for once, he was magnificently attuned to life and that everything about him was radiating a brightness and a glamour he might never know again.[8]

The prose anticipates Nick Carraway's account of Jay Gatsby's sense of wonder, but though Dexter Green is presented to us as a romantic dreamer, he is also clearly portrayed as a calculating young man with his eye on the main chance.

Once he has acquired the 'particular reserve' that his Eastern college gives its alumni as a sort of social passport, Dexter sets about acquiring a fortune. Social graces and poise are not enough—as he realizes—for a man whose mother was a Bohemian peasant and still speaks broken American, so he 'made money'. The narrator announces this fact in one stark phrase and then adds, 'It was rather amazing', though whether it amazed Dexter Green, the rich fathers of less enterprising sons in the city where he makes his fortune, or the narrator himself, is not made clear. In fact, our narrator seems to approve of Dexter's ambitions. He defends the young man from any possible suspicion of snobbery with the unembarrassed assertion that Dexter did not merely want association with glittering things and people—'he wanted the glittering things themselves.' If in this Dexter anticipates the young Gatsby, who will find Daisy desirable because she 'gleams like silver' and because there is money in her voice, at least Gatsby's dreams will be dignified by Carraway's metaphor when we are told that Gatsby had 'committed himself to the following of a grail' and by his apparent indifference to the glittering things he has acquired when they are not associated with his love for Daisy. In 'Winter Dreams', in contrast, we learn that the meteoric rise to riches was due to Dexter's skill in laundering the expensive golfing clothes of the patrons of the club at which he had worked as a caddy. Not only is the process of money-making unheroic, or even servile; the laundry business also connects with Dexter's acute awareness of the importance of clothes for social success. He imagines the young men who have loved Judy Jones before him as men who had entered college 'from the great prep schools with graceful clothes'. Once he has money, it is time for him to 'wear good clothes', so he frequents the best tailors in America. When he is 'fabulously wealthy' and so able to enter the social sphere of the Jones family, Judy appears to him as 'a slender enamelled doll in cloth of gold'.

'Winter Dreams' belongs to Scott Donaldson's category of stories in which the young man is rejected in his quest for the rich girl. Although he is eminently successful in his quest for money, Dexter loses Judy Jones. When he learns years later that she has become a faded beauty, married to a man who does not love her, he also loses 'the country of illusion'. In a mawkish conclusion, the rich Dexter Green laments the loss of 'something' in himself that was associated with the image of the beautiful rich girl, yet the story has left no doubt that his idea of himself has been constructed on the solid base of money. When Judy Jones had asked the newly-rich Dexter 'Who are you, anyhow?', he had replied 'I'm nobody' and then added 'My career is largely a matter of futures'. The financial metaphor—and the identification of self with career—is significant. Though he believes that it is 'beautiful and romantic' to tell Judy Jones that he loves her, after one of her displays of fickleness Dexter puts her behind him 'as he would have crossed a bad account from his books'. He relents enough to jilt the unglamorous Irene Scheerer when Judy favours him again, but—we are told— 'Dexter was at bottom hard-minded.' On the evidence of the story, Dexter is only the creation of his fortune; he has been given no independent character at all. The comparison with *The Great Gatsby* is instructive. When Tom Buchanan feels threatened by a potential rival for Daisy's loyalty he asks 'Who are you, anyhow?' and answers that question himself, defining Gatsby as a bootlegger and gangster. Just before this, Buchanan insults Gatsby by calling him 'Mr. Nobody from Nowhere'. In a sense, of course, Buchanan is right. Gatsby *is* a social nonentity and he *is* an associate of Meyer Wolfsheim and the thugs who sell grain

117

alcohol in drug stores. In a profounder sense than Buchanan could understand, Gatsby is a nobody, a non-entity, because he is an impossible conjunction of adolescent fantasy, adult hoodlum, and Carraway's romantic phrases. In 'Winter Dreams'—as in the obviously commercial love stories—the emptiness of the characters who aspire to win a rich lover is not disguised but is blatant.

When he summarized 'Winter Dreams' for A. W. Brown, the illustrator for the *Metropolitan*, Fitzgerald said, succinctly, that it was the story of 'a poor boy, his rise and his attempts to win a rich girl'.[9] In saying that, he was condensing the narrative to its essential magazine-worthy story stuff and at the same time foregrounding the ambiguous status of the central metaphor: to 'win' a rich girl can sound crudely mercenary rather than romantic. If we read this story in the context of other versions of the money and marriage theme that Fitzgerald produced in the early 1920s, the cumulative effect may well be to demythologize the glamorous rich girl (or boy) much earlier in Fitzgerald's career than we expected. Before turning to the *Post* variations on the theme, I want to look briefly at 'May Day' (1920), since this is an early story on the theme of money—or the lack of it—and the impossibility of loving without it.

'May Day' (1920) is an ambitious experiment in which Fitzgerald attempts to interweave the story of Gordon Sterrett's collapse and suicide with his analysis of the condition of America in 1919. The whole gamut of social class is included, from the very rich, extravagant, self-indulgent Yale men partying at Delmonico's to the moronic common soldiers at the very bottom of society. The physical proximity of the diverse characters is used as a means of bringing the classes into contact, though not into mutual comprehension, so that the ugly, ill-nourished, stupid Rose and Key share the scene with the affluent, pampered, Philip Dean and Peter Himmel when the soldiers blunder into Delmonico's. Fitzgerald uses the setting of Childs' restaurant, Fifty-ninth Street, to provide the occasion for explicit social commentary. The time gap between four o'clock in the morning, when the college boys, débutantes and their hangers-on hilariously crowd the place and eight o'clock, when the poor are there with sleep in their eyes, becomes a metaphor for the gulf between the rich and privileged and the poor and defeated. Money, or the lack of it, is the unifying theme of the various strands of the story. The main protagonist, Gordon Sterrett, announces that dollars damn him. Unable even to exercise his talent as an illustrator when discouraged by his poverty, he declares that moral and financial bankruptcy go together. To prove the point, he is in the clutches of a 'low' woman who has sufficient evidence of his moral bankruptcy to be able to blackmail him into marriage. The confrontation between the destitute and suppliant Sterrett and the wealthy and impatient Philip Dean, his former room mate at Yale, in the latter's rooms at the Biltmore Hotel, is a memorable one. Dean's suspicion, discomfort and—when he realizes that Sterrett is desperate for help and actually begging—his outright contempt and hostility, are vividly portrayed. In contrasting the condition of the two men, Fitzgerald focuses on the clothes of each of them. Sterrett notices a heap of rich, thick shirts littered on the chairs of his friend's room. Acutely embarrassed by his own frayed shirt-cuffs, Gordon picks up one of Dean's shirts and examines its heavy silk, which is yellow with a pale blue stripe. Shirts acquire a fetishistic quality in Fitzgerald's fictions, both novels and short stories. Always an index of wealth and success, the silk shirt becomes a talisman. Characters are judged—and define themselves—by the quality of the shirts they wear and possess in Fitzgerald's tales of social aspiration. Here, the luxuriousness of Philip Dean's clothing is the keynote in a scene that dramatizes his indifference to the fate of his former friend. The point is reinforced by a later visit to Rivers Brothers to buy collars and ties. Dean, who will refuse to lend Sterrett $300 to save him from collapse, buys not one but a dozen neckties.

The Gordon Sterrett of 'May Day' is not one of Fitzgerald's poor young dreamers of romantic dreams in which the beautiful rich girl represents all the glamour of the glittering world. Sterrett does sometimes think of Edith—the rich socialite with whom he spent a romantic evening at the Harrisburg Country Club—but he is obsessed only with his own failure. Noting that the character of Sterrett derived from Frank Norris' Vandover in *Vandover and the Brute*, Robert Sklar argues that his story is merely a thread used to draw together the other elements in the tale.[10] Since, however, the theme is the relationship between love and money, Gordon Sterrett's conviction that nothing fine or even decent is possible to the man condemned to poverty gives his story a central place in the group of tales on that topic.

The first of Fitzgerald's *Saturday Evening Post* stories on this dual theme is 'Myra Meets his Family' (1920), which takes as its material a woman's quest for a rich husband. Though Fitzgerald had a low opinion of this—his second—contribution to the *Post*, as Matthew Bruccoli points out it 'stakes out' the fictional territory that was to become his—that of the Eastern rich.[11] In terms of plot, this is a rather silly and unamusing tale in what is apparently intended to be a hilarious mode. Myra, the husband-and-fortune-hunting protagonist, is insulted and humiliated by Knowleton Whitney, the very rich and eligible bachelor she has schemed to marry, in a farcical episode in which actors grotesquely play his parents in order to frighten her into breaking off their engagement. She gets her revenge by duping Knowleton into a false marriage ceremony and then leaving him to take their honeymoon journey to Chicago alone. Neither character enlists the reader's interest or sympathy and the story reveals nothing about Fitzgerald apart from his premise that where vast wealth is involved marriage is a cruel business.

'The Popular Girl'—published in the *Post* in two instalments in February 1922—is another story for which Fitzgerald had no great enthusiasm, as he confided to Harold Ober. In essence, this too is a tale of a woman's hunt for a rich husband, but the theme is not treated flippantly here, though the happy ending is patently devised 'for the trade'. It tells of Yanci Bowman, who is an 'exquisite little beauty' in the eyes of the members of the country club which she and her father frequent in their Middle Western city. Appearances are everything in this story, for we learn that the Bowmans are the 'handsomest people' in their city and that the father is so conscious of his looks that he devotes his life to exhibiting his handsome profile. Yanci admires her father for his fine appearance and his social graces (he had been a popular Bones man at Yale), but when he dies suddenly, after years of alcoholism, she is left with a pittance and with no resources for making a living. Yanci is 'the popular girl' in the sense that she cannot live without the support of admiring men and the company of gay, amusing girl friends.

Yanci is also in love with glittering things in a way that is more real—because more detailed—to the reader than was Dexter Green's longing. On her annual visits to New York with her father, she had spent her time at fashionable dances and restaurants and had dreamed of what she might have bought 'at Hempel's or Waxe's or Thrumble's', if her father's income had been adequate. She adored New York and 'felt her soul transported with turbulent delight' in the 'gaudy bazaars'[12] of the city. Unable to face the prospect of a meagre existence of genteel poverty, she decides to stake her remaining dollars on a gambit to win a fabulously wealthy husband. In Scott Winfield, an admirer from her days as a popular girl, she finds 'a personification of all the riches and pleasure she craved'. To the now desperate Yanci, he is 'so good-looking . . . and marvelously well-dressed'. In short, Yanci visits New York, where Scott Winfield lives in splendour, and puts on a pretence of being 'popular' in order to get him to propose. In her endeavour to make him think that all New York is at her feet, she invents bogus engagements and spends her afternoons on Park Avenue, where she indulges her fantasy of 'acquiring and acquiring, ceaselessly and without thought of expense', or hides in the cinema, where she rejoices in the beauty of Mae Murray's clothes and furs, her gorgeous hats, her 'short-seeming French shoes'. This sordid story has a 'happy' ending. Scott Winfield has seen through the pretence from the start and is there to forgive, comfort and marry the erring girl just when she faces humiliation and disaster, her last dollar gone.

In this *Post* story on the poor-girl-wins-rich-man theme, there is no hint of idealism to counterbalance the acquisitive, consumerist yearnings of the woman, yet the romantic idealism of the poor young men seeking to win the rich women in Fitzgerald's early fictions can easily be overestimated. Shortly after *The Great Gatsby* was published, Fitzgerald wrote 'Presumption'—a story about a successful pursuit of the rich girl by a once-poor boy. This story seems to have been tailored quite precisely for the commercial magazines (it was published in the *Post* in January 1926).[13] San Juan Chandler is a young man of higher social class than the Dexter Green of 'Winter Dreams'. His father is not rich—he is a retired clergyman in a small Ohio town—but he has a cousin who owns a house at

Culpepper Bay, a fashionable New England resort, and who humiliates her poor relation when he is her guest. Juan has met and fallen in love with the infinitely desirable and fabulously rich Noel Garneau while both were on a dude ranch where casual clothes disguised class differences. When he meets her again at Culpepper Bay, Juan is acutely aware that his clothes are not right and that he is an outsider in the social set where Noel is at home. In an agony of injured self-esteem and jealousy, the young Juan makes a fool of himself and leaves the resort in shame. His embarrassment, agonizing self-consciousness and deep humiliation are vividly portrayed in a story that—up to this point—is authentic and realistic. The plot then revolves around a chance meeting between Juan and Noel's father, in which the latter unwittingly encourages the young man to risk his future in order to get rich quickly and win the rich girl. The rise to riches is, we are told, one of those 'mad, illogical successes' upon whose foundations ninety-nine failures are later reared, but we do not see the failures, only the magical, improbable accumulation of a fortune through a speculative investment in an enterprise that pays Juan 400 per cent in the first year. This 'fairy tale'—as Fitzgerald calls it—is 'too immoral to be told'; it is followed by another: that of 'winning' the rich girl.

Realism survives when the newly-rich Juan discovers that he is still an outsider in the world of the social élite. By the time he is ready (and rich enough) to introduce himself to Noel Garneau again, she is engaged to a man with a 'Harvard-Oxford drawl' whose engagement is announced in the *Boston Evening Transcript*. Though Juan is convinced that he is 'a nobody no longer' and that there is 'something solid behind him' (that is, money), he is met by a wall of family hostility when he attempts to persuade Noel to break off her engagement with Brooks Fish Templeton, the Harvard man, and marry her one true love, that is, himself. The 'presumption' of the title is the presumption of all poor boys who are in love with wealthy girls, in Juan's opinion, and he rejects the label, until finally confronted by an imposingly aristocratic aunt of his beloved, a Mrs. Poindexter, who really *is* somebody: she has a place in the *Social Register* and a five-storey house on a Fifth Avenue corner. The twist to the plot, presumably included to suit the needs of the trade, comes when Juan is at last defeated on receipt of a note from Noel stating that she has never loved the 'intolerable bore' who has been pestering her with his 'presumptuous whining'. Crushed and abject, he then learns that the note was intended for his rival—the 'presumptuous' Harvard alumnus. Since everything the reader has been allowed to see of Juan Chandler after his adolescent humiliation makes him an unmistakable bore and since his assurance that the rich girl must really love him cannot be anything but presumption, the dénouement is so patently false to its own fictional premises that the story has been regarded as a lapse on Fitzgerald's part into a jejune and immature mode, or—as Robert Sklar forcefully puts it[14]—as a capitulation to the requirements of the slick magazines by an author who has returned to short pants after achieving artistic maturity (in *Gatsby*). It is possible, however, that the flagrant implausibility and inconsistency of the story is a deliberately parodic inversion of its own norms.

In the 1920s Fitzgerald wrote a number of stories for the *Post* in which a magician's wand is waved to create instant fortunes and remove class barriers that would otherwise block the way to 'happy' marriages. Yet in some of his *Post* love stories published before the Wall Street Crash there is a clear-eyed recognition that the gulf between the very rich and the poor cannot be bridged by romantic yearnings. One of these—'The Love Boat'—was published in the *Post* in October 1927 and has now been collected in *The Price Was High*. It is the story of three young Harvard men who intrude on a high-school boat trip, disrupt the fun of the obviously working-class youngsters, and flirt with the prettiest girl, a certain Mae Purley who is virtually engaged to Al Fitzpatrick, an ambitious worker at the Hammacker Mills who intends to become shops manager. One of the Harvard men—Bill Frothington—wears 'one of those New England names that are carried with one always' and is destined for a career in banking, but he allows himself to indulge in romantic dreams involving Mae Purley and he visits her in her 'rural slum', a dingy flat where her 'soiled mother' and 'anaemic, beaten' father live in squalor. Though he flirts with Mae, Bill knows 'that it was impossible to marry Mae Purley'. Once she has been driven past his family estate, Mae herself knows that the 'wide acres' of his property will 'lie between them all her life'. Though Bill broaches the possibility of such a marriage in conversation with his mother, he puts up little resistance to her peremptory statement that 'common women are common for life' and therefore Mae would always be impressed 'by cheap and shallow people, by cheap and shallow things'.[15] Bill, therefore, marries one of his own set, after falling 'romantically in love with her' and visits Mae Purley (now Fitzpatrick) eleven years later to find that she is absorbed into her world of upward social mobility: her husband has done so well at the works; they have bought an old barn and improved it to make it worthy of *Home and Country Side* magazine. Everything contributes to the sense of class in a story where the romantic impulse is reduced to an indulgence that has no consequences. There are no heroics here, and no illusions about the conquering power of love when confronted with the walls of caste.

Though it remains an adolescent love story (the hero is only 16 years old), 'Forging Ahead' is the Basil Duke Lee story that most nearly impinges on the fantasy world of the 'boy gets rich, gets girl' theme. Published in the *Post* in March 1929, not long before the Wall Street Slump, it tells of Basil's romantic attachment to a teenage Southern beauty, but it also confronts the young boy with the prospect of poverty when his middle-class family suddenly loses $80,000. Basil's plans to go to Yale are put in jeopardy by the financial disaster. To avoid the indignity of attending the unglamorous State university, he determines to earn his way to Yale. He takes down his Alger books from the shelf, only to find that all his attempts to find work in the real world lead to humiliation and frustration. A labouring job at the Great Northern railroad car shops lasts three days and earns him a pittance, though it costs him his pride and his illusions. At the end of the first half-day, to his surprise

> The president's little daughter had not come by, dragged by a runaway horse; not even a superintendent had walked through the yard and singled him out with an approving eye.[16]

Basil quickly learns that even to make a few dollars a week he must use his family connections, and even this proves degrading, because he is exploited socially by the uncle who employs him. He is saved from the sordid actualities of a world in which he tried to rise to riches by the authorial magic wand: the family's sale of its Third Street block to the Union Depot Company raises $400,000. Consequently, Basil Duke Lee's rude awakening will have no effects in this fictional world. The Alger myths are exploded, only to be replaced by the '20s' version: a real estate windfall.

In the Depression years, Fitzgerald became irked by the tendency of magazine editors to expect him to produce stories of young love when he knew, as he put it in a letter written in 1939, that that particular well had run dry for him. He believed that he had made 'a sort of turn'[17] in his writing in the '30s, and that he had opened a new vein of material. The forty-two stories Fitzgerald wrote between 1930 and 1936—when the 'turn' became apparent—seem, to Ruth Prigozy, to illustrate the struggle of a new style and new fictional forms to emerge: means adequate to express the ideas of the mature Fitzgerald. Prigozy finds the plots of many of these transitional stories outworn, stale, mechanical—unintentional parodies of those stories of young love that had been very popular in the boom years.[18] If my theory is correct, the note of parody was there from the start and the later rehearsals of the theme are not different in kind but in degree. In some, at least, of the transitional stories, the self-parody is deliberate.

The last two stories on the poor boy rich girl theme that I propose to discuss were both published in the *Post*; neither was selected for *Taps at Reveille*. 'The Bridal Party', which appeared in August 1930, has recently been treated as the product of the maturer Fitzgerald who had come to realize that the pursuit and capture of the rich girl was really not worth the trouble and heartache,[19] or even as a tale in which a Fitzgerald version of the 'code hero' is introduced to teach the love-sick protagonist the lesson of self-reliance.[20] The yearning lover is Michael Curly, who strongly resembles the Gordon Sterrett of 'May Day'. He is poor and believes that he has lost the rich girl he loved 'because he had no money and could make no money; because . . . he could not find himself' (*Stories*, p. 271). In contrast to this weak and resentful outsider, Hamilton Rutherford— the supposed 'code hero' of the story—is so strong a character that even when he loses his entire fortune in the Wall Street slump on the eve of his wedding, he undauntedly—even blithely—spends his last dollars on the sumptuous reception.

Yet this hero is also a male chauvinist who believes in keeping women in their place. He expounds his views on marriage for the pathetic Michael Curly's benefit: if the man stands any nonsense from the woman, she will gobble him up after five years, or he will have to get out before then. When a 'low' woman, with whom he has obviously become sexually involved, attempts to interrupt his wedding, he quickly frightens her off. Such strength is rewarded. The very girl who rejected Michael Curly now chooses to stay with Rutherford, even though he has lost his money. But before we take Caroline's sacrifice as morally instructive, we should note that Rutherford has been offered a job at $50,000 a year. As a friend predicts, 'in another year he'll be back among the millionaires.' Clearly, we are meant to believe that women like Caroline respond to strong men, but Rutherford is a post-Slump version of Anson Hunter of 'The Rich Boy'. He is a man with a firm sense of self, but hardly admirable.

The interesting development in this late variation on an old theme is the treatment of the poor young man. Initially, Curly feels the resentment of all Fitzgerald's poor boys humiliated by their poverty. His inability to afford expensive clothes makes him an outsider in the smart set in which the fascinating Caroline moves. But when the death of a grandfather converts the poor boy into the prince with $250,000, he immediately makes a change of costume, ordering costly clothes, and these change his character:

> Michael was surprised to find what a difference his new dinner coat, his new silk hat, his new, proud linen made in his estimate of himself; he felt less resentment toward all these people for being so rich and assured . . . he felt that he was part of all this. (*Stories*, p. 279)

The story ends with Michael cured of his yearning love for the unattainable Caroline and cured—we are told—by the 'ceremonial function' of the wildly extravagant wedding party. No longer jealous of the people who are 'at home in their richness with one another', Michael decides that 'This is our way of doing things. . . . Generous and fresh and free; a sort of Virginia-plantation hospitality, but at a different pace now, nervous as a ticker tape. . . .'

Far from teaching that money has its limits and cannot achieve everything, this bleak story offers yet another example of character defined in terms of money and its insignia. Michael Curly is the creature of his money and the clothes it can buy; he is a nobody without them. As far as we are allowed to see him in the story, he is a man who lacks an inner self.

If 'The Bridal Party' is a new departure in the sense that it offers as the story of a poor and resentful outsider suddenly metamorphosed by money into a rich and complacent insider, his yearning love at once transformed into a sense of well-being by the donning of expensive clothes, this is not different in kind from 'Winter Dreams' but only in degree; the late version of the theme is a simplified reworking of its early plot. Similarly, 'The Rubber Check', which appeared in the *Post* in August 1932, rehearses the old story of the poor boy in search of the rich girl, but does so in a new mode, restating, in hyperbolic terms, many of the ideas that had been part of all the stories. The young man here starts in an anomalous social position, for his mother is a socialite who has married three times and is about to enter on her fourth marriage. At 21, Val Schuyler has an allowance of $25 a month and a family name (adopted from his second step-father) that is an asset to a young man of social ambitions. His social career began three years earlier, when he bluffed his way into the world of the affluent Mortmain family. When the 16-year-old daughter of the family becomes attracted to Val, her mother quickly gauges his social rating, but is tolerant because he is no true threat:

> By the time Mrs. Mortmain had identified him as a nobody she had accepted him, at least on the summer scale. . . . Mrs. Mortmain knew that Ellen adored Val, but Val knew his place and she was grateful to him for it. (*Price*, p. 419)

Once Val has got himself on the invitation lists of New York society, thanks to his connection with the Mortmains, his main interest in life is dancing with débutantes; his 'career' in the brokerage business is a mere interlude between dances and parties. The callow young man is delighted at the prestige of his rôle as Ellen Mortmain's escort. Appropriately, the narrator treats him with indulgent contempt: 'He hated the reproach of superficiality. . . . Actually he cared deeply about things, but

127

the things he cared about were generally considered trivial.'
The minor tragedy of Val's life occurs when he finds himself
obliged to pay the $80 bill for a luncheon party at which he had
imagined himself to be a guest. The rubber check of the title is
one that bounces when his mother refuses to honour it, and thus
compromises her son's reputation for honesty, since he has used
an eminently respectable and very rich Philadelphia family—
the Templetons—as a reference. As always in Fitzgerald's
stories, the humiliation and embarrassment are described with
conviction. So, too, is the cruelty of the rich Mrs. Templeton,
who spreads the story of Val's financial untrustworthiness, with
the result that his social career is ruined. After a series of snubs
by young women at the society dances he so loves, Val confronts the formidable Mrs. Templeton, accusing her of unfairness, but she shows no compassion and no remorse. No longer
persona grata at the balls, or in New York society generally, Val's
sense of himself is undermined:

> No longer did the preview of himself in the mirror—with gloves,
> opera hat and stick—furnish him his mead of our common
> vanity. He was a man without a country. (*Price*, p. 427)

He is, one could even say, a man without a self, for his self has
been defined in terms of his social acceptability, and he realizes
that, after years of effort, he has reached 'exactly no position at
all'.

The turning-point in the young man's career is the now-
routine transformation from relative poverty to wealth when he
inherits $20,000 from his mother's estate. No longer a suppli-
cant, Val regains his confidence, and with that social acceptability. We next see him in London in 1930 and as yet untouched
by the Crash. We are invited to regard him as he walks down
Pall Mall, tall and even stately in his expensive clothes. He
meets an American friend who notices

> how his shirt sleeve fits his wrist, and his coat sleeve incases his
> shirt sleeve like a sleeve or valve; how his collar and tie are
> moulded plastically to his neck. (p. 432)

If this seems just a repetition of 'The Bridal Party', when Val
finds that he has lost everything in the Crash and that his
wonderful clothes will be attached because he cannot pay his

hotel bill, the mode modulates to farce. The young man swathes himself in layers of clothes, putting on four shirts over two sets of underwear and stuffs his pockets with ties, socks, studs, gold-backed brushes, and toilet articles. Here is the epitome of consumerism in a ludicrous form. Where the popular girl just dreams of acquiring and acquiring, this popular man *is* his possessions. Clothes make the man in a shockingly obvious way.

The crude reduction of the success story and the emptying of character that occur in 'The Bridal Party' and 'The Rubber Check' can hardly be unintentional. Fitzgerald could, of course, create plausible characters in the realist mode when he wished to, and he demonstrated that ability in evoking the anguish of his poor young men when humiliated and frustrated by their poverty. The blatant manipulation of both character and plot in the love stories does not, in my opinion, indicate a readiness to tailor his fictions to the requirements of the magazine trade. In his increasingly parodic rehearsals of the story of love as a form of social aspiration, Fitzgerald exposed the conventions on which that story depended and created radical tales of alienation— stories of men without countries and without selves.

NOTES

1. *The Letters of F. Scott Fitzgerald*, ed. Andrew Turnbull (New York: Scribner's, 1963; Bantam, 1971), p. 120.
2. *Bits of Paradise: Twenty-one Uncollected Stories by F. Scott Fitzgerald*, selected by Scottie Fitzgerald Smith and Matthew J. Bruccoli (London: Bodley Head, 1973; Harmondsworth: Penguin Books, 1976), pp. 13–14.
3. Introduction to *The Price Was High: The Last Uncollected Stories of F. Scott Fitzgerald*, ed. Matthew J. Bruccoli (New York; Harcourt Brace; London: Quartet Books, 1979), p. xii.
4. *Correspondence of F. Scott Fitzgerald*, ed. Matthew Bruccoli and Margaret M. Duggan (New York: Random House, 1980), p. 406.
5. *Bits of Paradise*, p. 14.
6. Scott Donaldson, 'Money and Marriage in Fitzgerald's Stories', in Jackson R. Bryer (ed.), *The Short Stories of F. Scott Fitzgerald: New Approaches in Criticism* (University of Wisconsin Press, 1982).
7. *Letters*, p. 192.
8. *The Stories of F. Scott Fitzgerald*, ed. Malcolm Cowley (New York: Scribner's, 1951), p. 133.
9. *Correspondence*, p. 114.

10. Robert Sklar, *F. Scott Fitzgerald: The Last Laocoön* (New York: Oxford University Press, 1967), p. 74–5.
11. *The Price Was High*, p. 11.
12. *Bits of Paradise*, p. 27.
13. 'Presumption' has been reprinted in Bruccoli's *The Price Was High*.
14. *The Last Laocoön*, pp. 215–16.
15. *The Price Was High*, p. 245.
16. *The Basil and Josephine Stories by F. Scott Fitzgerald*, ed. Jackson R. Bryer and John Kuehl (New York: Scribner's, 1973), p. 149.
17. *Letters*, p. 596. The letter was addressed to Kenneth Littauer.
18. Ruth Prigozy, 'Fitzgerald's Short Stories and the Depression: An Artistic Crisis', in Bryer (ed.), *The Short Stories*.
19. Donaldson, 'Money and Marriage', pp. 82; 86–7.
20. James J. Martine, 'Rich Boys and Rich Men: "The Bridal Party" ', in Bryer (ed.), *The Short Stories*.

7

'The most poetical topic in the world': Women in the Novels of F. Scott Fitzgerald

by ELIZABETH KASPAR ALDRICH

1

'They are all Zelda': we say this facetiously, but we might do so in earnest, as Fitzgerald himself did often, in tones ranging from reverent devotion to the most extreme bitterness. What is striking about Fitzgerald's case—and what is particularly challenging to criticism of his work—is how little we seem to be able to avoid saying it one way or the other. The challenge looks at first all negative: to conflate the life and the work is to violate a sacred tenet of the New Criticism to which many of us went to school, to commit that intentional fallacy against which we were so stringently warned. And at its worst, committing the fallacy simply means descending to the kind of gossip which, in this particular case, is and always has been far too common.[1]

Yet the very prevalence of such gossip is telling. More than any other American writer who comes to mind, Fitzgerald is associated in criticism as well as biography with a particular, real woman who was at once wife, muse, model and sometimes literary rival. The highly public and well-documented career of his marriage served always as addendum to or even gloss on the work. And as the revelations of Nancy Milford's 1970 biography have made plain, Fitzgerald not only wrote with Zelda as

131

model, he wrote with and from Zelda as *text*: her diaries and letters, essays and short fiction, even medical records relating to her, found their way into his work.[2] Immortality conferred or exploitation committed, Fitzgerald's use of Zelda in his fiction, like his non-literary advertisements of their life together, amounted to an extraordinary kind of collaboration, one which calls for the most careful reconsideration—here is the challenge in its positive sense—of the relationship between text and context and how we interpret it.

Now the context to which a writer's text is related may be either circumstantial or literary. Probably the most demanding if not grandiose definition which we have of the latter sort is to be found in T. S. Eliot's 'Tradition and the Individual Talent', (1919) where he pronounces on the 'historical sense' which compels the poet to write

> not merely with his own generation in his bones, but with a feeling that the whole of the literature of Europe from Homer and within it the whole of the literature of his own country has a simultaneous existence and composes a simultaneous order.

Eliot's purpose is surely revisionary of the other sense of context: that is, he wishes not only to exhort the artist to that famous 'escape from personality', but also to exhort the critic to escape from the artist's biography.[3] Of course the shift from the circumstantial to the literary-traditional opens up for us another, in academic terms still more traditional sense of context as con-text, an area better known as source studies: a text may have, may literally transcribe, another or ante-text. Zelda writes to Scott (ca. April 1919), complaining of how much women

> love to fancy themselves suffering—they're nearly all moral and mental hypo-crondiacs [sic]—If they'd just awake to the fact that their excuse and explanation is the necessity for a disturbing element among men—they'd be much happier. . . .

Rosalind, the heroine of *This Side of Paradise* (1920), 'once told a roomful of her mother's friends that the only excuse for women was the necessity for a disturbing element among men'.[4] Rosalind 'is' Zelda in ways which bring together all three senses of context mentioned above, and which may illuminate not only Fitzgerald's work but the tradition in American letters of which he forms a part.

2

If it is a commonplace of Fitzgerald criticism that he had only one story to write, that all of his novels are autobiography, it is equally true that they were first read as a sort of social history. At the time of Fitzgerald's death in 1940 the dominant note of the memoirs and obituary evaluations that appeared was lament at the persistence of that inaccurate and reductive label, 'Chronicler of the Jazz Age'; nevertheless, this was precisely the title and public function which the author courted and profited from at the start of his career.[5] Yet even if we assume that his own life, as he performed and recorded it, could contain and exemplify the *zeitgeist*, the two functions in his writing were not really compatible. For Fitzgerald the self-chronicler was a Romantic of the most lyric stripe, and Fitzgerald the Chronicler of the Jazz Age wanted above all to be a sociologist of the finest accuracy and the weightiest *authority*. This dual attitude is nowhere more prominent than in *This Side of Paradise*, where the hero is characterized as a 'cynical idealist', and the work warrants more scrutiny than its now agreed-upon place in the whole *oeuvre* might suggest. The dual attitude with all the problems it entails persists throughout that *oeuvre* in the writer's treatment of women; nowhere is his need more urgent for the authority of a 'primary text'.

This is precisely what Fitzgerald found for his first novel in Zelda who, entering (and temporarily departing from) his life midway through the composition, refocused the work and provided in her own diary and letters the text for its heroine's characterization:

> Rosalind is—utterly Rosalind. She is one of those girls who need never make the slightest effort to have men fall in love with them. Two types of men seldom do: Dull men are usually afraid of her cleverness and intellectual men are usually afraid of her beauty. All others are hers by natural prerogative.

Like the passage quoted earlier but far more closely, this comes from a letter of Zelda's. 'One of those girls who . . .' is the locution of that perennial bore, the Authority on Women: indeed, the earlier passage begins still more pompously: 'The education of all beautiful women is the knowledge of men' and

133

so forth. Although pronouncements like this can be found till the end of the career, they are for the most part sins (if they are sins) of youth. What is important is that they work best when taken from Zelda's own text and attributed to the 'Zelda-character', who may well serve to liberate or license the Romantic in hero and narrator alike. Curious breakdowns occur in the sociologically-authoritative tone when the supporting female authority is displaced, as in the late novel *Tender is the Night* (1934), where both omniscient narrator and protagonist/Doctor are given to more questionable generalities: 'Like most women, she liked to be told how she should feel' is typical; but this is to anticipate.[6]

This Side of Paradise ostensibly chronicles the progress of its hero from Romantic Egotist to Personage (to invoke alternate titles of early drafts); but with remarkable self-consciousness the novel confesses on page after page its real subject: the use of women in the making of a writer. It begins with a wonderfully ambiguous first sentence on what 'Amory Blaine inherited from his mother'—whether it is 'every trait . . . that made him worth while' or every trait '*except* the stray inexpressible few' that did so depends on the placement of a comma—and proceeds through a series of infatuations, courtships, disappointments and departures to the emergent artist's independence from:

> Women—of whom he had expected so much; whose beauty he had hoped to transmute into modes of art; whose unfathomable instincts, marvellously incoherent and inarticulate, he had thought to perpetuate in terms of experience. . . .

Now they have become, the women in Amory's life, merely:

> consecrations to their own posterity. Isabelle, Clara, Rosalind, Eleanor, were all removed by their very beauty, around which men had swarmed, from the possibility of contributing anything but a sick heart and a page of puzzled words to write.

The posterity is, of course, to be literary. Each woman character, once desired and considered as potential wife, can contribute more, it seems, by her absence (causing the sick heart that enables the page of words); her service, in other words, is to impress and attract by her beauty and then to be gone. But this has been true at every stage. After being let down by his childhood sweetheart, Isabelle, Amory 'took a sombre satisfaction in thinking that perhaps all along she had been nothing except what he had read into her'—in realizing however negatively his own primacy in the creation of the character of the beloved. With Clara, his beautiful, widowed cousin, Amory comes still closer to an acknowledgement of her, let us say, archetypal utility; after his confession, 'if I lost faith in you I'd lose faith in God' and her rejoinder that five men have already made this announcement to her, Amory realizes that this is Clara's very fate:

> His entity dropped out of her plane and he longed only to touch her dress with almost the realization that Joseph must have had of Mary's eternal significance. But quite mechanically he heard himself saying:
>
> 'And I love you—any latent greatness that I've got is . . . oh, Clara, I can't talk. . . .'

Her eternal significance is the enigma his latent greatness will unfold—again *once she is in the past*, 'translated to the steady realm of thought' (to take a phrase from one of Fitzgerald's masters, James), whence her posterity will come forth.[7]

Although Rosalind is at the emotional centre of Amory's story, the crescendo of what I will call Romantic Attitudes continues after her defection (because of Amory's lack of money and prospects: a direct reflection of what Fitzgerald felt his situation to be with Zelda at the time of writing). It reaches a peak with Eleanor, last in the procession of muse/models and most prominently in Fitzgerald's work, I think, the posterity of a particular literary ancestor (a master preceding James himself):

> For years afterward when Amory thought of Eleanor he seemed still to hear the wind sobbing around him and sending little chills into the places beside his heart. The night when they rode up the slope and watched the cold moon float through the clouds, he lost a further part of him that nothing could restore. . . . But Eleanor—did Amory dream her? . . . Was it the infinite sadness of her eyes that drew him or the mirror of himself that he found in the gorgeous clarity of her mind?

Eleanor first identifies Amory, 'I know who you are—you're the blond boy that likes "Ulalume" ', thus indirectly identifying herself, the girl descended from 'Ligeia'. There are several clues to Poe's presence in the chapter on Eleanor: her very name, the Maryland setting (Poe died, famously, in Baltimore), her promise to 'be Psyche, your soul', the small detail of the 'tell-tale' white line over her lip, most significantly perhaps the protagonist's 'sense of coming home' in her presence. She is the one character in the novel who has the distinction of out-posing Amory—to the extent of riding her horse breakneck on a dark, moonless night until 'some ten feet from the edge of the cliff she gave a sudden shriek and flung herself sideways', barely saving her own life as the horse plunges to its death.[8] The gesture has been in response to a taunt from Amory (about a probable deathbed recantation of her present atheism), but it bears a close relation to her own earlier promise to be his Psyche; it enacts, 'allegorically' we might say, the implications of that essentially suicidal promise in a manner of which Fitzgerald himself may have been only half-aware.

This half-awareness emerges in a curious reflection of Amory's on some sentimental verses he has written to his (unnamed, abstracted) love:

> he pondered how coldly we thought of the 'Dark Lady of the Sonnets,' and how little we remembered her as the great man wanted her remembered. For what Shakespeare *must* have desired, to have been able to write with such divine despair, was the lady should live . . . and now we have no real interest in her. . . . The irony of it is that if he had cared more for the poem than for the lady the sonnet would be only obvious, imitative rhetoric and no one would ever have read it after twenty years. . . .

I say curious because the consideration of art's relation to its real or once-living subject, while in keeping with earlier moments cited above, is unexpectedly explicit here; and curious for Amory's conviction—patently Fitzgerald's own at this point—that *the subject must predominate* in the artist's devotion *over the art*. Leaving aside the fairly breathtaking revisionism (Shakespeare must write from personal circumstance or produce imitative rhetoric—a magnificently displaced self-reference, reflecting uneasiness with this obvious and very book-inspired lady), we should notice the latent bargain at work here; if the artist cares more for his subject than his art, then and then only he will be rewarded with the greater art. A corollary, still more deeply buried in the passage but also present, is that the subject, the living woman, is sacrificed to the art, becoming 'ironically' indifferent, of no interest. Eleanor's willing offer to be Amory's Psyche is self-sacrificial, an offer to be poetic subject made by a character out of Poe, who himself celebratedly pronounced, in 'The Philosophy of Composition' of 1846, that 'the *death* . . . of a beautiful woman is, unquestionably, the most poetical topic in the world.'[9]

At the end of *This Side of Paradise* we find Amory heroically alone, 'determined to use to the utmost himself and his heritage from the personalities he had passed'; closing his text and beginning the career it proclaims, he cries 'I know myself . . . but that is all.' And that, the whole tone of this ending suggests, is enough: 'Isabelle, Clara, Rosalind, Eleanor'—the heritage of memory—are all, always especially Rosalind, translated to the realm of thought, become a part of that self which he knows and which will remain the inexhaustible material of his art.

With hindsight we can see the irony of this first novel's great success, which won for its author the once-unattainable bride and left him indeed wedded to his idealized subject, who is retranslated, or we might better say de-translated, to the original. Happy endings are notoriously, in real life, quite different as beginnings, and the damnation of the marriage chronicled in *The Beautiful and Damned* (1922) is predictable enough, given Fitzgerald's insistence on Romantic excess in whatever direction. There is nothing particularly noteworthy for our purposes about the character of the wife Gloria in this work—however unflatteringly depicted, she is still Rosalind *recidiva*, the beautiful golden girl, reckless and self-absorbed— save that here she is even more conspicuously identified as the subject of the hero's art, as finding her *raison d'etre* in that rôle. Gloria brings Anthony Patch 'an understanding remembered from the romancings of many generations of minds. . . . [she is] the fragment of a sentence to that part of him that cherished all beauty and all illusion'; indeed, her past 'was an old story to him . . . for he was going to write a book about her some day'.[10] But by the close of this book (less 'about' Gloria or Zelda than about her use as subject-of-book) there has been a change in the

137

hero's hopes and certainties caused, it seems, by the subject/ wife's failure of or rebellion against this version of herself. Although he can still dream that money might bring him a Keatsean romance of blue canals and golden hills 'and of women, women who changed, dissolved, melted into other women and receded from his life, but who were always beautiful and always young', nevertheless the reality of marriage has shown him:

> that there should be a difference in his attitude. All the distress that he had ever known, the sorrow and the pain, had been because of women. It was something that in different ways they did to him, unconsciously, almost casually—perhaps finding him tender-minded and afraid, they killed the things in him that menaced their absolute sway.

And Anthony ends unimaginably rich but childish, or mentally 'killed', while his triumphant wife—once muse/model but now mere vulgar mannequin—parades her husband's fortune on her back.

As before, Fitzgerald used Zelda's diary and letters, although since most of the originals are lost we cannot determine how extensively: very, if the authoritative tone is any guage. Zelda herself, invited to review the novel, made joking reference to 'a portion of an old diary of mine which mysteriously disappeared shortly after my marriage' as well as 'scraps of letters' which she recognized (almost certainly major sources of authority), concluding that the author 'seems to believe that plagiarism begins at home'. What is of especial interest and relevance in this review is Zelda's evaluation of Gloria's character in terms embracing both literary comparison and personal self-reference. 'I think Gloria is most amusing', she writes, feeling (according to her biographer) at once wounded and defensive:

> I have an intense distaste for the melancholy aroused in the masculine mind by such characters as Jenny Gerhardt, Antonia and Tess [of the D'Urbervilles]. Their tragedies, redolent of the soil, leave me unmoved. If they were capable of dramatizing themselves they would no longer be symbolic, and if they weren't—and they aren't—they would be dull, stupid and boring, as they inevitably are in life.[11]

There is a distinction made here which amounts to mutual exclusion: on the one hand we have the woman who is capable of dramatizing herself; on the other, the woman who is symbolic to the masculine mind. As with Scott's allegorical use of Eleanor, we cannot be sure how far Zelda was aware of the implications of this division. But they are there and chilling enough. Some struggle is inevitable between the artist and *this* subject over the very issue of authorship/authority: who may determine dramatic or symbolic meaning, the woman 'in life' or the masculine mind in art?

That it must be one or the other emerged some years later in the real and ugly struggle that arose between husband and wife over their relative rights to the 'material' of their life together, in some sense of their respective identities. The story has been told many times now: taken unawares by Zelda's autobiographical novel *Save me the Waltz* (1932), on which he demanded extensive revision, and feeling intolerably menaced by her projected novel on the insanity (hers) which was the subject of his own disastrously blocked and delayed work-in-progress, Fitzgerald was forced, as it were, into the open: 'Everything we have done is my [material] . . . I am the professional novelist . . . . . . That is all my material. None of it is your material.'[12]

Perhaps defensible or even logical, if one is concerned with competing shares of a limited market. But there is something far more fundamental at stake which we can sense in a complaint Fitzgerald made at this time to one of Zelda's psychiatrists about her fictional use of him. 'My God', he wrote, 'my books made her a legend and her single intention in this somewhat thin portrait is to make me a non-entity.' Whether or not Fitzgerald considered the portrait thin and Zelda 'a third rate writer' is irrelevant to his distress. This last term should, I think, be given its full, literal weight of non-being; it seems that the portrait, once made, takes a kind of ontological precedence over the model, drains it of its own being. Art does not simply copy the life of its subject, it draws *on* that life, or draws it *out* and into its own. Entity is, like blood, a limited quantity and Art, vampirish; we are once more in the world of Poe.

To an extent not fully appreciated, I think, and in varying senses of the term Poe provides us with a context for reading Fitzgerald, or at least Fitzgerald's women, and I would like to leave the latter briefly to try and pursue it. Poe is a fairly constant source in the fiction, although most directly acknowledged in the early works (the allusions in the Eleanor episode described above amount to quotation). And there are coincidences in the biographies which led some contemporaries of Fitzgerald—and critics after them—to refer to him as 'our Poe'. The reference was principally to an often public, always self-destructive dissipation, aggravated perhaps by the martyrdom of the Serious Artist to the philistine demands of the New York magazine world or, as the case may be, Hollywood. But a more fundamental coincidence is of real consequence to the writing: Poe, like Fitzgerald later, was noted for—could be said to have originated a tradition of—fictions of women within a literary culture understood to be inimical to them.[13] And whether or not he was actually obsessed by the real woman, his very young cousin Virginia, who was his wife and muse, Poe nevertheless made that circumstance the subject of his art.

It is here that Eliot's ideas of tradition and order intersect, paradoxically enough, with our use of biography as context for the work. We can better see how this is so by applying the modification of Eliot's 'ideal order' proposed by Frederic Jameson in *Marxism and Form* (1971): 'the smaller idea of limited sequences which are modified by the addition of a new term, itself perceived against the continuum of which it is a part'.[14] Jameson's examples, such as the sequence Richardson–Fielding–Scott for the English novel, are national and generic in character and designed to show how one writer's 'specificity' may best be perceived in such relative terms. The intersection mentioned above occurs when we define such a sequence less according to genre than to subject: the internalization of circumstance—the artist's use of a living model—as subject. It is this we find in the work of Poe (the model his child-bride Virginia), as well as Hawthorne (his fair bride Sophia; perhaps his dark elder sister also)[15] and Henry James (his forever-mourned cousin, Minny Temple, who was translated to the steady realm of his thought). To see Fitzgerald critically within such a sequence can be of tremendous help in our efforts to escape his own biography—would that he had done so better himself!—while still recognizing that this writer's use of his life, especially the woman in his life, was not simply the condition of his art but its very substance. With this perspective we may even redeem for criticism such flippancies as 'they are all Zelda.'

3

In order to gain the perspective, of course, we must at least glance back over the sequence itself, particularly at Poe, who establishes a pattern for the subject against which we may measure the variation, hence specificity, of Fitzgerald's work. In 'The Philosophy of Composition', where Beauty is pronounced 'the sole legitimate province of the poem' and, as we noted above, 'the death of a beautiful woman' the indisputably greatest poetical subject, a corollary goes unexpressed: that is, that the dying of the woman is prerequisite to the art of which she is subject. Although Poe detested allegory, as he announced in one of his reviews of Hawthorne (as James did some thirty years later in the same context), he produced one for this corollary in the brief tale 'The Oval Portrait' (1845; as is sometimes the case with poets, the corollary precedes the proposition). Here a 'desperately' wounded narrator, seeking shelter in a deserted house, is startled by a portrait of and reads an explanatory text about 'a young maiden of rarest beauty' who in 'an evil hour' weds a painter with 'already a bride in his art'; she sits as model to him 'for many weeks' until at the portrait's completion the painter, 'very pallid and aghast', cries of his painting ' "This is indeed Life itself!" ' and turns to see that his model/wife is dead. The art is vampirish: the tints on the canvas were drawn 'from the cheeks of her who sat', although we must note that it seems to have drained the artist as well.[16] Manifestly, Poe exposes the lie of the artist's exaltation of his subject which the naïveté of Amory Blaine espoused: in so far as she is model, she is not wife; in so far as she is the subject of art, she is not beloved of the artist, she is cannibalized. As Daniel Hoffmann has shown in his now-classic work on Poe, 'The Fall of the House of Usher' is a less starkly allegorical but far more complete exploration of this same theme, the relation of artist (or poet) and subject, and it is from this tale that we can complete an archetype for our sequence.[17]

Indeed, it is archetypal for Poe's *oeuvre*. In 'Usher', as generally in Poe's tales, we have a male protagonist whose internally-divided nature is externalized in the presence of another—double or opposite and here, as is usually true, narrator. (Thus the narrator of 'Usher' is 'ushered into the

141

presence' of its protagonist at the start of the tale; consider also the anonymous narrator of the exploits of Dupin, the detective who is both poet and mathematician, 'creative and resolvant'; or the eponymous William Wilson, the often intoxicated criminal-narrator who is haunted by, until he murders, along with himself, his always sober conscience, William Wilson— this last tale, I think, of unusual importance to Fitzgerald.) The female subject, Roderick's sister the Lady Madeline, completes what is a characteristic triangle. (The variant of this pattern is to be found in another archetypal tale already mentioned, 'Ligeia', where we have one husband-narrator and two ladies: Ligeia and, after her death, the second wife Rowena, whose body is taken over by the returned spirit of the first.) With the arrival of the narrator and the splitting of the central con- sciousness we can follow the treatment of the subject/woman through three parts or stages which may be labelled as follows: (1) the *translation* of the subject (the Lady Madeline 'succumbs' and is placed by Roderick in the tomb); (2) translation transmuted to *transgression* (at the moment of inhumation, which amounts to murder, Roderick confesses his unnaturally sym- pathetic twinship with his sister or, by displacement, their incest); (3) catastrophe, the *return of the dead* (Madeline rises up from the tomb to fall with her brother in a mortal embrace).

Although we seldom find exactly this pattern repeated in our sequence, these elements—splitting or doubling and translation, the crimes of murder or self-murder and incest, resurrections ghostly and otherwise—are remarkably constant, and constant in their clustering around the theme of the artist's use of life embodied in the living woman. Even the apparently truncated allegory of 'The Oval Portrait' can be 'completed' if we imagine the subject as having escaped from her frame (this is the impression of the narrator on first seeing the portrait) and 'returned' to account for the otherwise unexplained desperate wound; if, in other words, we shift the referent of the text- within-the-text from portrait to frame, from being an account of the subject to accounting for the condition of narrative (thereby arriving at what I would call the latent, in contrast to the manifest, content of the allegory). Hawthorne's version of 'The Oval Portrait' is his tale of 1846, 'The Birthmark', where an austere, similarly 'already-married' husband uses his arts to draw from the cheek of his bride an imperfection of nature, thereby killing her.[18] The youthful James, in his first full-length novel *Roderick Hudson* (1876) shows himself very much within the worlds of Hawthorne and Poe but seems to reverse the terms of the allegory. Obsessed by Christina Light, the model on whom art cannot improve, who is 'Beauty itself', the artist Roderick is not only blocked—he loses his inspiration even as he insists he has found his muse—but eventually killed, perhaps by himself. (Christina herself does 'return from the dead' ten years later to be heroine of *The Princess Casamassima* (1886) and a factor in another hero's self-murder.) Like Rosalind after her, Christina has refused to marry the relatively poor or as-yet-unmade hero. Were we to imagine another version in which she consented, we might find ourselves in the world of *The Beautiful and Damned*. In either case, she is a muse very close to the Fitzgerald type: idealized in the most Romantic terms, indeed adored, she is in her human aspect at once cool and confiding, contradictory, perverse, yet withal appealing; and in her divine aspect—a Medusa.

Two years after *Roderick Hudson*, James earned his first and perhaps greatest celebrity by proving that for American and English readers the death of a beautiful woman was still the most poetical topic in the world. 'Daisy Miller' (1878) is a fiction outside or at least to the side of our sequence, except for this value which inheres in its heroine, and which permeates the idea—if not the solidly alive body—of her namesake Daisy Fay, the symbolic centre of Fitzgerald's masterpiece.

I would like to defer our consideration of *The Great Gatsby* (which will in any case be brief), since we can, I think, learn more about certain of a writer's problems from failures or partial successes than from the more nearly perfect work. For instance, although we find the pattern of splitting, translation, transgression and return in Hawthorne's masterpiece, *The Scarlet Letter* (1850), it is far more obtrusive and revealingly unresolved in his last published romance, *The Marble Faun* (1860), a troubled and almost (it seems) wilfully *un*masterful work which is centred on a murder and haunted by incest. *The Marble Faun* appeared eight years after Hawthorne's previous romance, as *Tender is the Night* followed the preceding *Gatsby* by nine years. Each work was continually revised, even after initial

143

publication; indeed neither was ever, to the satisfaction of its author, really completed. Since I find the analogies between these two both remarkably close and illuminating of our subject, I propose concentrating on two 'mirror' scenes—in each a woman regards herself in a work of art—which occur in early chapters of both fictions. There is a closely parallel moment in James's late work *The Wings of the Dove* (1902; containing neither murder nor incest, it is nevertheless the sole novel which James identified as the portrait of a once-living model—*his* model, his beautiful cousin Minny who died) which belongs with these two and will form a bridge in the comparison.

There are two women in *The Marble Faun*, both servants to Art. Hawthorne's fair maiden, Hilda, is a completely self-abnegating and almost supernaturally gifted copyist of the Old Masters. His dark lady, Miriam, would be an 'original'; she paints mythologi-cal and Biblical scenes of 'women acting the part of a revengeful mischief towards man', all of them from 'stories of bloodshed'. One day Miriam visits Hilda's studio and is shown the recently completed, miraculously perfect copy of Guido's Beatrice Cenci—*the* figure for the nineteenth century of the double crime of incest/murder—which she contemplates as the two women discuss the character it represents. Hilda, interpreting the portrait alone, sees only 'sorrow so black . . . it oppresses her . . . as sin would'; but when Miriam directs her attention to 'the deed for which she suffered' the Puritan maiden recoils:

> 'Ah!' replied Hilda, shuddering, 'I really had quite forgotten Beatrice's history, and was thinking of her only as the picture seems to reveal her character. Yes, yes; it was terrible guilt, an inexpiable crime . . . Her doom is just!'

Hawthorne, through his characters, demands a great deal of portraits; as in *The House of the Seven Gables* (1851), where a central portrait serves as mystical oracle, what is expected from them is no less than the essential truth of the subject/model. Miriam, protesting against Hilda's sword-like and merciless innocence, cries out

> passionately, 'If I could only get within her consciousness!—if I could but clasp Beatrice Cenci's ghost and draw it into myself! I would give my life to know whether she thought herself innocent, or the one great criminal since time began.'

As Miriam gave utterance to these words, Hilda looked from the picture into her face, and was startled to observe that her friend's expression had become almost exactly that of the portrait. . . .[19]

It is a 'magical picture', as the characters acknowledge, and it is clear that within Hawthorne's romance-world the story of Beatrice Cenci is meant to stand in for Miriam's own; there is a dark secret pursuing her from her past, but she is never permitted to speak it (it is the American sculptor, Kenyon, who suppresses her) and the author gives us only this scene as sufficient to identify and even, as it were, interpret it.

Apart from or beyond the allegorical correspondences of the romance-world, however, a debate proceeds over the relationship of the work of art to its referent (Hilda, as we have seen, interprets the two antithetically); and inseparable from this is the question, passionately engaged throughout the romance, of sexual spheres: who may determine symbolic meaning? Miriam wonders if Guido might not 'be jealous of [Hilda's] rivalship', although the copyist protests that she is mere instrument: 'Guido . . . wrought through me.' But Miriam goes on to wonder 'if a woman had painted the original picture, there might have been something in it which we miss now', and considers making a copy herself 'to give it what it lacks'. What it lacks, of course, is *her own version of herself*, for whom this picture is mirror. Hawthorne could resolve this debate only at the level of a plot with which he was clearly dissatisfied: Hilda is dispatched to woman's proper domestic sphere with Kenyon as husband; Miriam is consigned to an explicitly asexual marriage-of-shared-guilt with the 'faun' Donatello. But whose is the guilt for which she pays? If hers, might it not be simply the guilt of trying to be her own 'original'?

Our bridge can be short: in an extraordinary and very Hawthornean moment in *The Wings of the Dove* the beautiful and foredoomed heroine, Milly, finds herself amidst the Great World at the country estate of Lord Mark, where she is brought before a 'mysterious portrait' by Bronzino and, through her tears, recognizes her double:

> a young woman, all magnificently drawn, down to the hands, and magnificently dressed; a face almost livid in hue, yet handsome

145

in sadness and crowned with a mass of hair rolled back and high, that must, before fading with time, have had a family resemblance to her own [which is bright red]. The lady in question, at all events . . . was a very great personage—only unaccompanied by a joy. And she was dead, dead, dead. Milly recognised her exactly in words that had nothing to do with her. 'I shall never be better than this.'[20]

The moment of recognition itself is 'as good a moment as she should have with any one, or have in any connection whatever'. According to the logic of James's plot, Milly responds to the revelation that the 'hero', Densher, would have feigned love for the sake of her gold by turning her face to the wall to die. But according to a deeper logic (what we could call a latent content in the work) of which the above scene is interpretative sign, she succumbs neither to injury nor to the illness which has condemned her; she succumbs, rather, to the imperative of Art. The Bronzino portrait, like the Guido, seems to stand as 'original' to a living 'reproduction'. It prefigures the fiction of which it forms a part, the work of art for which the living subject is fated to be model. What we see here is that subject's willing *consent* to such a translation.

4

Although my justification for this admittedly lengthy excursus into a sequence of writers has been that it would help us to view Fitzgerald's work from an angle other than biographical, with *Tender is the Night* this is only partially feasible. In this novel Fitzgerald internalized circumstance as subject so radically that he seems to have defeated whatever end of mastery—over either—he might have hoped to achieve. We simply cannot escape the fact, and this no matter what our sympathies, that in assuming exclusive rights to the 'material', living and textual, of Zelda's illness—*the* tragic catastrophe of her life, after all, and one that is as much 'in progress' as her husband's work— Fitzgerald exploited his often helpless subject in a way that really can seem vampirish. He himself could not escape it. We may attribute the years of delay and the incoherencies of the end result to drink (as Zelda did; Fitzgerald also blamed, even as he charted for his translation, the illness itself) but ambivalence

146

and guilt had to play their part; they are evident throughout the book. What seems to me remarkable is how the elements of our Poe-esque pattern tend to rise up to structure or simply punctuate it as if automatically, apart from the author's volition. There is, to give one brief example of what I mean, a dream-like quality to the murders scattered throughout—from the dead Negro in Rosemary's bed, to the shooting of a lover by Nicole's old schoolmate, to the fatal off-stage beating of Abe North, of which Dick hears casual mention towards the end; they seem to perform a sort of dream work, standing in for or displacing the otherwise unimaginable, though not unattempted, murder of husband by wife or wife by husband. Or to take another example, Fitzgerald's attribution of Nicole's schizophrenia to the trauma of rape by her father is an invention, incest as poisonous first cause, that vitiates the 'authenticity' of the medical history—which he does not, in fact, seem to have understood very well.

What he does seem to have understood is the value of a mirror scene which might contain and 'solve' the seemingly insoluble problem of artist and subject. So we have the screening of the film *Daddy's Girl*, arranged by its young star Rosemary, who is hopelessly in love with the psychiatrist-husband (saviour, Pygmalion, and so forth) of the 'Zelda-character' Nicole:

> There she was—the school girl of a year ago, hair down her back and rippling out stiffly like the solid hair of a tanagra figure; there she was—young and innocent—the product of her mother's loving care; there she was—embodying all the immaturity of the race, cutting a new cardboard paper doll to pass before its empty harlot's mind. She remembered how she felt in that dress, especially fresh and new under the fresh young silk.
> Daddy's girl.

This is not Fitzgerald at his best, although the weaknesses (bad endings to phrases or aphorisms promisingly begun) are typical. How can the immature race have an empty harlot's mind? If Rosemary embodies it, how can she show, as described a few lines further on, 'fineness of character . . . courage and steadfastness'? The inconsistencies may indeed result from the ambivalence mentioned above, for Rosemary is standing in here for Nicole, later described in parallel terms as embodying 'the

147

essence of a continent'. This function, in fact, is the strength of the entire episode. Although the analogy may seem incongruous, the film—or rather the conjunction of Rosemary and film— serves the purpose of the portrait by Guido: it *stands in* for Nicole's history, as the Guido subject did for Miriam's. With the difference that, as the virtually parodic title indicates, in this case we are substituting comedy for tragedy. *Daddy's Girl* represents a successful or guilt-free translation of life to art, one which gives the freedom or licence of reversibility. The celluloid image can be living without being vampirish, without drawing its tints from the cheek of the living actress, who sits in the darkened room enjoying it along with the rest of the audience, remembering (and by implication feeling again) how 'fresh and new' she had felt when it was made.

Rosemary is the actress, in other words, *of* Nicole, who is wife and model. It would seem at first that Fitzgerald has split the woman/subject along the pattern of 'Ligeia', with Rosemary playing the part of Rowena. She does offer to replace Nicole as Dick's wife, as she has previously tried to draw him into her celluloid world by offering him a screen test. But each of these attempts seems more *faux pas* than serious threat. Nicole does return to and from insanity rather like Ligeia from the dead, but the body she enters is not that of her rival Rosemary.

> A wave of agony went over him. It was awful that such a fine tower should not be erected, only suspended, suspended from him. Up to a point that was right: men were for that, beam and idea, girder and logarithm; but somehow Dick and Nicole had become one and equal, not apposite and complementary; she was Dick too, *the drought in the marrow of his bones*. (My emphasis)

Dick is very much a writer here, if not a poet of the Roderick Usher stamp. The antidote to this possession-by-vampirish-twin is described in the passage where Fitzgerald comes closest to presenting the strategies of the writer under the guise of the professionalism of the doctor.

> Having gone through unprofessional agonies during her long relapse following Topsy's birth, he had, perforce, hardened himself about her, making a cleavage between Nicole sick and Nicole well. This made it difficult now to distinguish between his self-protective professional detachment and some new coldness in his

heart. As an indifference cherished, or left to atrophy, becomes an emptiness, *to this extent he had learned to become empty of Nicole.* . . . (My emphasis)

The passage describes a process of splitting (Nicole sick, Nicole well; Dick husband, Dick doctor) which represents the writer's alternative self-protective strategy. It is occasioned by the husband's current preoccupation with the rival woman and points to what I read as the strategic split at the novel's start between author-surrogates: between, that is, the protagonist Dick and the narrative point of view, which is Rosemary's. This results in a different sort of mirror scene (to paraphrase one critic's fairly snide summing up: Fitzgerald-as-Rosemary gushing over Gerald Murphy-as-Fitzgerald).

The point I would like to emphasize is that, just as Fitzgerald boasted of (when he did not agonize over) a feminine half of himself and claimed all his feminine characters as feminine F. Scott Fitzgeralds (that they are Zelda Fitzgeralds, too, is no contradiction), so he tended to expropriate to his heroes, or male fictional selves, the traditional *rôle* of the beautiful woman: the one who is devotedly contemplated becomes the one too-late mourned. So as Rosemary fades away from the novel and Nicole rises up into health and a new husband, Dick Diver ends in exile (that is, upstate New York) and terminal, or at least interminable, decline. In the end it is *he* who has been sacrificed to Art.

Although critics have made much of the differences and new directions they find indicated in the final, unfinished novel *The Last Tycoon* (1941), I am myself more struck by the almost schematic continuities with what went before. The initial narrative perspective is, like Rosemary's, that of a young woman openly adoring of the hero. And the hero seems a logical extension, perhaps we could say 'correction' of Dick Diver and his predecessors. This artist-figure is a successful movie-maker, and we should recall the liberating usefulness of film as portrait-medium, who combines effectiveness and power in the market-place with high aesthetic achievement. (His name, Monroe Stahr, strikes me as both crudely denotative and uncannily predictive of the woman who was shortly to become the star of the century, a golden girl, weighted with impossible symbolic

149

significance by an ultimately vampirish public, who might have come out of a Hollywood novel by Fitzgerald.) Stahr's beautiful actress-wife-subject is dead, and the text we have centres on her benign 'return' in the person of a strangely pliant or receptive surrogate (named Kathleen and presumably based on the mistress of Fitzgerald's last years, Sheilah Graham). The hero's by-now understandable hesitation to embrace this surrogate-woman in marriage leads to her temporary loss but no real alteration of identity or rôle. The hero's by-now inevitable destruction or sacrifice—a plane crash is planned—will end the work.

Zelda's written reaction to the posthumously published fragment reveals, amidst the general praise and admiration of Scott's work, a jealousy of the heroine; whether or not she knew of Sheilah Graham she certainly, as Milford writes, 'sensed and resented the intrusion of another feminine model in Fitzgerald's prose'. It also reveals the kind of self-referential acuity which we saw in her sadly prescient review of a novel much closer to her own life:

> I confess that I don't like the heroine [Kathleen], she seems the sort of person who knows too well how to capitalize the un-welcome advances of the ice-man and who smells a little of the rubber shields in her dress. However, I see how Stahr might have found her redolent of the intimacies of forgotten homely glamours, and his imagination have endowed her with the magical properties of his early authorities.[21]

When in 'The Philosophy of Composition' Poe reserves the soul for Beauty and Beauty for Poetry, he assigns the faculties of intellect and truth to prose:

> Truth, in fact, demands a precision, and Passion a *homeliness* (the truly passionate will comprehend me) which are absolutely antagonistic to that Beauty which ... is the excitement, or pleasurable elevation, of the soul.

Wittingly or not, in assigning homeliness as well as glamour to her own magical feminine authority (for, of course, the final term is meant to be singular and self-referential), Zelda points to a central problem of Fitzgerald's ideal woman-in-prose: cherished, like Anthony's Gloria, as 'all beauty and all illusion', she often seems to belong elsewhere than in the 'realistic' novel—in the ethereal, abstracted verse of Poe or his descendant Amory Blaine, perhaps; she promises or inspires an 'excitement, or pleasurable elevation of the soul' which verges on the inhuman, which humanity, in any case, cannot sustain.

Which is of course what happens in and what brings us back, finally, to *The Great Gatsby*. Daisy 'in life' (the character who lives in the world—both satirically comic and sociologically accurate—of Nick Carraway's narrative) cannot sustain Gatsby's faith in and demands on her as symbol. This is the subject of the work: as it has always been in Fitzgerald, the transmutation or translation of living woman to symbol. In *Gatsby* the translation is of the Daisy whose history and affective life are 'only personal' to the inhuman green light to which Gatsby stretches forth his arms. The difference in this work is that the subject is liberated for once into full clarity and full congruence with its artistic form. Several factors combine to make this possible.

First of all, as several critics have noticed, Fitzgerald is brilliantly served by the split between narrator Nick Carraway and hero (double and profoundly opposite) Gatsby. Not only does this free him from the inconsistencies of one 'cynical idealist' consciousness, it frees him from the Authority (hitherto an area of simultaneous dependence and rebellion) of the woman/subject. Nick is the mildest of cynics, but his world is definitely prose and authoritative ('dishonesty in a woman is a thing you never blame deeply' is one example of the old aphoristic mode). Gatsby is the Romantic idealist, and Fitzgerald had the genius to make him a *bad* poet (hearing Gatsby's version of his life 'was like skimming hastily through a dozen magazines'). When Nick, on the other hand, presents Daisy through Gatsby's perspective—whether he shares or only appreciates it—he rises to lyricism; when at the end he meditates on Gatsby's death, he rises to true poetry (Fitzgerald's models are Keats and especially Eliot).[22]

Second, the rôle of heroine is split, not into two women characters over whom one man is divided (as in *Tender is the Night*) but among three women, each of whom is, as it were, assigned to one man. Of course heroine is the wrong term, but we should not discount the extent to which the characters reflect and reflect on each other. Jordan Baker, first presented as indistinguishable from Daisy ('two young women . . . in white') turns out to represent a sort of masculine aspect or alternative: she has, along with name and (sporting) activity, taken on the masculine function of lying about the woman, that is herself. And Myrtle, Tom's vulgar mistress who is presumably beneath illusion or even the right to speak Daisy's name (she is slugged for doing so), nevertheless reveals her twinship in her own flower name, not to mention her sharing of Daisy's husband; she is a heroine in the *poetical rôle* which she, like Gatsby, finally plays: she dies, and in death achieves the dignity at least of surrendering her 'tremendous vitality'. But her closest link to Gatsby, and the most important if least remarked clue to the centrality of doubles in the fiction, lies in her other name. Myrtle 'returns' from the dead in the person of her avenging husband, who murders the hero and then himself, thereby duplicating the action of Poe's eponymous double—Wilson. *The Great Gatsby* acknowledges itself on every page tied to the tradition we have been examining; what astonishes is its masterful containment and transformation of it.

Finally, Fitzgerald's masterpiece owes much to the unprecedented distance he achieved in it from the immediate realities of his own life. True, he reproduced his myth of his own courtship and seduction of Zelda in Gatsby's of Daisy, but it is here not only relegated to the past but rendered in a manner frankly legendary. The profounder autobiographical truth which he seizes in *Gatsby* comes from what must have been a personal realization, that his survival as a pure Romantic would have depended on his *not* winning his bride. For the irony is that Fitzgerald, that incessant brooder on women and Woman, was not particularly good at rendering full or convincing women characters in his long fictions (he is, in this respect, far more the descendant of Poe than, say, of James), and only in this work can he transcend—by rendering explicit—his entrapment by one model who must symbolize *all* beauty and illusion—an all which must end as none. It is tempting to regard *Gatsby* as a kind of valedictory to one phase of the career, and the project that became *Tender is the Night* (originally planned as the history of a man who kills his mother) as a departure into realism of a different sort. If this is so, then the renewed and more extreme recourse to the primary text of Zelda takes on an irony of its own. He could not prevent himself, it seems, from asking the resulting character to be a 'prototype' of his idea, to embody for example 'the essence of a continent'; she could not help failing.

In her discussion of *Gatsby* in *The Resisting Reader* (1978) Judith Fetterly sees the transmutation of the woman as working in the other direction—from symbol to human—and terms the process 'investment/divestment', one 'through which the golden girl is revealed to be a common weed'. But this does seem to me backwards; although her argument has brilliant insights and is valuable for the feminist challenge it poses to received critical wisdom, its conclusion that Fitzgerald imposes the 'cultural double standard' in his relative treatment of men and women does not seem to take us very far.[23] Of course Fitzgerald was not only product and chronicler but to some extent prisoner of his culture (to a greater extent, I think, than we look for in pre-eminent writers). Poe's concept of intellect was far less gender-bound, for instance (witness Ligeia); a strong trait of Hawthorne's nature sympathized with and assumed guilty responsibility for the suppression of any, especially artistic, female strength and independence; and if James had a double standard, it weighed more heavily on his men. But Fitzgerald belongs with these writers, both by tradition and achievement. Like each of them he seems to us an originator: inventor of a character archetypal in American culture; like them, he actually draws on and enriches a tradition that has always been there.

NOTES

1. The most notorious case is Hemingway's *A Moveable Feast* (New York: Charles Scribner's Sons, 1964), where Ernest details Scott's inability to hold his liquor, his domination by a jealous and insanely destructive Zelda, the anatomical anxieties she causes him.
2. Nancy Milford, *Zelda* (New York: Avon, 1971); this work still provides the most systematic exposition of and commentary on Scott's borrowings. A more recent work by James R. Mellow, *Invented Lives: F. Scott and Zelda Fitzgerald* (New York: Ballantine Books, 1984), treats much of the same material from a slightly different perspective.
3. T. S. Eliot, 'Tradition and the Individual Talent' in *Selected Prose of T. S. Eliot*, ed. Frank Kermode (New York: Harcourt, Brace, Jovanovich, 1975), pp. 38, 43.

4. *This Side of Paradise* (New York: Charles Scribner's Sons, 1920), p. 171. Quotations from this and all subsequent novels and stories by Fitzgerald are from the Scribner Library editions. Zelda's letter is quoted in Milford, p. 78.

5. For an excellent sampling see Alfred Kazin (ed.), *F. Scott Fitzgerald: The Man and his Work* (New York: Collier, 1951), pp. 108–46 especially.

6. *Tender is the Night* (New York: Charles Scribner's Sons, 1934), p. 58. The new element I detect here is D. H. Lawrence, who is mentioned a few paragraphs before the remark quoted. Lawrence's tones are unmistakable in passages like the following: 'Dick didn't want to talk—he wanted to be alone so that his thoughts about work and the future would overpower his thoughts of love and to-day. Nicole knew about it but only darkly and tragically, hating him a little in an animal way, yet wanting to rub against his shoulder' (p. 169). Perhaps under this influence, Fitzgerald is more explicit about his protagonist's generalizing habits of thought, with some occasionally curious results, for example: 'as the woman who served him pushed up with her bosom a piece of paper that had nearly escaped the desk, he thought how differently women use their bodies from men' (p. 89). I have discussed this passage with women friends, colleagues and students on three continents and their verdict has been unanimous that Fitzgerald is on the evidence *absolutely* off on how women use their bodies.

7. The phrase appears in a long letter written by Henry, then 26, to his brother William on hearing of the death of their cousin, Minny Temple: 'The more I think of her the more perfectly satisfied I am to have her translated from this changing realm of fact to the steady realm of thought. There she may bloom into a beauty more radiant than our dull eyes will avail to contemplate.' Leon Edel (ed.), *The Letters of Henry James* (Cambridge, Mass.: Harvard University Press, 1984) I, 226.

8. In Poe's tale 'Eleanora' the heroine sees that 'she had been made perfect in loveliness only to die' (*Complete Works*, (New York: G. P. Putnam's Sons, 1902), IV, 310; hereafter *Works*). 'Psyche' is Poe's term for the soul, particularly in the form of ideal woman/muse, as in 'To Helen': 'Ah, Psyche, from the regions which/ Are Holy Land!'; or in 'Ulalume' itself, where the poet and his muse/soul ('Thus I pacified Psyche and kissed her') pass a night in a dark haunted woodland to which Amory's and Eleanor's seems indebted. For the relevance of Amory's sense of coming home, see the whole of the poem 'To Helen' ('Thy Naiad airs have brought me home' and so forth). A possible precedent for Eleanor's equestrian gesture can be found in the tale 'Metzengerstein', where a possessed steed and doomed rider plunge to their deaths together, the latter giving only one 'solitary shriek' while doing so (*Works* II, 221).

This might be the place to remark that, according to one biographer, the favourite writers of Fitzgerald's father were Byron and Poe (see Mellow, p. 17). Amory Blaine's father is given only half this predilection—'an ineffectual, inarticulate man with a taste for Byron' (p. 3)—perhaps because the other half was reserved for author and son. The title of Fitzgerald's first published story, 'The Mystery of the Raymond Mortgage', suggests an influence ('The Mystery of the Rue Morgue') so pervasive as to be unconscious.

9. *Works* I, 287; my emphasis.

10. *The Beautiful and Damned* (New York: Charles Scribner's Sons, 1922), p. 73.

11. Quoted in Milford, pp. 89–90.

12. Quoted in Milford, p. 273.

13. This century's image of American literature has been remarkably faithful to the model of D. H. Lawrence's *Studies in Classic American Literature* of 1925. Lawrence formulated there the 'Natty and Chingachkook myth' of white man paired with red man in a flight from woman and society, and it has been regularly repeated and elaborated since that time—most faithfully, perhaps, by Leslie Fiedler in *Love and Death in the American Novel* (1960). Hemingway (*Men Without Women*) was of course the embodiment of, if not high priest to, this tradition in Fitzgerald's lifetime; Norman Mailer is most conspicuously so in ours.

14. Frederic Jameson, *Marxism and Form: Twentieth-Century Dialectical Theories of Literature* (Princeton, N.J.: Princeton University Press, 1971), pp. 314–15.

15. This is one part of Philip Young's argument in *Hawthorne's Secret* (Boston: David R. Godine, 1984); the secret Young uncovers is a 'somehow' incestuous relation between Hawthorne and his sister which later haunts the writer and becomes encoded in his work. Although I too deplore the occasionally perfervid tone of the book, I take it more seriously and find it more convincing than some of my dismissive colleagues and its reviewers.

16. *Works*, IV, 320–25.

17. Daniel Hoffman, *Poe Poe Poe Poe Poe Poe Poe* (Garden City, N.Y.: Doubleday, 1973), pp. 295–315. Hoffman summarizes the theme of 'Usher' (which he finds stated even 'less equivocally' in 'The Oval Portrait') as follows: 'Madeline is Usher's twin, his sister, his lover, and—but this is true *only when he can think of her as dying*—his muse. It is as though her dying is a precondition for the exercise of his creative impulse. The notion that the artwork outlives its subject is indeed an old one, but Poe makes the artist a cannibal or vampire whose subject *must die* so that there may be art' (pp. 310–11; emphases in text).

18. Nathaniel Hawthorne, *Selected Tales and Sketches*, ed. Hyatt H. Waggoner (New York: Holt, Rinehart and Winston, 1950), pp. 203–21. Aylmer is nominally a scientist, but the analogy he uses for himself is to Pygmalion, and it is clear that he is the sculptor—or, since again only the face is in question, the portraitist—of his model/wife; he is a portraitist, in fact, who works on the 'material' of her own flesh, rather than on canvas, to realize his vision.

19. *The Complete Novels and Selected Tales of Nathaniel Hawthorne*, ed. Norman Holmes Pearson (New York: Modern Library, 1937), pp. 615, 627–28; the passages later cited are from p. 629.

20. Henry James, *The Wings of the Dove* (New York: Modern Library, 1930), p. 242.

21. Milford, pp. 418–19.

22. *The Great Gatsby* (New York: Charles Scribner's Sons, 1925), pp. 59, 67. Fitzgerald's attachment to Keats is well-documented and attested to in the title (from 'Ode to a Nightingale') of the novel which follows this one.

Indeed, some of the lush imagery and even rhythms of that ode are discernible in the 'fresh, green breast of the new world' passage which ends the book. But more strongly the passage, especially its final sentence— 'So we beat on, boats against the current, borne back ceaselessly into the past'—echoes, I think, the last lines of Prufrock:

> I have seen them riding seaward on the waves
> Combing the white hair of the waves blown back
> When the wind blows the water white and black.

> We have lingered in the chambers of the sea
> By sea-girls wreathed with seaweed red and brown
> Till human voices wake us, and we drown.

Fitzgerald, who hero-worshipped Eliot rather embarrassingly, made immediate use of 'not only the title, but the plan and a good deal of the incidental symbolism' of *The Waste Land* in *Gatsby*, particularly in the image of the valley of the ashes, but also to such details as his having his scapegoat hero meet, if not death by water, then at least death in the swimming pool (T. S. Eliot, *Selected Poems* (New York: Harcourt, Brace, Jovanovich, 1934), pp. 16, 68).

23. Judith Fetterley, *The Resisting Reader: A Feminist Approach to American Fiction* (Bloomington and London: Indiana University Press, 1978), pp. 73, 94.

8

'A Touch of Disaster': Fitzgerald, Spengler and the Decline of the West

by JOHN S. WHITLEY

How much F. Scott Fitzgerald knew about and was influenced by Oswald Spengler's work, *The Decline of the West*, and at what points in his career that influence became most profound have been matters of some debate.[1] Writing to Maxwell Perkins on 6 June 1940, Fitzgerald enquired:

> Did you ever read Spengler—specifically including the second volume? I read him the same summer I was writing *The Great Gatsby* and I don't think I ever quite recovered from him. He and Marx are the only modern philosophers that still manage to make sense in this horrible mess—.[2]

Fitzgerald's memory was probably at fault here, perhaps because, as André Le Vot points out,[3] Marx and Spengler seem to have been powerful influences on the novelist in the 1930s: first Marx when the Depression became really bad and then back to Spengler with the threat and then the onset of the Second World War. His closeness to the German historian at the time of his letter to Perkins perhaps suggested that *The Decline of the West* must have influenced his own masterpiece, a novel full of Spenglerian images of decline. Robert Sklar pointed out years ago, attacking R. W. Stallman's notion that *The Decline of the West* was a major influence on *The Great Gatsby*, that

157

Spengler's first volume was not published in English until 1926 and that Fitzgerald did not read German.[4] Perkins sounds as if *he* is introducing Fitzgerald to Spengler's work in a letter of 27 April 1926:

> I'm almost afraid to tell you about a book that I think incredibly interesting—Spengler's 'Decline of the West'—for you'll tell me it's 'old stuff' and that you read it two years ago;—for it was published eight years ago in Germany and probably six in France, and has been a long time translating into English.[5]

Fitzgerald appears not to have responded to this point in any of his subsequent letters to Perkins, and his editor may have been the first person to prompt Fitzgerald to look at *The Decline of the West*. However, Fitzgerald could have been alerted earlier through his relationship with Princeton professor, Christian Gauss, or through various magazine articles about Spengler prior to the first English edition, such as W. K. Stewart's 'The Decline of Western Culture: Oswald Spengler's "Downfall of Western Civilization" Explained' in the July 1924 *Century*.[6]

Certainly the importance of the German historian's ideas to Fitzgerald, right to the end of his days, is confirmed by Sheilah Graham in her account of the novelist's attempts to educate her in Hollywood in the late 1930s:

> 'Spengler and Modern Philosophers' was to be the culmination of my education, as it had been for Kathleen and her ex-king in *The Last Tycoon*. 'When you have completed Spengler you will know more of history than Scottie at Vassar,' he promised me. After he explained Spengler to me, I wondered whether I could ever read him. How could one man know so much of cultures and civilizations? And how alarming he was, with his prophecies of wars that would ravage Europe, then America, and spiral across the Pacific until Asia was master of the world.[7]

Sheilah Graham never got to Spengler and seems to have found H. G. Wells's *Outline of History*, almost a polar opposite of Spengler's book, a much more interesting companion. Kathleen's progress, in *The Last Tycoon*, mirrors Sheilah's:

> He made out schedules. . . . He wanted me to read Spengler—everything was for that. All the history and philosophy and harmony, was all so I could read Spengler, and then I left him before we got to Spengler. . . .[8]

There are critics for whom Kathleen's failure to read *The Decline of the West* is a crucial factor in any understanding of Fitzgerald's last, unfinished novel.[9]

Sklar remarks, perceptively, that Fitzgerald's interest in Spengler was 'yet one more aspect of his curious reversion to the moods and attitudes that shaped his intellect and art at the very start of his career',[10] and certainly one could argue that what drew the novelist most directly to Spengler's book was its very title. One of his most famous statements about his art occurs in the 1937 essay 'Early Success':

> All the stories that came into my head had a touch of disaster in them—the lovely young creatures in my novels went to ruin, the diamond mountains of my short stories blew up, my millionaires were as beautiful and damned as Thomas Hardy's peasants.[11]

'Disaster', 'ruin', 'damned'; the words are appropriate to much of Fitzgerald's fiction both before and after Spengler came into his life. In telling him that the civilization of the West was in decline, the German historian was, in a sense, merely giving form and scholarship to something the American novelist had always known.

In this essay I wish to concentrate (though not exclusively) on some of the fiction prior to *The Great Gatsby* and consider aspects of that fiction both in terms of Spengler's ideas and in terms of other influences on Fitzgerald's basic pessimism. These influences include both the Romantic poets, especially Keats, who contributed to a persistent theme whereby ideals repeatedly came into contact with obdurate reality, thus causing disillusionment and disintegration, and the American naturalist writers, particularly Frank Norris, for whose work Fitzgerald early conceived a relish, writing to Perkins in 1920: 'There are things in *Paradise* that might have been written by Norris—those drunken scenes, for instance—in fact, all the realism. I wish I'd stuck to it throughout!'[12] That is perhaps why he makes Dick Caramel say, near the end of *The Beautiful and Damned*:

> Everywhere I go some silly girl asks me if I've read *This Side of Paradise*. Are our girls really like that? If it's true to life, which I don't believe, the next generation is going to the dogs. I'm sick of all this shoddy realism.[13]

As Sheilah Graham notes, Fitzgerald retained his admiration for Norris and the better writers of social realist novels throughout the rest of his life.[14] There is, of course, a strong sense of decline in these writers. Influenced both by Zola and by Nordau's *Degeneration* (1895) the particular flavour of their *fin-de-siècle* pessimism comes from a dark view of the evolutionary process, a feeling that the spiritual and brutal sides of man's nature are near aligned, witnessed by the almost Gothic 'otherness' of the 'beast' in Norris's work and by the more horrific yoking of man to animal in H. G. Wells's *The Island of Dr. Moreau* (1896) and restrained civility to unrestrained appetite in R. L. Stevenson's *The Strange Case of Dr. Jekyll and Mr. Hyde* (1885). In much of this work there is a strong sense of civilization tottering on the brink of some abyss, like the fragile world of Stephen Crane's *Maggie: A Girl of the Streets* (1893), constantly exploding into fragments before the bewildered participants.

A third influence would be the general pessimism of American literature between the two world wars. Leon Howard, for instance, asserts that those writers most typical of the '20s generally wrote with a sense of '*après moi la déluge*'.[15] Whether much of this feeling resulted from a fashionable following of people like H. L. Mencken or can simply be dismissed as 'sophomoric',[16] it was pervasive and was much stimulated, in 1922, by the publication of *The Waste Land*. The opening of that poem, with its inversion of the opening lines of *The Canterbury Tales*, suggests that the natural rhythms linking body to nature to spirit are no longer working, one of the key indices of decline in Spengler's account. The relation of this kind of pessimism and the distrust of the new physics to Fitzgerald's early work will be explored a little later in this essay. Fitzgerald was also concerned with what he considered to be a decline in moral values in the American society around him. He was fascinated by the rich and by the spectacle of a 'whole race going hedonistic, deciding on pleasure',[17] but he was also acutely aware of the stern moral rebukes carried regularly by leading newspapers and journals throughout the 1920s. For example, he cannot have been unaware that the increasing incidence of 'petting' was linked, in the minds of many, to a boom in automobile sales. By the mid-'20s many campuses were banning student-owned automobiles, partly because of traffic problems, but mainly because they were seen as agents of moral disintegration. 'Fast' cars provided opportunities for misbehaviour by 'fast' boys and girls; by the time that Isabelle Borge enters *This Side of Paradise* she has acquired a reputation as a 'speed'.[18] In *The Great Gatsby* there are many references to cars and driving, often gaudy cars and very bad driving. The ability to 'steer' becomes an important moral metaphor.

All the above factors coalesce in Fitzgerald's treatment of love, marriage, motherhood, promiscuity and male/female relationships generally. Writing to Perkins in 1940, Fitzgerald seemed to indicate that the second volume of Spengler had more importance for him than the first. At one point, quite early in the second volume, in the chapter 'The Soul of the City', Spengler takes as a principal item of evidence for the decay of the West the sterility of civilized man. He wishes, in part, to use the word 'sterility' literally: 'Children do not happen, not because children have become impossible, but principally because intelligence at the peak of intensity can no longer find any reason for their existence.'[19] Man, giving overdue emphasis to his intelligence, has lost his connection with the eternal rhythms of Nature:

> When the ordinary thought of a highly cultivated people begins to regard 'having children' as a question of *pro*'s and *con*'s, the great turning-point has come. For Nature knows nothing of *pro* and *con*.[20]

What follows, in the city-civilization which ends each thousand-year cycle, is a great emphasis on contraception. This has been accompanied, in the West, by women's desire for 'freedom', by ideas of companionate marriage, by the Ibsenite and Shavian heroines who have soul-conflicts rather than children and who want to belong to no one other than themselves. The concept of motherhood, central to Spengler's notion of 'culture', that period of creative activity in society where Nature and man are in harmony, is now rejected. The decline of the West is signified in sexual and familial sterility.

In Fitzgerald's work there are few depictions of parent/offspring relations. In the five novels, the only major figures to become parents are Dick and Nicole Diver who succeed, prior to their separation, in having appalling scenes in front of their children, and Tom and Daisy Buchanan who '. . . were careless people . . . they smashed up things and creatures and then retreated back into their money or their vast carelessness. . . .'[21] Despite the warmth and great charm that constantly characterizes Fitzgerald's relationship with his daughter, Scottie, the short story that comes closest to describing their relationship, 'Babylon Revisited' (1931), describes the father as a repentant ex-drinker whose escapades killed his wife and gave his sister-in-law and her husband custody of his daughter. An unfortunate accident prevents him regaining custody and he *is* portrayed sympathetically, but the reader is left with the clear impression that bad parents may very well lose, and deserve to lose, their children.

This almost fairy-tale morality structure is followed in an early story, 'The Cut-Glass Bowl' (1920). There the fragile, meretricious nature of American life (the story begins in the 1890s but there is little attempt to give a meaningful historical location) is summed up in its love of cut-glass ornaments: artifacts doomed, like those Huckleberry Finn sees in the Grangerford house, to undergoing the full process of decline. In one paragraph, during the 'struggle for existence', they are 'knocked', 'chipped', 'fractured', 'scarred' and 'maimed' and a number 'disappeared'.[22] Their fragility mirrors the fragile moral nature of Evylyn Piper who is given the ornament of the title by a discarded admirer, almost as an act of enmity, and for whom marriage offers little hindrance to a continuing succession of such admirers. The bowl acts as a witness to the deterioration of the marriage ('. . . she and Harold had drifted into a colourless antagonism . . .'),[23] increasing lapses into drunkenness, the deformity of Evylyn's daughter (blood poisoning, following the cutting of her thumb on the bowl, leads to the loss of her hand) and the death of her son in the Great War. The moral pattern is completed firmly when Evylyn, trying to throw the bowl away, falls and dies at the same time as her ornament; the final image being specifically one of disintegration:

> And all over the moonlit sidewalk around the still, black form, hundreds of prisms and cubes and splinters of glass reflected the light in little gleams of blue, and black edged with yellow, and yellow, and crimson edged with black.[24]

Spengler's fears of population suicide could be aligned with the tremendous attention given to contraception in the early years of the twentieth century: an interest which allowed births to be spaced according to financial needs, rôles within marriage to be changed, often quite drastically, and female sexuality to be recognized and sanctioned to a much greater extent in the 1920s than ever before. That Fitzgerald shared with Spengler a view (however naïve and romantic) of the cultural importance of motherhood long before the crucial connection between cultural sterility and incest in *Tender is the Night* (1934) can be seen by brief examinations of his first two novels. In *This Side of Paradise* (1920) Amory Blaine is surrounded by 'vamps' and 'speeds' and shows an alarming propensity to equate sex with evil. A brief alternative is provided by his third cousin, Clara Page, whom Monsignor Darcy describes as 'rather a remarkable woman' (129). One can see why: 'she was alone in the world, with two small children, little money, and, worst of all, a host of friends' (130). When told that she is remarkable, she emphatically denies this: 'I'm really most humdrum and commonplace. One of those people who have no interest in anything but their children' (131). Amory, of course, falls in love with her, but *reverently*, and writes a poem for her and about her called 'St. Cecilia': 'But she was the first fine woman he ever knew and one of the few good people who ever interested him' (133). She helps people, gives them excellent advice, provides a restful ambience for the weary of spirit, and so on, and so on. Naturally she takes on, for Amory, a strongly religious aura:

> She was very devout, always had been, and God knows what heights she attained and what strength she drew down to herself when she knelt and bent her golden hair into the stained-glass light. . . . (135)

Amory longed 'only to touch her dress with almost the realization that Joseph must have had of Mary's eternal significance' (136). She declines to marry Amory because

> I've got my two children and I want myself for them. . . . I assure you that if it weren't for my face I'd be a quiet nun in the convent without my precious babies, which I must go back and see. (137)

Of course, it can be argued that one of the delights of Fitzgerald's first novel is the accuracy with which he chronicles how it felt to be young in the early years of the century, an accuracy capable of making the reader squirm with sympathy and embarrassment. Amory is young, naïve, romantic and therefore quite apt to divide the women he meets into angels and devils, but the Clara episode is treated without irony and she does not appear in the novel after that. Moreover, if Amory's views of women seem limited there is little authorial correction of this (though Rosalind is shown to be less vampish than Amory seems to believe). Women in this novel, as in much of Fitzgerald's work, seem to have difficulty in growing up. Rarely operating as mother-figures, they are offered as emblems of that materialism into which Spengler insisted that Western civilization had declined: shoddy products, like the cut-glass ornaments, manufactured by their era. With Clara, by contrast, Fitzgerald carefully interweaves references to physical beauty, kindness, motherhood, Mary-worship and a more general 'religious' aura to establish a significant difference between Clara and the other women in Amory's world. There are few clearer indications of Fitzgerald's essential conservatism.

In his second novel, *The Beautiful and Damned* (1922), more obviously under the spell of the Naturalists, one strong index of the appalling degeneration of the Patches is their unwillingness to have children. The primary refusal is seen to be Gloria's. Anthony prefers Gloria because, beside her, most other women were 'so many *females*, in the word's most contemptuous sense, breeders and bearers, exuding still that faintly odorous atmosphere of the cave and the nursery' (89). Gloria herself echoes this: 'What a fate—to grow rotund and unseemly, to lose my self-love, to think in terms of milk, oatmeal, nurse, diapers . . .' (124). She is appalled when she believes she is pregnant and when she is informed that she is not she sleeps 'untroubled', nursing a child's doll (187). Much later in the novel she remains adamant: 'She knew that in her breast she had never wanted children. The reality, the earthiness, the intolerable sentiment of child-bearing, the menace to her beauty—had appalled her' (319). Small wonder she turns out to be a very bad driver— '. . . Gloria was a driver of many eccentricities and of infinite carelessness' (147)—or that she cares little for people in general: 'Millions of people, swarming like rats, chattering like apes, smelling like all hell . . . monkeys! Or lice, I suppose' (320).

Small wonder, too, that Anthony's mother dies when he is very young and Gloria's is a vain, prattling creature whose only legacy to her daughter is the lunatic tenets of Bilphism. The only other mother briefly mentioned, Dorothy Raycroft's, is described as 'tired' and 'spiritless' (275).

I have already pointed out that the increasing (and increasingly successful) use of contraception in the United States in the 1920s meant that greater emphasis than before was placed on female sexuality and woman's place in the marital relationship. She was now much less the sub-ordinate partner for, as Paula S. Fass points out: 'Contraception freed women from that rôle assignment and its necessary constrictions at the same time that it permitted a fuller expression of women's total personality and emotional needs.'[25] Yet this freedom caused much suspicion and concern to be directed at young women in this decade. Dancing, smoking, automobiles, petting, these activities coalesced, for many older people, into an alarming picture of debauchery and loss of values. According to Professor Fass it was thought that:

> Once released from previous controls and well-defined rôles, women risked the danger of succumbing to impulse, of entering upon a path from which there was no return, of teetering on the edge of sexual promiscuity.[26]

By 1930, Fitzgerald could write that the contemporary girl 'is our finest and most representative product from the point of view of beauty, charm and courage . . .',[27] and his early work, especially, rarely fails to register effectively the glamour and excitement of the 'flapper'. However, he remains always very clear that the 'flapper' is an index of possible degeneration and decay. If his overt attitude is sometimes that of the celebrants of the Jazz Age, his covert attitude seems to be consistently Victorian.

It could be argued that this covert attitude emerges often as a cumulative effect of a host of minor references. In *This Side of Paradise* Isabelle is compared to Thaïs and Carmen. Just before Amory meets Eleanor ('the last time that evil crept close to Amory under the mask of beauty' (200)) he loses his way in the wood in a most Comus-like manner: 'He stumbled blindly on, hunting for a way out, and finally, through webs of twisted branches caught sight of a rift in the trees . . .' (201). In the story 'May Day' (1920) the girl who both leads Gordon Sterrett astray and represents the declining values in New York is called Jewel Hudson (Fitzgerald had as great a delight in naming his characters as Henry James). In *The Beautiful and Damned* Gloria is viewed as being without mercy, 'la belle dame sans merci', the familiar Keatsian figure who persistently recurs in Fitzgerald's work. Gloria makes men miserable; she 'struck to kill' (69). This relates to Rosalind Connage in *This Side of Paradise* who, according to her sister Cecelia, is 'a sort of vampire' who treats men in an appalling manner: 'she abuses them and cuts them and breaks dates with them and yawns in their faces— and they come back for more' (155); just as much as to Evylyn Piper as well as later *femmes fatales* such as Ailie Calhoun in 'The Last of the Belles' (1929) or even Nicole Diver. Some of these figures are placed in more serious contexts than others but the family relationship is clear. The influence of Keats and other Romantic poets on Fitzgerald has been carefully chronicled, but not always in relation to his concern for decline. If women, for Fitzgerald as well as Keats, represent mystery, beauty and sometimes, as in Poe's work, the eternity which only art can envisage, they also represent the terrible passing of time and the approach of death as well as the brutal intrusion of reality upon the dreams and ideals of the hero. Almost at the end of *This Side of Paradise*, only two pages before Amory cries 'I know myself . . .' (254), he comments on just this aspect of the Romantic heritage:

> Inseparably linked with evil was beauty—beauty, still a constant rising tumult; soft in Eleanor's voice, in an old song at night, riding deliriously through life like superimposed waterfalls, half rhythm, half darkness. Amory knew that every time he had reached toward it longingly it had leered out at him with the grotesque force of evil. (252)

Thus, in Fitzgerald's writings, women in general become easily associated with the cheap, gaudy and distasteful in life. In *This Side of Paradise* the changing terms for young women imply degeneracy: 'The "belle" had become the "flirt", the "flirt" had become the "baby vamp" ' (61). Each term is a little worse than the one before. Shortly afterwards, Isabelle is called a 'speed' (63). Eleanor, despite her magical qualities, was part of a rather fast crowd 'who drank cocktails in limousines' (209).

Amory is depressed by the ugliness of city life and dwellers, an ugliness signalled by 'the fetid sensuousness of stale powder on women' (229) and by an inversion of the values represented by Clara: '. . . where even love dressed as seduction—a sordid murder around the corner, illicit motherhood in the flat above' (230). In *The Beautiful and Damned*, Anthony and Gloria's horror at the working-classes seems directed less at their male representatives than 'their giggling, over-gestured, pathetically pretentious women' (61), and Anthony remembers lectures being given to undergraduates on 'the ever-present menace of "women" ' (65). Travelling by train through the upper East Side of New York, Anthony's vision of tenement life seems much narrower than that of *How the Other Half Lives* or *A Hazard of New Fortunes*:

> From the tenement windows leaned rotund, moon-shaped mothers, as constellations of this sordid heaven; women like dark imperfect jewels, women like vegetables, women like great bags of abominably dirty laundry. (232)

Fitzgerald may very well be poking fun at Anthony Patch's egotism when he has him feeling, almost at the end of the novel, that 'All the distress that he had ever known, the sorrow and pain, had always been because of women' (360), but the direction of the book, while paying due regard to Anthony's weakness of character, tends to suggest that it might not have been so disastrous a life if he had avoided Gloria and continued a 'safe' batchelor. In his essay, 'The Crack-Up', Fitzgerald made a general observation: 'the test of a first-rate intelligence is the ability to hold two opposed ideas in the mind at the same time, and still retain the ability to function.'[28] This sounds rather like a cut-price version of Keats's 'negative capability', but despite his attempts to maintain the balanced view of women, between beauty and evil, Fitzgerald had too deep a sense of decline not, frequently, to allow one idea to assume a certain dominance. This is particularly the case when the ticking of the clock becomes loud.

Fitzgerald brilliantly demonstrates, throughout *The Great Gatsby*, how well he understands and recreates the Keatsian belief that the arch enemy of the Romantic sensibility is Time. Frequently, in his early work, the remorseless movement of

Time is linked to an equally remorseless sense of moral and material decline and this, in turn, is measured by the ageing process in women. In 'Early Success' he laughs at such apprentice pretensions as 'she was a faded but still lovely woman of twenty-seven',[29] but equally he is not interested in the progress to anything approaching *old age*, only in the decline of beauty, of ideals, of a capacity for wonder. Time's ravages constitute a moral decline. In 'The Cut-Glass Bowl' the movement of the narrative to its awful conclusion is signposted by Evylyn Piper's changes of age and appearance. She begins the story at 27, 'beautiful'[30] with 'young, dark eyes'[31] and lips 'like tearings from a rose'.[32] We next see her at 35 when 'the mystery had departed' and 'Her mouth also had lost . . .'.[33] Finally, at 46: 'A tentative outlay of wrinkles on her face suddenly deepened and flesh collected rapidly on her legs and hips and arms.'[34]

The same kind of pattern informs *The Beautiful and Damned*. Although emphasis is placed on the physical degeneration of both Anthony and Gloria, hers tends to predominate and operate metronomically in the narrative, like Evylyn's. Gloria enters the narrative at the age of 22: 'She was dazzling—alight; it was an agony to comprehend her beauty in a glance' (51). As she nears 24 she goes into 'an attractive but sincere panic . . .'. With more drinking she moves less with a sinuous motion and more with 'a tremendous effort of her nervous system . . .' (181). She looks well but her stomach hurts her. At 26 the serenity had become grey, things 'had been slipping perceptibly' and 'both of them seemed vaguely weaker in fibre . . .' (228). Outwardly 'Gloria at twenty-six was still the Gloria of twenty' (243) but this is described as a 'shell' (292). Approaching her twenty-ninth birthday her beauty is 'faintly tired' (318). Following a bout of double pneumonia, slightly underweight, she takes a screen test but does not get the part because a younger woman is needed. She is, instead, offered the small character part of 'a very haughty rich widow' (327) and, for the first time, she perceives 'tiny wrinkles' (328). She takes to smeering her face at night with 'some new unguent which she hoped illogically would give her back the glow and freshness of her vanishing beauty' (337) and her hair changes from a rich reddish-gold to 'an unresplendent light brown' (344). At the end when she and a broken Anthony, having finally acquired $30,000,000 from the will of Adam Patch, take a sea-voyage, Fitzgerald, using a technique later brought more sophisticatedly to prominence by Faulkner in *Light in August* and Golding in *Pincher Martin*, introduces brand-new characters solely to give a new and jolting view of the Patches. Much earlier in the novel Gloria had divided women into 'clean' and 'unclean': 'By uncleanliness she meant a variety of things, a lack of pride, a slackness in fibre and, most of all, the unmistakable aura of promiscuity' (194). Despite the fact that the last charge cannot reasonably be laid at Gloria's door, it does seem entirely appropriate, in the closing moments of the novel, that the 'pretty girl in yellow' should say of Gloria: 'I can't stand her, you know. She seems sort of—sort of dyed and unclean . . .' (363).

Enforcing this view of women as the catalysts of decline is a variously reiterated notion of certain distinctions between men and women in their response to life's vicissitudes. Gloria Patch herself becomes a mouthpiece for this idea:

> Women soil easily—far more easily than men. Unless a girl's very young and brave it's almost impossible for her to go down-hill without a certain hysterical animality, the cunning, dirty sort of animality. A man's different—and I suppose that's why one of the commonest characters of romance is man going gallantly to the devil. (194)

and on the very next page we meet a minor validation of this statement when we are told that the Patches' Japanese servant, Tana, was fond of Anthony and instinctively, like all their servants, detested Gloria. Fitzgerald once complained, early in his career, about the over-emphasis, in American fiction, on the development-of-the-young-man theme:

> This writing of a young man's novel consists chiefly in dumping all your youthful adventures into the reader's lap with a profound air of importance, keeping carefully within the formulas of Wells and James Joyce.[35]

But his first novel uses this fully (as he acknowledged in the same letter), there are strong elements of it in his second, and Lionel Trilling once suggested that *The Great Gatsby* follows a typical European fictional process in regard to this theme.[36]

Fitzgerald follows a well-used American writing pattern in viewing the course of his country's civilization through the *Bildungsroman* form, and a useful clue to Fitzgerald's adherence may be found in *This Side of Paradise*.

Monsignor Darcy, expressing his hopes for Amory's development, makes an important distinction between a 'personality' and a 'personage':

> Personality is a physical matter almost entirely; it lowers the people it acts on—I've seen it vanish in a long sickness. But while a personality is active, it overrides 'the next thing'. Now a personage, on the other hand, gathers. He is never thought of apart from what he's done. He's a bar on which a thousand things have been hung—glittering things sometimes, as ours are; but he uses these things with a cold mentality back of them. (100)

'Personality' is defined as 'it', 'personage' is a 'he'. Book Two is then called 'The Education of a Personage' to enhance this theme, and when Amory and Rosalind are in the last throes of their novelettish relationship we are told that 'There is a difference somehow in the quality of their suffering' (177). The significant differences in the development of men and women crystallize in the Basil Duke Lee and Josephine Perry stories, as their editors, Jackson R. Bryer and John Kuehl, point out.[37] Fitzgerald published eight of the nine Basil stories in the *Saturday Evening Post* between April 1928 and April 1929 and all five Josephine stories in the same magazine between April 1930 and August 1931. That is, they all occur between the publication of *The Great Gatsby* and that of *Tender is the Night*. The stories, taken individually, are slight affairs, relying on the novelist's well-known ability to remember and accurately reproduce the behaviour and feelings of adolescence. Taken as two series, however, they demonstrate an important distinction in authorial attitudes. In the story 'He Thinks he's Wonderful' there is a moderately ironic relation of Basil's experience to such campus stories as *Stover at Yale*:

> He believed that everything was a matter of effort—the current principle of American education—and his fantastic ambition was continually leading him to expect too much. He wanted to be a great athlete, popular, brilliant and always happy.[38]

170

and the title of another story, 'Forging Ahead', pays suitably ambiguous tribute to the Horatio Alger tradition. Yet, despite multiple ironies and setbacks, Basil *does* forge ahead, becoming a popular athlete, making academic progress, being adored by various girls. He is a 'personage' capable of profound development:

> Time after time, the same vitality that had led his spirit to a scourging made him able to shake off the blood like water not to forget, but to carry his wounds with him to new disasters and new atonements—toward his unknown destiny.[39]

To put it another way, Basil's destiny is envisaged by Fitzgerald as being more like those of Dink Stover or Paul Morel than those of Henry Fleming or Martin Eden. In contrast, the five stories involving Josephine, although they only carry her age from sixteen to eighteen, chronicle a steady decline. In 'A Nice Quiet Place' she is styled a 'principal agent of corruption',[40] and we are told, at the end of 'A Snobbish Story', that 'she threw in her lot with the rich and powerful of the world forever.'[41] The concluding story is titled, significantly, 'Emotional Bankruptcy' and takes place in the Fall of 1916, not long before the entry of the United States into the Great War. Life is seen by her as 'a game played with technical mastery, but with the fire and enthusiasm gone',[42] and she ends the story on a note of all passion spent: 'She was very tired and lay face downward on the couch with that awful, awful realization that all the old things are true. One cannot both spend and have.'[43]

It is not surprising that, in his early work, Fitzgerald intensifies this anti-woman, anti-sex feeling with passages of a more melo-dramatic nature, passages which tend to link him quite strongly with those Naturalistic writers, like Norris and Frederic, whom he so admired and which Amory Blaine discovers to be excellent 'through a critic named Mencken' (189). For writers such as Norris, Crane, Frederic, Bierce and London the pessimistic side of Darwinian evolutionary ideas is that if man is climbing steadily away from the level of brute beast he has not, in the long view of history, yet travelled very far, and it seems all too easy for him to slip back to that ancient condition. For them, consequently, man is very often a victim of the beast within himself (Vandover's nemesis in Norris's *Vandover and the Brute*)

171

which demands release in drunkenness (alcoholism was coming to be a major problem in American cities by the closing years of the nineteenth century) or bestial sexual behaviour. Crane wrote of the horrors of alcoholism in *George's Mother*, and the worst aspect of Theron Ware's journey through the hell of the city in Harold Frederic's novel is his inability to obtain oblivion in drink when he so desperately wants it. In *The Beautiful and Damned*, likewise, one major point in the decline of the Patches comes with the 'realization that liquor had become a practical necessity to their amusement . . .' (228) and the path downhill is strewn with empty bottles: 'Added to this was the wretched aura of stale wine, with its inevitable suggestion of beauty gone foul and revelry remembered in disgust' (242). Certainly this last passage, with its faint hint of Keats, has the right kind of melodramatic vulgarity to link it directly to Norris.

Of far greater significance are those moments, especially in Fitzgerald's first two novels, where revulsion against women/ sex on the part of the central protagonists assumes the status almost of something numinous, a sense of an overpowering evil alive and beyond human capacity for control. Amory Blaine becomes conscious of some sort of wrongness, 'like weakness in a good woman' (108), and feels sick amid the noise and 'painted faces' (111) of Broadway. His memory of a 'sidelong, suggestive smile' (112) on a woman's face makes a sudden blackness flow around him, and on the train for Princeton the sight of 'a painted woman' (112) makes him feel sick again. Later, when he rides with Eleanor, an 'evil moon' (200) looks down on them. Again, one must accept that Fitzgerald is trying, often with remarkable success, to recreate for his readers the facile mentality of the undergraduate, but when, almost at the end of the novel, Amory links the problem of evil with the problem of sex, the reader is bound to admit that the drift of the narrative has been towards a validation of that linking: 'Amory knew that every time he had reached toward it [Beauty] longingly it had leered out at him with the grotesque face of evil' (252).

In *The Beautiful and Damned*, during the night before his wedding to Gloria, a union which is to bring more disaster to him than to her, Anthony is feeling quite happy when he hears the noise of a woman's laughter which intrudes 'jarringly' on the rest of the city's noises. It starts low and whining then becomes high-pitched and hysterical. Starting again, it sounds coarse, then 'strangely terrible'. It reaches the point almost of being a 'scream' and then it stops, impressing its 'animal quality' on Anthony. Not for the first time does Fitzgerald make the association between women and animality, thus suggesting that women are more predatory in sexual matters and hence closer to the 'beast' of Darwinian fears. Occurring when it does in the novel, this experience of terror has to act as a kind of premonition, a warning to Anthony of what is to follow the marriage ceremony. Anthony is greatly upset by his experience and full of 'his old aversion and horror toward all the business of life . . . Life was that sound out there, that ghastly reiterated female sound' (125/26). Anthony could have been affected by any kind of sound, but not merely is the female sound reiterated, Fitzgerald makes sure that its *female* nature is also reiterated.

The language used to describe these experiences in both novels is routinely Gothic: 'horror'; 'darkness'; 'leering'; 'evil'; 'blackness'. Its Gothic flavour, oddly enough, also links it to Naturalist fiction, for in both brute nature, particularly of a sexual inclination, exists as a kind of 'otherness' flowing beneath normal existence, ready to snare the unaware, unlucky innocent. Thus poor Haight, in *Vandover and the Brute*, cuts his lip on a chipped glass, is kissed by a whore and contracts syphilis. Such a feeling of 'otherness' is powerfully *there* in Fitzgerald's first two novels and helps to explain one of Fitzgerald's rare excursions into the supernatural, 'A Short Trip Home' (1927). I have already mentioned strong notions of degeneration and perversion in novels of the end of the century in both England and America.

One prominent example of the concern is Henry James's *The Turn of the Screw* (1898), the work of a writer familiar with literary interests on both sides of the Atlantic. In this tale, James's response to the decadent 1890s is to outline a threat to the well-being of two beautiful small children, either from the ghosts of promiscuous servants or the prurient mind of their governess. The horror is generated less by the possibilities of the supernatural than by the possibility that the 'innocents' possess a knowledge of sexual deviance which they should never have had. They are objects both of beauty and horror. In Fitzgerald's story, shorn of Jamesian ambiguity, the ghost is that of a minor hoodlum: 'His eyes were a sort of taunt to the whole human family—they were the eyes of an animal, sleepy and quiescent in the presence of another species.'[44] His trick is to get money from girls travelling alone on the train. We are never told exactly how, but there is a clear implication of sexual knowledge that such girls ought not to have. As in the work of Norris and others of his time, such corruption is imaged as being just beneath the daylight world, ready to show itself once the guard has slipped:

> I tried to think how lucky we were to be comfortably off and taken care of, but all the warm, respectable world I had been part of yesterday had slipped away from me. There was something we carried with us now that was the enemy and the opposition of all that; it was in the cabs beside us, the streets we passed through.[45]

Moreover, the threatened girl, Ellen Baker, in her enthralment to this malignant presence, gives way to the brute within herself. She speaks with 'almost a snarl'[46]; her face is 'contorted with mirthless, unnatural laughter'[47] and she keeps showing an 'expression of low-animal perspicacity'.[48] She becomes part of what the narrator describes as a 'contagion of evil'[49] but is saved by the narrator who has a 'solid foothold in the past'[50] and a 'faith in the essential all-rightness of things and people'.[51] In other words, a young man with a sense of tradition and development.

Fitzgerald's work, then, represents, in its treatment of women, motherhood and sex, a configuration of influences from Romanticism, Naturalism and contemporary social comment, quite apart from the writer's own personality. We should also remember that Spengler saw as a feature of the decline of the West, as well as a lack of interest in motherhood and an increase in contraception, an intensification of the Puritan conception of sex as a sin. For Fitzgerald, like the Naturalists, there is also a sense that people are safest when sex is no longer an issue, when all passion is spent. In Norris's *McTeague* (1899) the important characters who remain unscathed are the elderly couple, Old Grannis and Miss Baker, who end in this position precisely because they are old. They are left in 'a little Elysium of their own creating',[52] happy and passionless, happy *because* passionless, amid the debris of marital/sexual breakdowns which surround them. A not dissimilar ending occurs in Fitzgerald's 'The Lees of Happiness' (1920), a story which the author described, in a letter to Burton Rascoe, as 'perhaps a little gloomy'.[53] The plot concerns the relationship between Roxanne, married to novelist Jeffrey Curtain who suffers a cerebral haemorrhage, the first sign of which is to treat his wife as an enemy, and who then remains a vegetable for years, and Jeffrey's friend, Harry Cromwell, who is married to Kitty, a slut and a bad mother. Divorced, Harry persists in a platonic relationship with Roxanne, both growing older without the conflict of marriage and children. Yet the ending, though muted, is calm and conciliatory:

> To these two life had come quickly and gone, leaving not bitterness, but pity; not disillusion but only pain. There was already enough moonlight when they shook hands for each to see the gathered kindness in the other's eyes.[54]

One final influence remains, which links Fitzgerald's early work to the Spengler he did not then know. In the 1920s, as later in American literature, the concept of 'entropy' was to prove of considerable importance. The term, and its application to the notion that the universe was running down, came from Rudolph Clausius in 1845 and was then developed by John Clerk Maxwell in the 1860s into the form that became known as the Second Law of Thermodynamics. By the 1920s this had been converted to a notion that the universe was doomed. People talked of the 'heat death of the universe', a hypothetical situation which would come about when the disordering tendency expressed by the Second Law of Thermodynamics, acting over aeons of future time, resulted in the absence anywhere in the universe of energy in a form which could be converted into work by organisms. The initially ordered system of the universe is randomizing and running down as time proceeds. The English version of Max Nordau's *Degeneration* (1895), a powerful influence on *fin-de-siècle* writing, maintained that society's capacity for order was doomed because of loss of energy which has been syphoned off into technology and city life. Henry Adams, in his 'Letter to American Teachers of History' (1909), transformed the notion ('nothing would be left except a dead ocean of energy at its lowest possible level')[55] into a kind of law of history.

Spengler, believing, like Nordau, that Western civilization was approaching the end of a thousand-year cycle, emphasized the loss of energy involved in the shift to world-cities and the dominance of money:

> Now the giant city sucks the country dry, insatiably and incessantly demanding and devouring fresh streams of men, till it wearies and dies in the midst of an almost uninhabited waste of country.[56]

For him, the true mark of the sterility of civilized man is 'an essentially metaphysical turn towards death'.[57] The effects of the notion of entropy on American literature in the inter-war years can be seen at their most pessimistic in the poetry of Robinson Jeffers:

> For man will be blotted out, the blithe earth die, the brave sun
> Die blind, his heart blackening

and their most brilliant in the uses of reification in Nathanael West's *The Day of the Locust* (1939).

Fitzgerald's most obvious use of this idea occurs, as Tony Tanner points out, in the Valley of Ashes section of *The Great Gatsby*: '. . . and, finally, with a transcendent effort, of ash-grey men who move dimly and already crumbling through the powdery air'[58] and in its most important denizen, Wilson, '. . . a bland, spiritless man, anaemic . . .'.[59] Wilson reminds the reader of the mechanistic Bitzer in Dickens's *Hard Times* (1854) who looked as though 'he would bleed white'.[60] The Valley of Ashes owes an obvious debt to *The Waste Land*, but it could be argued that Fitzgerald's most concerted description of an increasingly entropic state occurs in *The Beautiful and Damned*, first published in the same year as Eliot's poem. The representatives of their world, Anthony and Gloria Patch, are repeatedly characterized by such words as 'lethargy' and 'inertia'. Their behaviour was 'a triumph of lethargy' (178). Gloria, like the ash-grey men of the Valley of Ashes, finds that everything becomes a 'tremendous effort' (181). Anthony can, at one point, be seen as a clear representative of Spengler's sterile civilized man, moving only towards extinction:

> Listlessly Anthony dropped into a chair, his mind tired—tired with nothing, tired with everything, with the world's weight he

176

had never chosen to bear. He was ineffectual and vaguely helpless here as he had always been. One of those personalities who, in spite of all their words, are inarticulate, he seemed to have inherited only the vast tradition of human failure—that, and the sense of death. (181)

It is worth remembering, too, that Nordau attributed the decline of his contemporaries not merely to the strains of industrial and city life but to their consumption of alcohol and tobacco, a consumption about which Fitzgerald knew only too well and which, as we have already seen, continually signposts the joint decline of the Patches. Small wonder that Frederick E. Paramore, paying a surprise visit to Anthony and Gloria at the grey house in the country, could be lingering there 'in order at some future time to make a sociological report on the decadence of American life' (222).

In his admirable biography of Fitzgerald, André Le Vot suggests that the novelist was only the second major male American writer (Henry James being the first) to oppose the American imagination's rejection of women and create successful, independent, victorious American girls: 'With *The Great Gatsby* and *Tender is the Night*, the romance of chivalry for a while dethroned the epic.'[61] This seriously overstates one side of the case. There emerges from Fitzgerald's work, both early and late, a deep distrust of women. How much of this was created by his own personality, by that instinctive male hatred of women examined so caustically by Germaine Greer in *The Female Eunuch*, by an updated version of that Victorian attitude in which, according to Kate Millett:

> The disparity between the good and the evil, chaste and sensuous woman, figures older than Christianity, becomes far more overt than it had ever been previously, partly because the cover of religious sanction afforded by the figures of Eve and Mary had pretty well collapsed.[62]

or by the complaint of H. L. Mencken, voiced in the same year as *The Beautiful and Damned* and presumably referring at least as much to his fellow-countrymen as to anybody else:

> Men do not demand genuine beauty, even in the most modest doses; they are quite content with the mere appearance of beauty. That is to say, they show no talent whatever for differentiating between the artificial and the real.[63]

it is impossible to say. What is clear is that Fitzgerald had, from his earliest days as a writer, a very strong sense of decline and decay, a sense neither originated nor changed, only enhanced, by the influence of Oswald Spengler, and that a prominent aspect of this was his treatment of women and related themes of sex and motherhood. Recognizing the ease with which discussions of possible sources and influences can easily paint the artist as a kind of talented magpie, I hope that the foregoing discussion will have offered sufficient illustration to make quite clear that whatever F. Scott Fitzgerald took from various currents of his time, he made entirely and brilliantly his own.[64]

NOTES

1. I am grateful to my colleague, Dr. Peter Nicholls, for his helpful advice during the writing of this article.
2. Andrew Turnbull (ed.), *The Letters of F. Scott Fitzgerald* (Harmondsworth: Penguin, 1968), p. 310.
3. André Le Vot, *F. Scott Fitzgerald* (Harmondsworth: Penguin, 1985), p. 270.
4. Robert Sklar, *F. Scott Fitzgerald: The Last Laocoön* (New York: Oxford University Press, 1967), p. 135.
5. John Kuehl and Jackson R. Bryer (eds.), *Dear Scott/Dear Max* (London: Cassell, 1973), p. 139.
6. See Matthew J. Bruccoli, *Some Sort of Epic Grandeur* (London: Hodder and Stoughton, 1981), pp. 206–7.
7. Sheilah Graham, *College of One* (Harmondsworth: Penguin, 1969), p. 78.
8. F. Scott Fitzgerald, *The Last Tycoon* (Harmondsworth: Penguin, 1963), p. 111.
9. See, for example, Kermit W. Moyer, 'F. Scott Fitzgerald's Two Unfinished Novels: The Count and the Tycoon in Spenglerian Perspective', *Contemporary Literature*, XV (Spring, 1974), 238–56.
10. Sklar, p. 223.
11. F. Scott Fitzgerald, *The Crack-Up* (Harmondsworth: Penguin, 1965), pp. 59–60.
12. *The Letters*, p. 162.
13. F. Scott Fitzgerald, *The Beautiful and Damned* (Harmondsworth: Penguin, 1966), p. 341. All subsequent parenthetical page references are to this edition.
14. Sheilah Graham, pp. 116–17.
15. Leon Howard, *Literature and the American Tradition* (Garden City, N.Y.: Doubleday and Company, 1960), p. 274.
16. See Ernest Earnest, *The Single Vision* (New York: New York University Press, 1970).

17. *The Crack-Up*, p. 11.
18. F. Scott Fitzgerald, *This Side of Paradise* (Harmondsworth: Penguin, 1963), p. 63. All subsequent parenthetical page references are to this edition.
19. Oswald Spengler, *The Decline of the West* (New York: Knopf, 1928), II, 104.
20. Ibid.
21. F. Scott Fitzgerald, *The Great Gatsby* (Harmondsworth: Penguin, 1958), p. 186.
22. F. Scott Fitzgerald, *The Diamond as Big as the Ritz* (Harmondsworth: Penguin, 1967), p. 7.
23. Ibid., p. 25.
24. Ibid., p. 30.
25. Paula S. Fass, *The Damned and Beautiful* (New York: Oxford University Press, 1977), p. 71.
26. Ibid., pp. 23–4.
27. F. Scott Fitzgerald, 'Girls Believe in Girls', *Liberty*, vii (February, 1930), 22–4. Reprinted in Matthew J. Bruccoli and Jackson R. Bryer (eds.), *F. Scott Fitzgerald: In his Own Time* (New York: Popular Library, 1971), p. 211.
28. *The Crack-Up*, p. 39.
29. Ibid., p. 60.
30. *The Diamond as Big as the Ritz*, p. 7.
31. Ibid., p. 8.
32. Ibid., p. 9.
33. Ibid., p. 13.
34. Ibid., p. 24.
35. Letter to Thomas Boyd on 9 February, 1921. Matthew J. Bruccoli and Margaret M. Duggan (eds.), *Correspondence of F. Scott Fitzgerald* (New York: Random House, 1980), p. 79.
36. Lionel Trilling, *The Liberal Imagination* (Garden City, N.Y.: Doubleday and Company, 1950), p. 242.
37. Jackson R. Bryer and John Kuehl (eds.), *The Basil and Josephine Stories* (New York: Scribner's, 1973), pp. vii–xxvi.
38. Ibid., p. 78.
39. Ibid., p. 98.
40. Ibid., p. 205.
41. Ibid., p. 269.
42. Ibid., p. 276.
43. Ibid., p. 287.
44. F. Scott Fitzgerald, *Bernice Bobs her Hair and Other Stories* (Harmondsworth: Penguin, 1968), p. 109.
45. Ibid., p. 121.
46. Ibid., p. 119.
47. Ibid., p. 120.
48. Ibid., p. 122.
49. Ibid., p. 120.
50. Ibid., p. 117.
51. Ibid., p. 123.
52. Frank Norris, *McTeague* (Greenwich, Conn.: Premier, 1960), p. 228.

53. Letter to Burton Rascoe on 6 August 1920. *Correspondence*, p. 65.
54. *The Diamond as Big as the Ritz*, p. 238.
55. Henry Adams, *The Degradation of the Democratic Dogma* (New York: Peter Smith, 1949), p. 145.
56. Spengler, *The Decline of the West*, II, 102.
57. Ibid., 103.
58. *The Great Gatsby*, p. 29. See Tony Tanner, *City of Words* (London: Jonathan Cape, 1976), p. 143.
59. *Gatsby*, p. 31.
60. Charles Dickens, *Hard Times* (New York: Norton, 1966), p. 3.
61. Le Vot, *F. Scott Fitzgerald*, p. xi.
62. Kate Millett, *Sexual Politics* (London: Abacus, 1972), p. 128.
63. From *In Defense of Women*, 1922. Reprinted in Alistair Cooke (ed.), *The Vintage Mencken* (New York: Vintage Books, 1955), p. 124.
64. As an afterword, I note that Robert Sklar interprets the 1929 story 'The Swimmers', which he correctly describes as 'neglected' and 'undervalued', in terms of Spengler's theories, making the triumph of Henry Clay Marston a triumph of Nature over money. It is, however, useful to note that it is also a triumph of an American man over his shallow, unfaithful, French wife who relinquishes the custody of their sons. See Sklar, *F. Scott Fitzgerald*, pp. 236–39.

9

The Lost Teigueen: F. Scott Fitzgerald's Ethics and Ethnicity

by OWEN DUDLEY EDWARDS

Tadhg, -aidhg, m., a poet (Dav.), personal name Teig, Teague or Thady, Tady (= Thaddeus) and equated with Timothy (*Tiamhtha*, early), the typical Irishman (*esp.* the plebeian type, while *Diarmaid* seems applicable to the upper class); *T. an mhargaidh*, the 'man in the street'; . . . *Taidhgín*, g. id., pl. -i, m., dim. of *Tadhg*, Tim, etc.; . . . *tuigeann Tadhg T.*, one rogue understands another . . .
—Rev. Patrick S. Dinneen, *Foclóir Gaedhilge agus Béarla: An Irish-English Dictionary*[1]

Yesterday I saw the film of *Tender is the Night*. I had never heard Fitzgerald's name until after his death, after the war, when a film producer remarked that I must have been greatly influenced by him.

(a) The American self-killers—Fitzgerald, Hemingway were apostate Catholics.

(b) *Litera scripta manet*. . . . The enormously expensive apparatus of the film studio can produce nothing as valuable as can one half-tipsy Yank with a typewriter. But we novelists should remember that our 'characters' and our 'dramas' are mere shadows compared with those of the real world.
—Evelyn Waugh, diary entry for 9 May 1962[2]

The historian interested in cultural evidence finds in F. Scott Fitzgerald an invaluable witness to the character of a decade

181

in the mind of the North Atlantic. The decade is that of the 1950s. Fitzgerald was actually too much the creator of the 1920s to epitomize them, and much of what he put into them was his distillation of experience before they began. But the 1950s responded to him with an enthusiasm far beyond any reflected in the sales of his books during his lifetime. At his death in 1940 his writings were out of print or out of demand. After the war they re-emerged, thanks in part to the editorial conviction, the personal devotion and the critical evangelism, of Edmund Wilson. In 1950 Budd Schulberg brought out his novel *The Disenchanted* based on his knowledge of Fitzgerald in his last years. In 1951 Arthur Mizener produced the first biography. Thousands of paperbacks of his novels were snapped up on both sides of the Atlantic throughout the decade, and as the more famous titles showed their appeal and staying-power publishers turned to all else that could be obtained.[3] Surviving contemporaries such as Malcolm Cowley noted the literary resurrection with misgiving and doubts as to its staying-power. Assessing Fitzgerald's stature in the vocabulary of the stock-exchange, Cowley somewhat sourly commented on the cult features:

> His stories were collected and published with a long intro-duction, and many of them were dramatized for television and radio. Professors of contemporary literature and fiction writing discovered that his work was extremely teachable because of the notes he left behind him, and that students could profit even from his mistakes. By that time students were indeed profiting, in more ways than the professors intended. At several American univer-sities—Princeton less than others—they were trying to relive the 1920s, acting with the romantic desperation of Fitzgerald heroes, and wearing their fathers' coonskin coats to football games. As for Fitzgerald stock on the Big Board, it attracted speculators, had a dizzy rise, and in the summer of 1951 it was being bought and sold at what I should judge to be two or three times its par value.[4]

Some observers, among them Kenneth Eble, agreed that it was part of a special '20s' cult in the 1950s: 'The older generation is old enough to feel nostalgia for it; the younger constrained enough to respond to its freedom.' But he saw it as the product of contrast.[5] MAD magazine, which was probably unrivalled in its expertise on youth cults of the '50s, saw fundamental similarities between the decades.[6] The 1950s certainly added its macabre interests: the generation which read Fitzgerald found a cult hero of its own in James Dean. 'Disenchanted' was a great vogue word of the decade. But Eble was essentially right in seeing an association between the Fitzgerald cult and yearnings for liberation in manners, sexual relations and human integrity. The Fitzgerald cult of the 1950s did not directly confront the prevailing socio-political consensus, but it sounded an early, uncertain trumpet in remote, almost unconscious rally to a future confrontation.

The cult may have passed, but the sceptical Cowley proved very wrong in assuming it had inflated Fitzgerald stock above par: his reputation among critics, and his popularity among readers, has continued to climb. This popularity certainly made some literary people a little nervous: witness the emphasis of so many critical analyses on the fidelity of Fitzgerald to the tradition of Henry James.[7] James E. Miller, for instance, went to great lengths to show that Fitzgerald, undeniably influenced by H. G. Wells in his first novel, came to accept James's position in his famous debate with Wells on literary form and structure.[8] But there was little surface evidence for such a conclusion. It would be hard to find two styles more at variance than the prolixities of James and the almost icy clarity and succinctness of Fitzgerald, particularly the Fitzgerald of *The Great Gatsby* where the Jamesian spirit was held to have conquered. Fitzgerald was ready enough to perform lip-service to the higher cultural ideals of the day, but in practice while deferring to his friend Edmund Wilson by thoughts of *Daisy Miller* and reading *What Maisie Knew* (and Zelda read *Roderick Hudson*)[9] he continued to return to Wells and similar influences of his adolescence, however surreptitiously. *This Side of Paradise* owed its final female rejection of Amory Blaine to the influence of George Ponderevo in *Tono-Bungay*, but if anything that work was stronger rather than weaker in its hold on him for later books. In *The Beautiful and Damned*—

> 'Memory is short', he thought.
> So very short. At the crucial point the Trust President is on the stand, a potential criminal needing but one push to be a jail-bird, scorned by the upright for leagues around. Let him be

acquitted—and in a year all is forgiven. 'Yes, he did have some trouble once, just a technicality, I believe.' Oh, memory is very short!

—might almost stand as a gloss on the fall of Uncle Teddy Ponderevo and the reflections of uncle and nephew thereon.[10]

What Fitzgerald did do was to bring much more forceful but constructive criticism to bear on his old literary icons, and thereby made them inspire fresh answers. *Tono-Bungay* has the artistic flaw that we never discover exactly how Uncle Teddy managed to make Tono-Bungay take off; Fitzgerald made a similar lack of discovery of the origin of Gatsby's wealth absolutely integral to the artistic unity of *The Great Gatsby*. And *Tono-Bungay* concludes: 'We are all things that make and pass, striving upon a hidden mission, out to the open sea.' While *Gatsby* directly responds to that challenge in its end: 'So we beat on, boats against the current, borne back ceaselessly into the past.' Even the very last word is inspired by the sound of Wells's confident progress 'make and pass': but 'pass' becomes 'past' as Wells's neo-Whig interpretation of history is literally thrown into reverse. 'Sea' similarly prompts the sound with which Fitzgerald affirms it as the unattainable: 'ceaselessly'. Wells, with the confidence of the late Victorian rebel, partly follows the assured imagery of Swinburne's *Poems and Ballads: First Series* (1866), in its 'The Garden of Proserpine':

> We thank with brief thanksgiving
>   Whatever gods may be
> That no life lives for ever;
> That dead men rise up never;
> That even the weariest river
>   Winds somewhere safe to sea.

Fitzgerald, like his Amory Blaine, had 'tried hard to look at Princeton through the satiated eyes of . . . Swinburne', and now in *Gatsby* was sure of none of those things. Above all, he knew what God might be, and was far beyond any form of thanking Him. Swinburne and Wells might offer a cheerful agnostic progress, even though it might be a progress towards oblivion; Fitzgerald saw a terrible survival and resurrection of a buried past. George Ponderevo looks back to produce his narrative of *Tono-Bungay*, but with a confident worldly-wisdom and control, distilled of his experience; Nick Carraway in *The Great Gatsby* is a haunted narrator.

From this it becomes easy to see the fantastic charade of Uncle Teddy's world of empty ostentation and frog-leaps in self-advancement transferred from its place as a detail in the *Tono-Bungay* canvas to its central position in *Gatsby*. Fitzgerald was acutely sensitive to charges of plagiarism, and grew increasingly uneasy at implications that he had given himself inadequate cultural foundations, but he remained a professional story-teller, and the major change in his work from the first two novels was in the surer hand with which he built. He strengthened his cultural base (with Conrad, for instance) but he did not discard the old bricks. Wells had also served him, it would seem, in 'The Diamond as Big as the Ritz'; the idea of a strange new country with different values, the ultimate assurance of social acceptance being consolidated by a supreme sacrifice, the flight of the hero from that sacrifice and its surrounding paradise, and the final alienation from the ethos of the new country, are all factors in 'The Country of the Blind'. The variants are obvious (and there are other sources), but it is a nice touch that where Wells at the end has the beloved girl becoming 'small and remote', Fitzgerald allows his hero to keep the girl while it is her diamonds that prove to have lost their grandeur.[11]

The critics in the 1950s, perhaps uneasy at finding themselves for once on the popular side, took their starting-point on the James trail from T. S. Eliot's tribute to *Gatsby*:

> . . . it has interested and excited me more than any new novel I have seen, either English or American, for a number of years.
> . . . In fact it seems to me to be the first step that American fiction has taken since Henry James.

Nobody seems to have commented on the curious resemblance the tribute holds to one written by Henry James about Compton Mackenzie's *Sinister Street* some twelve years earlier:

> He affects me at any rate as, putting one or two aside (or rather as putting Wells only . . .) as very much the greatest talent of the new generation. And the modernity of him! It is such a happy and unexpected change to be interested!

When the second volume of *Sinister Street* appeared a year later, James wrote to tell Mackenzie 'that I had emancipated the English novel'.[12]

Fitzgerald himself was gratified by Eliot's praise: a man from Minnesota receiving a tribute from a man from Missouri could hardly ask for a reference-point which would distance them more emphatically, than would this literary landmarking by invocation of James, from their own unfashionable Midwestern origins. Certainly nobody would reflect that it had been a very different James whose violent demise had been the most newsworthy event in Missouri six years before Eliot's birth. Even so, a Protestant birth in the state so recently identified with the deathplace of Jesse James conferred a higher status than a Catholic birth in the city of St. Paul, the name of whose most famous citizen symbolized the alien origin of his and Fitzgerald's people: the Roman Catholic Archbishop Ireland. Fitzgerald needed acceptance by those of a higher cultural, as well as social, ethnic and geographical origin than he possessed, as *Gatsby* reminds us, and his posthumous clinching of the acceptance should release rather than affirm the necessity to further his illusions.

Fitzgerald's mother was an Irish-American Catholic, with a background reflecting the confidence and opportunity of an Irish-dominated Midwestern city rather than the abrasive Northeastern ghettoes whence his fellow-Irish so abrasively and vulnerably struggled to rise. He was proud of the deep colonial Maryland roots of his paternal grandmother, and was quiet about her Irish husband, Michael Fitzgerald, of whose background nothing is known.[13] He may not even have been Irish: Omar's Fitzgerald had been English and so, too, had been that 'hoarse Fitzgerald' whose bawling provided Byron with the first line of 'English Bards and Scotch Reviewers'. But Michael Fitzgerald left a son Edward able to marry into the staunchly Catholic McQuillans of St. Paul without difficulty.[14] In any case Fitzgerald's Maryland legacy was more pointedly Anglophobic than any of his Irish forbears might supply. He was much less closely related to Francis Scott Key than he seemed to think,[15] but it was the ancestral link of which his family made the most, and it carried a bitter disdain for American truckling to British cultural or political ascendancy:

And where is that band who so vauntingly swore,
   That the havoc of war and the battle's confusion
A home and a Country should leave us no more?
   Their blood has wash'd out their foul footsteps' pollution.
      No refuge could save the hireling and slave
      From the terror of flight or the gloom of the grave,
      And the star-spangled banner in triumph doth wave
      O'er the land of the free and the home of the brave.

But the affirmation of the American credential thus given to the mid-nineteenth century (1842 and hence pre-Famine) immigrant McQuillans was broadly asserted on positive lines, and the fruit of the union of old and new families was duly saddled with the inescapably patriotic name of Francis Scott Key Fitzgerald. He wanted to escape from the visibility of the need for such proclamation, and he did it by the nonconformity of the habitual reduction to one first name and initial which he employed from an early stage. F. Scott Fitzgerald, unlike his mother, saw no need to assert an American identity. It may well have been the credential-seeking of the McQuillans which produced his initial alienation; it was only later that he would discover how deeply the crass Philistines of the new South wrapped themselves in a Confederate cult with which as a boy he had sought to distance himself from St. Paul conformity.

The first major literary influence on him was, not surprisingly, of Irish Catholic origin; his early tutors may not have been aware that it was also ex-Catholic. Arthur Conan Doyle first attracted him through the Sherlock Holmes stories, though later he was to read the deeply researched and cheerfully anticlerical medieval romances *The White Company* and *Sir Nigel*.[16] From Conan Doyle he would have received his first lessons in literary economy, in the structure of the short story deployed with scientific precision, and in the use of the commonplace for the creation of haunting atmosphere.[17] He would also have learned how wit, irony and the celebration of great literature could be integrated with narrative of force, pace, mystery and heightened emotion. His first surviving attempt at fiction is in the Holmes-and-Watson manner, although even at the age of 12 he grasped the unrealized possibilities his model handed to him. His 'The Mystery of the Raymond Mortgage' follows the pattern of *A Study in Scarlet* in having the Watson figure,

Egan, initially exhibit contempt for the Holmes character, but instead of private resentment Fitzgerald has it expressed as an outright insult: ' "I am not here", I interrupted coldly, "to tell every newspaper reporter or adventurer about private affairs. James, show this man out." '[18] Egan is in fact a chief of police (whose 'ablest detective in the force' is called Gregson, as is a comparable policeman in *A Study in Scarlet*—'the smartest of the Scotland Yarders . . . the pick of a bad lot'). Egan later makes a handsome apology for his rudeness, but the difficulty for the Holmes protagonist in winning *social* acceptance, and making little of its refusal, is suggestive (as is the extraordinary manorial *seigneur* style of the police-chief). In passing, the title draws on that of Conan Doyle's chief inspiration in the field of the detective story—Edgar Allan Poe's 'The Murders in the Rue Morgue'; and it may have been important that Fitzgerald so firmly identified his work with the American point of origin, while the text of his work derived from the Irish-Scots elaboration.

A slightly later story, 'The Room with the Green Blinds', also shows by its title that Fitzgerald was looking at another of Conan Doyle's sources, in this instance Stevenson's *New Arabian Nights*,[19] but for all of its setting as a sequel to the American Civil War the *dénouement* is deliciously Holmesian: ' "Gentlemen", said he, "Let me present to you John Wilkes Booth, the slayer of Abraham Lincoln" ' (the speaker indicating the corpse of the man he has just despatched). Compare Holmes in *A Study in Scarlet*: ' "Gentlemen", he cried, with flashing eyes, "let me introduce you to Mr. Jefferson Hope, the murderer of Enoch Drebber and Joseph Stangerson." ' The association of ideas will also be sufficiently obvious: the murderer in *A Study in Scarlet* has a first name which to a boy saturating himself in Confederate pieties would promptly suggest Jefferson Davis, but while the story is sympathetic to Confederates the villain is to be a villain, not a scapegoat, so hence John Wilkes Booth, presented as a far more villainous figure than Jefferson Hope or Jefferson Davis. Perhaps the young Fitzgerald felt his Northern audience would have wanted an unquestionably execrable Southerner as villain, however much good feeling might be deployed on defeated Confederates (who actually unmask Booth); perhaps he was asserting the limits of his Confederate sympathies.

And it is to Watson and Holmes that we have to look for the very earliest origin of Carraway's relationship with Gatsby. Conan Doyle had shown Fitzgerald how a narrator can bring the apparently inaccessible protagonist within the view of the reader while continuing to elude the reader's understanding. It is true that Henry James was to try such a plan in his later fiction, but as Marcus Cunliffe judiciously remarks of the James 'character-observer': 'The snag in James is that this person tends to seem ineffectual, unconvincingly dedicated to the well-being of others, and almost pruriently inquisitive.'[20] On this point at least Fitzgerald had no need of James; he had received his tutelage from the method's true Master.

This is the most important effect of Conan Doyle on Fitzgerald, but some elementary deductions on the relationship of *Gatsby* to the Holmes cycle may be added. The data, save when otherwise stated, are from *A Study in Scarlet*. Watson's initial *caveat* (as though anticipating Professor Cunliffe)—'The reader may set me down as a hopeless busybody, . . . Before pronouncing judgment, however, be it remembered how objectless was my life . . .'—is brilliantly worked into the opening of *Gatsby*, but then reversed: Carraway represents himself as having confidences thrust upon him rather than seeking them (although as becomes apparent he does seek them, at least in Gatsby's case), and Watson's warning to the reader against hostile judgement becomes Carraway's father's to Carraway. The initial hostility of Watson to Holmes, already worked on by Fitzgerald in the 'Raymond Mortgage', is here with the exquisite precision which marks all of *Gatsby* made an overture: 'Gatsby, who represented everything for which I have an unaffected scorn.' The delay in gaining any information on the object of enquiry is common to both, and the unexpected, apparently casual, offering of an opening is common also. Carraway's finding himself talking to Gatsby while under the impression his interlocutor is anyone else follows the various Watson meetings with a disguised Holmes from *The Sign of Four* onwards (most notably in the stories of Holmes's 'death' and 'resurrection', 'The Final Problem' and 'The Empty House'); it is a double twist in that Gatsby is not disguised at all, and it later emerges his whole life is a disguise. Carraway's apology for the incident is dismissed by Gatsby as alluding to something quite unimportant; so also is

189

Watson's compliment to Holmes in *A Study in Scarlet* masking his acknowledgement that Holmes is not a charlatan, only to have it swept aside. The sequel in both cases is an utterly unlooked-for invitation, and virtual demand, for Watson's and Carraway's hitherto unsought companionship on an exotic short journey.

General allusions to Holmes's European reputation and consequent decorations prefigure Gatsby's. The casual reference in the litany of Gatsby's guests to Edgar Beaver, 'whose hair they say, turned cotton-white one winter afternoon for no good reason at all', sounds like Poe's Maelstrom-survivor with a memory of Watson's allusions to unsolved cases of Holmes not recounted by him, satirically applied.

> Isadora Persano, the well-known journalist and duellist, who was found stark staring mad with a match box in front of him which contained a remarkable worm said to be unknown to science

seems the best candidate (there is a horrific nuance to Fitzgerald's satire, as there is satire in the horror of Conan Doyle); the Persano mystery is mentioned in the best of the last Holmes stories, 'Thor Bridge', which was published in *Hearst's International* in February and March 1922, and Fitzgerald, who had no doubt been studying the magazine in advance, contracted to write for it the following December.[21] Fitzgerald would have been interested in the confrontation of Holmes and the Gold King, Senator Neil Gibson. Watson's remark before he discovers Holmes's profession—'I was on the point of asking him what that work might be, but something in his manner showed me that the question would be an unwelcome one'—is characteristically sharpened by Fitzgerald into: 'when I asked him what business he was in he answered: "That's my affair", before he realized that it wasn't an appropriate reply.' Finally, Carraway's farewell to Gatsby, which he does not know is a final farewell, is given when Gatsby is a silhouette in colour, reminiscent of his silhouette at the end of the first party Carraway attended, and Watson's last sight of Holmes in 'The Final Problem' is also one of a lone form. Watson concludes that narrative, which he and his creator take to be a final conclusion, with the famous tribute adapted from Plato's *Phaedo* (where it refers to Socrates), 'the best and the wisest man whom I have ever known', and Carraway tells Gatsby in the last words he will ever speak to him: ' "You're worth the whole damn bunch put together." '

Fitzgerald quickly learned to avoid open allusion to writers whom his coevals were in the habit of discarding with the rest of their childhood playthings: only to the closest confidant of his later adolescence, Father Sigourney Fay, does he seem to have indicated a surviving involvement in Conan Doyle. But as a professional writer he would have noted how the old man continued to deliver for his readers. His own 'The Love Boat', for instance, appeared in the same number of the *Saturday Evening Post* as an instalment of Conan Doyle's 'The Maracot Deep'.[22] Ironically, his Princeton career might very well have brought him without interruption along the road to agnosticism, which Conan Doyle began at his Jesuit school, had it not been for that same confidant. The Sigourney Fay episode in Fitzgerald's life, together with all that swam in the train of Sigourney Fay (whose ultimate immortality was to supply the maiden name of Gatsby's Daisy)—Shane Leslie, Henry Adams, Cardinal Gibbons, Sir Cecil Spring Rice, Compton Mackenzie, A. J. Balfour, Oscar Wilde, Robert Hugh Benson, Algernon Charles Swinburne, St. John Ervine, W. B. Yeats, John Millington Synge, Pope Benedict XV, James Joyce, Bourke Cockran, Mrs. Winthrop Chanler, Charles Scribner, Rupert Brooke—reactivated Fitzgerald's involvement in a Catholic and Irish inheritance. It enabled him to taste the wine of that inheritance in a manner and at a moment of extraordinary excitement, when it seemed to tower in judgement over a Western culture towards which the McQuillans even more than the Maryland families had been striving for acceptance. And although he left his Catholic faith, it never left him; he was haunted by it as Joyce, whose cold usage of it is proverbial, was not haunted. Both in faith and culture its effects were to leave the values of his American contemporaries hollow at heart for him. Fitzgerald became the great interpreter of American society for his readers and critics of the 1950s, not because he won the immigrant goal of reaching its heights, but because he had stood above them.

The cartography of Fitzgerald's relationship with Sigourney Fay has been charted as clearly as the evidence permits.[23] It needs rather closer scrutiny for analysis. Commentators have handled Sigourney Fay somewhat gingerly, in part because non-Catholics are often uneasy in talking about Catholic priests beyond generalization, in part because Sigourney Fay seems a scarcely credible figure. In fact, he seems like a character in a novel. Waugh's Father Rothschild, S. J., in *Vile Bodies* might have been modelled on him, or on some aspects of him.[24] Perhaps it was not, but Waugh had imbibed much at the springs which had touched Sigourney Fay at a higher point; Fay was deeply involved by his reading of Compton Mackenzie's *Sinister Street*, which certainly influenced Waugh's *Brideshead Revisited*, and he greatly influenced Shane Leslie, whose novels of the 1920s were in the Mackenzie line and may also have affected Waugh.[25]

Sigourney Fay was extremely conscious of his own logical place in a novel, and went to some pains to ensure that the thing be done to his satisfaction; the most obvious result of his endeavours was *This Side of Paradise*. He seems to have been fascinated by the mingling of identities. He signed an article which he declared to have been chiefly the work of the dying Henry Adams[26]; he had notions of taking over Mackenzie's Michael Fane of *Sinister Street*[27]; he saw himself as father to Fitzgerald, but somehow equated both Fitzgerald and himself with Fane[28]; he carefully corrected Fitzgerald's fictional portrait of himself[29]; Fitzgerald even in the final text of *This Side of Paradise*, written after Fay's death, included much of Fay's own words in the letters and conversation of 'Monsignor Thayer Darcy', but Darcy was also the name of a character invented by Fitzgerald for a play before he met Fay and Darcy was a pseudonym he thought of using in his final years[30]; Fay projected articles by Fitzgerald and himself 'signed with any initials we care to put to it'[31]; Fitzgerald was convinced that Fay appeared to him at the moment of his death[32]; and so on. Sigourney Fay did not merely read certain novels and encourage Fitzgerald to do so; they possessed him, he entered them, he saw himself recreated by them and sought to induce creation himself in his turn. The result was that if Fitzgerald fictionalized Fay, Fay had also created Fitzgerald.

The process is most obvious in *This Side of Paradise*. Fitzgerald presumes that before taking orders his Fay figure had been the lover of the mother of Amory Blaine, the character based on himself; there is a slight implication that he could be Blaine's real father. But the use of Fay's actual words, especially in his letters to Fitzgerald, makes for a curious division in the character of Blaine. Darcy remains consistent: the memory of Fay, his letters and his own revisions had seen to that. But Blaine is not simply Fitzgerald; he is a working out of aspects of Fitzgerald's character and life-style to logical conclusions beyond reality, and he is also a confessional means of Fitzgerald's self-accusation. The result is that when Fay's actual correspondence takes over, *verbatim* or with tolerably faithful streamlining by Fitzgerald, the student whom Darcy is supposed to be addressing appears to be a much more likeable character than the Blaine who should be under assessment. And if Sigourney Fay relished self-fictionalization, he seems to have been a wise and realistic mentor in the moral instruction of Fitzgerald. In his letters he obviously loves him with a realism which knows the existence of a finer person than Blaine is otherwise supposed to be. Fay loved Fitzgerald; Fitzgerald did not love himself. Hence Amory Blaine splits into different people, that addressed by Darcy being more worthy of literary as well as human attention—in fact, something closer to Nick Carraway. Darcy's Blaine, otherwise Fay's Fitzgerald, may be closer to a real likeness of the author than his own.[33] But this is not enough; the Eleanor episode, for instance, is based on an experience of Fay's earlier life, not on anything that happened to Fitzgerald, and Fay went to some pains to ensure that Fitzgerald got it right.

So Blaine is not only split between Fitzgerald's self-portrait and Fay's protégé; he is also, albeit briefly, Fay himself.[34] He owes much to the suspiciously similar-sounding Fane of *Sinister Street*, but here Fitzgerald was much more master of his material than when he was dealing with sources from real life, since to him Fane was a character in a book (although to Mackenzie he possessed much of Mackenzie). He was right to reject accusations of plagiarism, since what he did was to rationalize Mackenzie's method for his purposes. For instance, *Sinister Street* may intend to draw a sympathetic portrait of Fane's mother, but it offers evidence that might justify a far less charitable interpretation whatever the author's intentions. Fitzgerald leaves his readers in no doubt of his view of Amory Blaine's mother, who is not so much derivative of Mrs. Fane as

Scott Fitzgerald: The Promises of Life

an acid rethinking of her implications. Above all, *Sinister Street* views its central protagonist from the inside, and reader as well as author are drawn within Fane; Fitzgerald and his reader remain severely outside Blaine.³⁵ It crudifies their opposition to term Mackenzie's Fane a case for the Defence, and Fitzgerald's Blaine a case for the Prosecution; the contrast is much more subtle, culminating in conclusions such that the reader is remotest from Fane in saying farewell to him, but is closest to Blaine at the same point. But for the course of the two novels the distinction may at least be helpful.

But if the sound of Fane disappears from Fitzgerald when he ceases to write about Blaine, the sound of Fay does not. In *The Great Gatsby*, Daisy is initially 'Daisy Fay', Gatsby (when he is Gatsby) is 'Jay', and his protector's dubious Madame de Maintenon is 'Ella Kaye'. Jordan Baker's aunt is 'Mrs. Sigourney Howard'. The ultimate purpose of all of this I suspect to be partly theological; it is an invocation of the spirit of Sigourney Fay sprinkled around various places in the work, much as Fay had liked blessing with holy water different rooms in the house of a friend. But the games Fay and Fitzgerald played of entering outside fictional characters into both of themselves, and themselves into Fitzgerald's characters, sometimes the same characters, are still evident in *Gatsby*.

Part of Fitzgerald is used for part of Gatsby, most notably in his point of origin (young Gatz is stated to be in South Dakota, but the father comes to the funeral from Minnesota and likens his son's infant potential to St. Paul's most prominent secular citizen James J. Hill, the railroad tycoon beloved of the McQuillans) but at another point Gatsby suggests Fay:

> The truth was that Jay Gatsby of West Egg, Long Island, sprang from his Platonic conception of himself. He was a son of God—a phrase which, if it means anything, means just that—and he must be about His Father's business, the service of a vast, vulgar, and meretricious beauty.

The description of the Father's business is not that of Fay's, except insofar as Fay's aestheticism led him to preach a beauty of a very different kind, but Gatsby's strange and far-flung organizations reflect Sigourney Fay's dazzling Odysseys ranging from World War I diplomacy in the Vatican and

194

Washington D.C., to cultivation of the mind (and, he hoped, the soul) of Henry Adams. Apart from this, Sigourney Fay's inculcation of rôle-playing and character-transference helped to give Fitzgerald his remarkable ability to throw himself and others, including Fay, into female parts. This could be physical as well as mental: 'all I could think of was how, when that certain girl played tennis, a faint moustache of perspiration appeared on her upper lip' is actually a quality of his own as described by Hemingway—'The sweat had come out on his long, perfect Irish upper lip in tiny drops.'[36] Both Fay and Fitzgerald played drag acts in amateur theatricals. 'Throughout all he said . . . I was reminded of something—an elusive rhythm, a fragment of lost words, that I had heard somewhere a long time ago.' On the evidence of influences of Conan Doyle and Wells in *Gatsby* it is appropriate to apply this remark of Nick Carraway to the circumstances of the book's composition as well as to Gatsby's impact on Carraway after the party to which the Buchanans come. Indeed, Fitzgerald tells us that he is harking back to his own ancient past as explicitly as the form of his novel will allow in his citation of his family's cult of James J. Hill in St. Paul, and in Carraway's recollection of night-train travel through Wisconsin in the last passages; the author in his writing is, like all else, 'borne back ceaselessly into the past'. Is Fay's part in *Gatsby* bigger than has been suggested up to now? Certainly it was true of Fay that 'A universe of ineffable gaudiness spun itself out in his brain'. And Sigourney Fay induces in the historian some of the reactions Carraway and others have to Gatsby at various points of epiphany. Fitzgerald may well have recalled his own reactions of wonder as to how, given Fay's fascination with fantasy, the claims he made for his career and influence could be true. Yet they do justify themselves on investigation, to us now as to Fitzgerald then, and it is possible to share Carraway's glee at the apparently impossible proving its credentials. Of course Gatsby achieves his effect on Carraway and the reader in part by a series of interlocking revelations of the genuine and the bogus. In Fay what was bogus—and in the last analysis this is also true of Gatsby—was his conviction that the past could be repossessed, in his fulfilment of Catholic dreams of religious reunion and restoration of the former domination of the civilized world; the conviction, in both cases, is sincere, but the dream is impossible. *The Great Gatsby* is rightly seen as verdict on the American dream, but it may also be verdict on *an* American dream—the dream of Sigourney Fay. Daisy—the world—was once, as Fay saw it, the world possessed by his Church; in externals she was once Gatsby's Daisy, as in name she was once Daisy Fay. This is not to provide the interpretation of *The Great Gatsby*; it simply adds to its layers of meaning.

Cyril Sigourney Webster Fay (he formally dropped his first Christian name as Fitzgerald dropped his last, 'Key', and as Gatsby shortened his given name and lengthened his surname—and Fay following Mackenzie thought of writing as 'Fane') was named (apart from 'Cyril') after an uncle; whether the uncle owed his name to Lydia H. Sigourney (1791–1865), otherwise 'the Sweet Singer of Hartford', 'the American Hemans' and 'the Christian Pindar', we do not know.[37] He made vague claims of Celtic antecedents unreflected by what we know of his Philadelphia parents; but it was not his fault that various biographers of Fitzgerald described him as having a dispensation to say Mass in 'Celtic' (which makes as much sense as saying it in Indo-European); the permission was for Greek. He certainly knew some Irish, and wrote a poem to Fitzgerald quoted in *This Side of Paradise* which makes good use of it[38]; the spelling is appalling, but he was, after all, writing to the worst speller in American literature since Petroleum V. Nasby.

He was ordained an Episcopalian priest in 1903, became a Roman Catholic in 1907, and was ordained priest in the Roman Catholic Church in 1910. He seems to have acquired an astonishing ascendency over almost everyone who encountered him: he became the secretary and envoy of Cardinal Gibbons, who had ordained him, and was made Monsignor by Pope Benedict XV, for whom he sought to obtain representation at the Peace Conference to follow World War I, and delighted Henry Adams, and even moved the hardened Cardinal William ('Gangplank Bill')[39] O'Connell of Boston. He had absolutely serious intentions of going to Russia in 1917 to convert the Russians to Roman Catholicism, and proposed to take Fitzgerald as his aide; their journey was to be through Vladivostok, but, as Fitzgerald's Princeton associate Edmund Wilson later pointed out, the future of Russia lay with envoys who came to the Finland Station. He won the confidence of significant figures in the Red Cross, in which he bore a Major's rank, he carried weight in the British Embassy in Washington, he enjoyed some friendship with Arthur James Balfour, and after his death the family of Mrs. Winthrop Chanler prayed to him as a saint and insisted they obtained miraculous favours through his intercession. Undoubtedly Mrs. Chanler won literary immortality through his intercession, since she is 'Mrs. Lawrence' in *This Side of Paradise*. Mrs. Chanler's own first name was Daisy.[40]

One relic of Sigourney Fay which does seem a Gatsby-like invention is the conviction he instilled in Mrs. Chanler that his 'mother came of a good Irish family and had transmitted to him the attractive speech of the cultivated Irish', and that he could, when he chose, as in amateur theatricals and story-telling, supply 'a most convincing Irish brogue'. Fitzgerald presumably knew better. Fay's mother was an Anglo-Saxon by descent, of ancestral celebrity in the American Revolution. But the alleged Irish origin probably assisted Fay's astonishing rise in the Roman Catholic Church. His motives may have been initially those of sentiment rather than career, and he produced an authentic Irish intellectual in his entourage in the person of John Randolph Leslie, heir to a Protestant baronet but himself a convert to Roman Catholicism and now calling himself 'Shane' (but not to rhyme with 'Fane' much though he, also, was a votary of *Sinister Street*: he pronounced it 'Shawn'). Fay was ten years Leslie's senior, and Leslie eleven years older than Fitzgerald. Here, too, there is a danger of being unduly sceptical, regarding Leslie's claims in his later memoirs. He lived long, and declined in literary quality and influence, and his ultimate comments on Fitzgerald were not such as to please the 1950s.[41] The hare is never likely to be capable of understanding the success of the tortoise, especially when the tortoise appears to have made his great spurt on alcohol and finishes the course victorious but dead.

Yet when Fitzgerald met him, Shane Leslie was a great man, in reality as well as in reputation. He came of old Irish Jacobite Protestant stock, he was educated at Eton and Cambridge (later recording these years, Mackenzie-fashion, in *The Oppidan* and *The Cantab*), he interviewed Tolstoi, was caught up in the exciting cross-currents of the Irish Renaissance, played with some folklore evidence with special reference to ghosts, mastered some Irish, wrote a little poetry (Chesterton was justly impressed by one or two of his efforts), and twice stood for Parliament in Derry, in the year of two elections 1910. His cause, the Irish Constitutional Nationalist, depended on a strong Catholic vote, and he showed courage in fighting a seat where his family's Unionist past would certainly invite bitter Unionist repudiation of his religious treachery. On one interpretation, he nursed the candidacy well enough to ensure that a Nationalist won in 1913 at the next opportunity; on another, he fled from the field, lost interest in it, or was eased out. But as one of the rising young aspirants in the Irish Nationalist Party, he would have known of other young poets who passed through it, and ultimately opted for stronger measures.

Leslie in 1916 found himself trying desperately to rally Irish-American sentiment to the Home Rule cause, now extended to include the cause of the Allies in World War I, in face of the revulsion against Britain prompted by the execution of the leaders of the Easter Rising. The huge response of sympathy to the victims came from people most of whom were wholly opposed to the Rising; but the martyrs, once dead, won converts whom they had no chance of swaying while alive. Leslie made no defence of the executions but continued to preach the Allied cause to the Irish-Americans. He had the advantage of being brother-in-law to W. Bourke Cockran, the silver-tongued orator of Tammany Hall (as well as its shop-window exhibit in culture and integrity); he himself was also grandson to Leonard Jerome, and hence first cousin to the British Cabinet Minister Winston Churchill (here less advantageous). Through the hospitality of Cockran, Leslie introduced Fitzgerald to wealthy Long Island society (where he would have found several Irish-Americans of the cultural delicacy and racial obsessiveness of Tom Buchanan).[42] Sigourney Fay, as secretary to the beleaguered but still pro-Ally Cardinal Gibbons, proved a valuable fellow-speaker and supporting writer for Leslie. Leslie's approach was at least original—to argue that the Irish-Americans should support the Allies as the least of two evils, the Germans being a more extreme version of their age-old English oppressor. This he sought to embody in a little book called *The Celt and the World*. It came out early in 1917, and Fitzgerald reviewed it in the *Nassau Literary Magazine* for May 1917, certainly at the request of Leslie and no doubt Fay (who, true to form, wrote at least one paragraph of the book).[43]

The Celt and the World did poorly, although it does not seem to have impaired Leslie's good relations with Charles Scribner's Sons, the publishers, to whom he later recommended Fitzgerald. The United States' entry into World War I made it not so much irrelevant, as disturbingly relevant; Leslie's mind had soared far beyond its propaganda cause, and produced theories of history and human destiny of a profundity and irony which sat uneasily with Wilsonian crusading. Its merit before the U.S.A. declared war was to offer a logic which allowed for Irish bitterness against Britain, but many of its assumptions would make Wilson as War President look either hypocritical or naïve. This would have suited the chief intellectual influence on it, Henry Adams, whose final phase was preoccupied with cycles of human history and the conflict of races. Leslie no less than Fay was drawn heavily under his sway, and the result is possibly the best book Leslie ever wrote. The racial bases may appear absurd, and the implication of Negro inferiority is very distasteful, though not obtrusive, but the prose is a fine mingling of grand play with historical forces, elegant appreciation of historical irony, and gentle and perceptive use of compassion. But Leslie did not simply absorb Adams into an Irish context like blotting-paper; his own capacities had been well established by his work of the previous year, *The End of a Chapter*, whose analysis of English power-structures and pre-war breakdown anticipated George Dangerfield's *The Strange Death of Liberal England* twenty years later. Now for Fitzgerald:

> After his most entertaining *End of a Chapter*, Mr. Leslie has written what I think will be a more lasting book. *The Celt and the World* is a sort of bible of Irish patriotism. Mr. Leslie has endeavored to trace a race, the Bretton [sic], Scotch, Welsh, and Irish Celt, through its spiritual crises and he emphasizes most strongly the trait that Synge, Yeats and Lady Gregory have made so much of in their plays, the Celt's inveterate

mysticism. The theme is worked out in an era-long contrast between Celt and Teuton, and the book becomes ever ironical when it deals of the ethical values of the latter race. 'Great is the Teuton indeed', it says, 'Luther in religion, Bessemer in steel, Neitzche [*sic*—Fitzgerald spelling] in philosophy, Rockefeller in oil—Cromwell and Bismarck in war.' What a wonderful list of names! Could anyone but an Irishman have linked them in such damning significance?

In the chapter on the conversion of the Celt to christianity, is traced the great missionary achievements of the Celtic priests and philosophers, Dungal, Fergal, Abelard, Duns Scotus and Ereugena. At the end of the book that no less passionate and mystical, although unfortunate, incident of Pearse, Plunkett and the Irish Republic, is given sympathetic but just treatment.

To an Irishman the whole book is fascinating. It gives one an intense desire to see Ireland free at last to work out her own destiny under Home Rule. It gives one the idea that she would do it directly under the eyes of God and with so much purity and so many mistakes. It arouses a fascination with the mystical lore and legend of the island which 'can save others, but herself she cannot save'. The whole book is colored with an unworldliness, and an atmosphere of the futility of man's ambitions. As Mr. Leslie says in the foreword to *The End of a Chapter* (I quote inexactly) we have seen the suicide of the Aryan race, 'the end of one era and the beginning of another to which no Gods have as yet been rash enough to give their names'.

The Celt and the World is a rather pessimistic book: not with the dreary pessimism of Strinberg and Sundermann, but with the pessimism which might have inspired 'What doth it profit a man if he gaineth the whole world and loseth his own soul'. It is worth remarking that it ends with a foreboding prophecy of a Japanese-American war in the future. The book should be especially interesting to anyone who has enjoyed *Riders to the Sea*, or *The Hour-Glass*. He will read an engrossing view of a much discussed race and decide that the Irishman has used heaven as a continued referendum for his ideals, as he has used earth as a perennial recall for his ambitions.

The citation of *The End of a Chapter*, with its fascinating conclusion describing a cultural decadence which links directly with *This Side of Paradise*, and *The Beautiful and Damned*, reminds us that Fitzgerald was describing in those books not the 1920s but the prewar society in which, for the most part, they are set. But the review indicates that Fay and Leslie gave Fitzgerald a vantage-point of contempt for 'Teuton' material success which he never lost, as well as a vision of 'Aryan' decline long before he became acquainted with Spengler. The emphasis on Irish purity may be Fay's—though the spelling affirms the review as Fitzgerald's (and no doubt it was much worse before it reached the editor)—but here we can see an ideal, no longer positive when he becomes a great writer, yet present as the negative ethics against which the society he described in his future work sinned. Fitzgerald has been made aware of a Celtic destiny of material failure far richer than the crass success his society, familial as well as contemporary, placed on its altar: the idea of the Messiah who cannot save himself as implicit in the Celticness he has embraced is all too self-prophetic. The quotation on loss of soul is basic to *The Beautiful and Damned*, dedicated to Leslie; it is also, of course, basic to *The Picture of Dorian Gray* which Fay recruited to the cause of appropriate Catholic intellectual reading for Fitzgerald and which so strongly influenced *This Side of Paradise*. For all that has been written about the Irish-American quest for assimilation and Americanization, eloquently symbolized by the gift of patriotic American nomenclature to Irish-American progeny, there lay at back of it the irony that good Catholics believed the Protestant American hosts to whose status they aspired were either damned to Hell, or 'invincibly ignorant'. Fitzgerald, charged with the exotic Catholic intellectualism of Fay and Leslie, expressed this in the sharpest cultural form it ever found.

The revelations of the Irish cultural influences which most attracted Fitzgerald are an important bonus. Synge's *Riders to the Sea* with its message of terrible acceptance when everything of value in a person's life has been wrecked, Yeats's *The Hour-Glass* with its idea of the fool Teigue holding on to religious beliefs which the wise teacher has sought to eradicate and then hopes against hope have been retained when he realizes his own soul is forfeit if he has destroyed them—these also offer their clues to Fitzgerald's bases for rejection of the conventional wisdom of American values. It is also noteworthy that where Leslie's book loses its melancholy in its own pyrotechnics, Fitzgerald's review restores a message of deep sadness. But it conveys the richness of what he described in 1922, reviewing Leslie's Etonian novel *The Oppidan*, when he recalled Fay and Leslie:

> he was a convert to the church of my youth, and he and another, since dead, made of that church a dazzling, golden thing, dispelling its oppressive mugginess and giving the succession of days upon gray days, passing under its plaintive ritual, the romantic glamor of an adolescent dream.[44]

It is this episode which in all sorts of ways liberated Fitzgerald from his background where offering a new, and dignified, intelligibility to it. Inevitably, it invited thinking and rethinking about the extraordinary men and ideas he had known, and the emotions they had aroused in him. If they bred Puritanism in Fitzgerald, they did not extol a joyless asceticism; Fay liked the good life of society, within reason, and Leslie showed some of its fascinations, and Henry Adams did not confine high thinking to plain living. Nor did he confine it to abstract ideas: in *This Side of Paradise* Fitzgerald offered a gratifying direction for it: ' "He's a radiant boy", thought Thornton Hancock, who had seen the splendour of two continents and talked with Parnell and Gladstone and Bismarck. . . .' ('Thornton Hancock is Henry Adams', wrote Fitzgerald to Maxwell Perkins on 4 September 1919. '—I didn't do him thoroughly of course—but I knew him when I was a boy.')[45] Their world seems to have reached far afield in its aesthetic enthusiasms: if Wilde did offer edifying poetry and a death-bed reconciliation to Catholicism in his final years, Swinburne merely became a suburban Tory, but Fay happily extolled his early work.[46] They did create an identification of homosexuality with Catholicism, to the extent that male friendship is good, entrapment by women is bad. The obvious case of this in Fitzgerald's writing is the short story 'One of my Oldest Friends' (1925) where the woman first betrays her husband and then incites him to betray his friend, whom he later saves from self-destruction by means of a vision of a cross.[47] English culture was ready enough to play with homosexual imagery, provided it was not called that (as in *Sinister Street*, in the cult of Leslie's acquaintance Rupert Brooke, in Robert Hugh Benson's novels, and in Leslie's own future novel *The Cantab* withdrawn under threat of public prosecution and condemnation by Cardinal Bourne but permitted to reappear after the deletion of what had been deemed unduly explicit *heterosexual* passages).[48] The happy and confident Fay rejoiced in the Catholicism of Oscar Wilde to an extent his English counterparts certainly would not (Leslie came to accept his outlook, but rejected it many years later).[49] But American obsessive concern with masculine virility wore it with much less ease. At the time, Fitzgerald, emancipated from such crudities by Fay, accepted it readily enough, as in his review of Leslie's *Verses in Peace and War*:

> . . . the brightest gem of the coffer is the poem 'The Dead Friend', beginning:
>
> > I drew him then unto my knees
> > My friend who was dead,
> > And I set my live lips over his,
> > And my heart to his head.[50]

But later he was vulnerable. His womenfolk, recognizing their enemy, taunted him. Zelda in a bad temper opined a homosexual relationship between himself and Hemingway (who may have been a little free in her presence with references to the beauties of Fitzgerald's Irish upper lip), and Sheilah Graham wondered why he was giving her so much Oscar Wilde to read (it 'made me uncomfortable, as does everything else that is not normal').[51] *This Side of Paradise* offers its final vision of Monsignor Thayer Darcy (apart from his funeral) in the attempt of his ghost to save Amory Blaine from a wicked woman.

The particular perspective of Irishness and Catholicism led Fitzgerald naturally to appreciate other and different denunciations of the world of material success; hence the ease with which he adopted Wells's lower-class critiques of that world. We think so much of the controversies of Wells with Belloc and Chesterton, that we forget how much they had in common in the attack which all three of them—all four, counting Shaw—mounted on the social ethics of their time. But it is important that the Irishness and Catholicism (whatever about the attendant homosexuality) were consciously realized by Fitzgerald. Leslie and even Edmund Wilson might see Fitzgerald's Irishness as being a natural consequence of his racial origin; but in the form it took, the great difference was made by his coming to regard it as a matter for gratitude rather than shame. It is for this reason that some of Fitzgerald's stories will deliberately inject a note of what he and Leslie might have called Celtic 'mysticism' or something else. Leslie would have taught him enough of Celtic revenge literature to supply the elation of the savage reprisal on which 'Bernice Bobs her Hair' ends, thereby raising itself to considerable stature; but the story in general is a nice metaphor on the worthlessness of the standards to which the immigrant is invited to aspire. 'The Cut-Glass Bowl' is in theme almost an Irish folk-story, of the preternatural kind beloved of Leslie, although the beginning reads like a parody of Great Historical Cycles ('There was a rough stone age and a smooth stone age and a bronze age, and many years afterward a cut-glass age . . .'). 'Two for a Cent' is again Irish folktale in its turning-point, although this time the folktale is brilliantly inverted to show the effects when looked at from the reverse end of its natural development: the good-luck cent explains how things have worked out instead of being the starting-point of a narrative of two destinies. 'The Pusher-in-the-Face' is the old story of the Irish fool with but one trick, and that normally useless, which somehow supplies the bases of a whole series of strokes of good fortune. Fay seems to have been even more drawn to stories of this kind than Leslie, and his influence has to be taken as working directly on both. For instance Fitzgerald's poem 'The Pope at Confession', and Leslie's story 'The Pope's Temptation', so similar to one another in point of departure, probably originated in a reminiscence of Fay's time at the Vatican when he was trying to win a place at Versailles for Benedict XV.[52]

F. Scott Fitzgerald, therefore, is an American *and* Irish and Catholic writer, all the more so because he expressed these last two qualities negatively for the most part, and conscious of his loss of formal allegiance. His tribalism, his intellectual, emotional and ethical legacy from his background and from his reappraisal of it under Sigourney Fay's direction, expressed themselves not in the usual immigrant pattern but working their way far below his formal expression of any message. *The Celt and the World*, Leslie's book but worked out in close harmony with Fay under Adams's influence (perhaps even including some of Adams's dictation), may have been a 'bible' for him, but it was not a bible to which any of his contemporaries had reference, and it even dropped from Leslie's horizon, never obtaining publication in his native British Isles; Fitzgerald's future recollection of its contours and ironies had to be entirely personal.[53] The change in Irish allegiance to Sinn Féin distanced him from Irish movements once more; he probably resembled Amory Blaine in being soured by the new protagonists, and Gloria Blanch in being bored by them (although in strict chronological terms she is premature in her boredom, since her annoyance with her Sinn Féin maidservant has to have been in the Fall of 1916, before the Irish rebellion survivors had taken over Sinn Féin). The enthusiasm of the Irish-American herd for the campaigns of Michael Collins would have done nothing to increase Fitzgerald's enthusiasm for them. Unlike Jewish writers who had lost their faith, he did not have an identity expressed through the cause of a homeland; his Celtic identity had been determined in a philosophy of success through failure. His Catholicism effectively lost its force with the death of Sigourney Fay on 10 January 1919 (he was unable to attend the funeral, and Amory Blaine's witness of Darcy's is drawn from Leslie's letter to him describing it—thus drawing in another source for Blaine if he had not in his turn supplied previous touches). Fitzgerald saw his former idols lose their attraction as they aged: Mackenzie disappointing him by supposed pursuit of comedy in place of spirituality (and he seems to have shared Fay's disgust at Michael Fane being led to abandon the hope of priesthood and marry Sylvia Scarlett at the end of the novel of her *Adventures*), Leslie growing increasingly and timorously clericalist. The memory of Fay alone remained eternally youthful and confident. Ironically, his new allegiance to Mencken after Fay's death would not have disturbed much of the Monsignor's ideology: Mencken revered Cardinal Gibbons and saw Catholicism at its best as aesthetically elevating in contrast to popular Protestantism.[54]

Fitzgerald's high moment of allegiance to Catholicism took place when he was about 21. Henceforward he found himself of an older generation, for all of his youth as a successful writer. 'Echoes of the Jazz Age' pointedly places the subject after him in time: 'the wildest of all generations, the generation which had been adolescent during the confusion of the War, brusquely shouldered my contemporaries out of the way and danced into the limelight.' His own work, so often looked on as the product of the Jazz Age, reflected both the perspective and the literary influences of an older time. ' "A chiel's amang ye takin' notes"—and, faith, he printed them; and became the Fatal Man of an era', asseverated Maxwell Geismar; but Geismar's Scots was faulty, for 'chiel' means 'man' rather than 'child' as Burns used it, and it was as a man that Fitzgerald anatomized his juniors.[55] Quite apart from the inability of the age to accept an old-fashioned moralist, particularly from so unfashionable and socially inferior a plane as Irish Catholicism, Fitzgerald's personal loss of faith made it impossible for him to express his outlook in formal terms. Nor would his chief literary derivations have won friends in the 1920s, and some of these went even farther back in time than those placed before him by Sigourney Fay. His most famous short story of all may owe its origin to a typical piece of schoolboy absurdist boasting ('My Father owns a diamond as big as a house!' '*My* Father owns a diamond as big as the Ritz!').

The actual point of his departure from Catholicism has been disputed, but in one critical respect it can be dated. Fitzgerald was married in a Catholic Sacrament, and his daughter baptized in another; but after that Zelda had an abortion. We know very little about it, and although he began to use it as material for *The Beautiful and Damned*, he could not bring himself to go through with it and left an unexplained allusion to pregnancy in the story without further resolution.[56] The abortive detail is instructive. It is from this event that a sense of being damned takes over, as indeed the title of the book says. Yeats's *The Hour-Glass* assumes a new significance as Fitzgerald moves from fool to teacher. Intellectually he could no longer accept Catholicism, he told himself; emotionally he found it increasingly hard to live with his action in having rejected it, particularly in this most dreadful of all repudiations. The self-destructive alcoholism becomes frighteningly explicable in these circumstances, and the meaning of *The Beautiful and Damned* is enormously strengthened if we read it with allowance for an abortion clearly required by the plot but too painful for him to confront in the act of creative writing. He might, and probably did, blame Zelda for it, and the impetus appears to have been hers: he very much wanted a son. He loved her, and he saw her as a source of damnation. It was virtually a recreation of the motives ascribed by Milton to Adam in eating the forbidden fruit, in *Paradise Lost*. I believe that this inherent conviction of damnation accounts for the terrible clarity of so much of his writing, as well as of his own tragedy.

It is unknown whether Fitzgerald ever read, or even heard of, Frederick Rolfe, although Rolfe had affected many of the literary influences on him, from Robert Hugh Benson, to Shane Leslie. He might have liked the end of *Hadrian VII*: 'Pray for the repose of his soul. He was so tired.'[57]

NOTES

1. This essay exists because of A. Robert Lee, and its concern about impetus and influence in Fitzgerald's writing enhances my pleasure in thanking him. He asked me to write it, prodded me to keep it up, made invaluable constructive comments, inspired me with his enthusiasm, and made the whole business a joy for me. His invitation was based on a generous recollection of my excitement about the discussion of Fitzgerald's Irishness in William V. Shannon, *The American Irish* (New York, 1963, 1966), pp. 233–44. This work is the starting-point for any enquiry, and it will be evident that my essay is largely a development of the perceptions of the future Ambassador to Ireland in his deeply perceptive book; my gratitude to Mr. Shannon is personal as well as historiographical. Dr. John Whitley is a Godsend to historians on any topic he takes up; my work here should be considered as deeply sympathetic to his essay in this volume, which I have read in writing my own. Professor W. W. Robson has been most helpful in suggesting areas for investigation and in his fascinating comments on the authors under discussion, famous and forgotten. Mr. Philip French has been a strong and shrewd adviser on sources. I have written under the inspiration of a superb impromptu lecture on *The Great Gatsby* by Professor Denis Donoghue at the first Conference of the Irish Association for American Studies, and I cherish the memory of the insights which the late Professor E. R. R. Green contributed to the discussion on that occasion. Ms Faith Pullin chaired a presentation of an earlier draft of this paper to the North American Studies Seminar at the University of Edinburgh, and my gratitude is due to her and to my other colleagues and the students who were most helpful in its discussion. My daughter Sara Dudley Edwards generously checked some important references for me at the Bodleian Library, Oxford, and my thanks are also due to its staff for courtesies far beyond the ordinary during my visit. The Library of the University of Edinburgh contributed much to my work, as did the Edinburgh City Library (especially Mr. Alan Taylor of the Reference

Room). The National Library of Scotland has been my patient and most helpful friend from start to finish. Mr. John Macfie lent me a very rare work by Shane Leslie, and was very helpful in discussions about him.

2. Michael Davie (ed.), *The Diaries of Evelyn Waugh* (London, 1976, 1979), pp. 787–88. The date is not absolutely certain; Waugh's diary-keeping was by then fragmentary and the entry may have been made between 9 May and 26 June. His recollection of never having heard of Fitzgerald until 1947 may not be a reliable memory. I have used the 1934 edition of Dinneen. (See also n. 24 below.)

3. *National* [i.e. U.S.] *Union Catalog Pre-1956 Imprints* (London, 1971), Vol. 174, pp. 263–67. *British Library Catalogue to 1975* (London, 1981), Vol. 109, 367–70. Jackson B. Bryer, *The Critical Reputation of F. Scott Fitzgerald* (Hamden, Conn., 1967).

4. Malcolm Cowley, *The Literary Situation* (New York, 1958), p. 126. Cowley subsequently came to terms with the situation by introducing and editing several collections of and about Fitzgerald.

5. Kenneth Eble, *F. Scott Fitzgerald* (New York, 1963), p. 7.

6. MAD repeatedly made this point in its analyses published 1960–63, drawing attention to the complaints about such phrases as 'I dig you the most, Daddy-oh' made by parents who in the 1920s had been addressing each other 'Boop-a-doop-boop, Baby', and '23-skidoo, no change'. This source must be the starting-point of any serious investigation of the question.

7. Bryer, *Critical Reputation*, pp. 362, 359, 63, 170, 258, 266, 278, 339, 88, 106, 240, 255, 303 lists several examples, many focusing on *The American*. The thing seems to have begun in the *New York Times Book Review*, 19 April 1925, with Edwin Clark, 'Scott Fitzgerald looks into Middle Age' which found a parallel with *The Turn of the Screw*. Gilbert Seldes, possibly prompted by Fitzgerald himself, saluted *The Great Gatsby* in 'Spring Flight' (*Dial*, August 1925) pointing out that it was written in a series of scenes, 'a method F. Scott Fitzgerald derived from Henry James through Mrs. Wharton'. The *Glasgow Herald*, reviewing *Tender is the Night* (20 October 1934), seems to have pioneered European perceptions along the same lines: 'this disciple of Henry James'. Sergio Perosa, *The Art of F. Scott Fitzgerald* (Ann Arbor, Mich., 1965), originally published in Italian in 1961, has references to James in 56 of its 225 pages of text and notes, beating all other authors (Hemingway is a bad second with 33).

8. James E. Miller, *F. Scott Fitzgerald: His Art and his Technique* (New York, 1964), pp. 2–11. James again romps home in index-references.

9. 'I certainly wouldn't begin Henry James with *The Portrait of a Lady* which is in his "late second manner" and full of mannerisms. Why don't you read *Roderick Hudson* or *Daisy Miller* first?' (Fitzgerald to his daughter Frances Scott Fitzgerald [July 1939]). 'Despite the fact that I am *not* quite as insane about *What Maisie Knew* as you prophesied I would be, I admire your judgments in almost every way more than those of anyone else I know' (Fitzgerald to Edmund Wilson, 6 February [1922]). Fitzgerald has been credited with reading James in the summer of 1917 (Matthew J. Bruccoli, *Some Sort of Epic Grandeur: The Life of F. Scott Fitzgerald*

(London, 1981), pp. 77, 611), but the reference is to reading philosophers, hence William James is the 'James' referred to (Fitzgerald to Wilson, 26 September 1917). Andrew Turnbull (ed.), *The Letters of F. Scott Fitzgerald* (Harmondsworth, 1968), pp. 74, 353, 338. Zelda's reading of *Roderick Hudson* (which may have supplied the basis of Fitzgerald's opinion of it) led to the Fitzgeralds' decision to winter in Rome in 1924 (Arthur Mizener, *The Far Side of Paradise: A Biography of F. Scott Fitzgerald* (London, 1951), p. 164). Fitzgerald recommended Scribner to reprint *The Turn of the Screw* (19 April 1922, *Letters*, p. 175) but there seems no other sign that he had read it, and this may simply have been to impress Scribner with his judgement and knowledge of Scribner's list. In any case Maxwell Perkins of Scribner's was unimpressed by another citation of James, writing on 12 April 1922 'I don't think Henry James had anything in the world to do with you at all, and so is not appropriate' (quoted Bruccoli and Margaret M. Duggan (eds.), *Correspondence of F. Scott Fitzgerald* (New York, 1980), p. 102n.).

10. *The Beautiful and the Damned*, Sect. III, subsection 'Wisdom'.
11. Amory Blaine's reading preferences at Princeton obviously follow Fitzgerald's, at least roughly: the reference to Swinburne is in *This Side of Paradise*, Sect. II ('Spires and Gargoyles'), fairly early. The snobbish embarrassment of critics at Fitzgerald's debt to Wells (and others with reputations wounded or missing in the wars of literary fashion) is amusingly reflected in Mizener's 'The Maturity of Scott Fitzgerald' (the defensiveness of the title is instructive): 'When he had . . . a need, he could learn from almost anyone. If he refers to Conrad's example in the letter to Kenneth Littauer about *The Last Tycoon*, he also refers, in his notes for the book, to H. G. Wells. He was even capable of learning from a movie magazine . . .' *Sewanee Review* (Autumn 1959), quoted Mizener (ed.), *F. Scott Fitzgerald: A Collection of Critical Essays* (Englewood Cliffs, N.J., 1963), pp. 160–61.
12. Eliot to Fitzgerald, 31 December 1925, quoted *verbatim* Edmund Wilson (ed.), *The Crack-Up with Other Uncollected Pieces . . . by F. Scott Fitzgerald* (New York, 1945); also quoted incessantly by the recipient. On Compton Mackenzie, see his *My Life and Times: Octave 4, 1907–1915* (London, 1965), quoting J. B. Pinker to Mackenzie, 5 January 1914 (itself quoting Henry James to Pinker, n.d.), also James to Mackenzie, 21 January 1914, and James to Mackenzie (paraphrased from lost letter) November 1914, pp. 210–13, 234.
13. 'Almost nothing is known about Scott's paternal grandfather, Michael Fitzgerald, who may have kept a general store in Maryland' (Bruccoli, *Some Sort of Epic Grandeur*, p. 11). André Le Vot tries to improve matters by making him 'a gentleman farmer . . . his family had lived for generations on Glenmary Farm near Rockville, Montgomery County', but it was his wife, Cecilia Scott, who inherited the farm (Le Vot, *F. Scott Fitzgerald* (Harmondsworth, 1984), p. 4). Michael Fitzgerald is supposed to have died in 1855, but desertion of his wife and three children seems a possibility, and an initial marriage induced by pregnancy more than that (given the obscurity of husband and lineage of wife). Much is made

of Fitzgerald's awareness of the plebeian roots of his maternal ancestry; the mystery of the ancestor whose name he bore seems much more suggestive.

14. But was Edward Fitzgerald a Roman Catholic? His mother's people showed a strong sense of responsibility to the religion of the deceased or defaulted husband if he was. 'That Mollie was married in Washington may indicate something about the McQuillans' uncertain social position in St. Paul', observes Bruccoli (*ibid.*, pp. 12–13) and goes on to lay down the law on the social position of the Irish and the Swedes. In fact, it may say something about their certain religious position: a Nuptial Mass and church wedding would be expected in St. Paul and would not be easily forthcoming if there were problems about the bridegroom's religion. A house wedding in Washington, D.C., disposed of awkward questions. Has anyone investigated the Archdiocesan records of Washington, D.C., on the point? It seems extraordinary that we do not know, and it would be important in reflections on Fitzgerald's legacy from his parents. Joan M. Allen, *Candles and Carnival Lights: The Catholic Sensibility of F. Scott Fitzgerald* (New York, 1978), a valuable if not over-imaginative special study, seems to miss out here: 'one of the few things the McQuillans and the Fitzgeralds had in common, their Roman Catholicism' (p. 4) in default of supporting evidence begs rather than answers the question. Even Harry Dan Piper, *F. Scott Fitzgerald: A Critical Portrait* (London, 1965), in many ways the most inspirational of Fitzgerald biographies, simply anticipates the Le Vot error about 'Captain' Michael Fitzgerald, supporting it by loose reference to clippings about the Maryland Fitzgeralds in scrapbooks in the Fitzgerald papers at Princeton. It is difficult to see how this might hold evidence on anything more than Edward Fitzgerald's maternal ancestry, especially since Professor Bruccoli, most indefatigable of authorities on Geraldiniana (as no doubt Fitzgerald would have liked it to be termed), is quite clear that only the maternal relatives of Edward Fitzgerald can be discussed with any confidence.

15. See the essay by Fitzgerald's daughter Frances, now Scottie Fitzgerald Smith, included in Bruccoli, *Some Sort of Epic Grandeur*, pp. 496–509. This valuable piece of original research is also significantly silent on Michael Fitzgerald. Bruccoli is surprised (pp. 164–65) that Fitzgerald wrote to Edmund Wilson in January 1922 (*Letters*, p. 351) 'incidentally, though it doesn't matter, I'm not Irish on Father's side': 'His claim is curious as well as incorrect because his paternal grandfather, Michael Fitzgerald, was Irish.' It may mean that he was not, as far as anyone knew; it may simply mean that Fitzgerald knew of no Catholic element in his father's origin, either because Edward was brought up a Protestant after Michael's death or departure, or because Michael himself was not a Catholic.

16. *This Side of Paradise*, Sect. I ('Amory, Son of Beatrice'), subsections 'Preparatory to the Great Adventure' and 'Incident of the Well-Meaning Professor'. On this evidence, Fitzgerald's reading of Conan Doyle's medieval romances was encouraged by Father Sigourney Fay.

17. I explore this in my *The Quest for Sherlock Holmes: A Biographical Study of Sir Arthur Conan Doyle* (Edinburgh, 1983).

18. Published in the St. Paul Academy school journal, *Now and Then* (October 1909), and subsequently in John Kuehl (ed.), *The Apprentice Fiction of F. Scott Fitzgerald* (New Brunswick, N.J., 1965), pp. 17–25. For other reprints see Bruccoli, *Supplement to F. Scott Fitzgerald: A Descriptive Bibliography* (Pittsburgh, 1980), pp. 171–72. My thanks to my friend and graduate student Colin Nicolson for pointing out the Poe allusion in the title; Fitzgerald mentions a Poe story among his earliest reading (or rather Amory's) in *This Side of Paradise*.

19. Published *Now and Then*, June 1911, and reprinted by Kuehl, ibid.

20. Marcus Cunliffe, *The Literature of the United States* (Harmondsworth, 1986: 4th edn. revised), p. 265.

21. Richard Lancelyn Green and John Michael Gibson, *A Bibliography of A. Conan Doyle* (Oxford, 1983: Soho Bibliographies, XXIII), p. 201. Bruccoli, *Correspondence of Fitzgerald*, p. 124n.

22. Bruccoli, *Some Sort of Epic Grandeur*, p. 109n. Green and Gibson, *Bibliography of Conan Doyle*, p. 207.

23. W. K. Dunn, 'FAY, CYRIL SIGOURNEY WEBSTER, diplomat', *New Catholic Encyclopedia*. [Margaret] Mrs. Winthrop Chanler, *Autumn in the Valley* (Boston, 1936), pp. 29, 78–86, 124–25. Mizener, *Far Side of Paradise*, pp. 42–5, 59, 65–6, 71, 319–20. Piper, *Fitzgerald*, pp. 37–8. Andrew Turnbull, *Scott Fitzgerald* (New York, 1962), pp. 39, 77–84, 90, 157. Sara Mayfield, *Exiles from Paradise: Zelda and Scott Fitzgerald* (New York, 1971), pp. 34, 39–42, 75. Allen, *Candles and Carnival Lights*, pp. 32–70. Bruccoli, *Some Sort of Epic Grandeur*, pp. 36–8, 52, 61, 74–7, 83–4, 86, 95–6, 129, 229, 278. Bruccoli, *Correspondence of Fitzgerald*, pp. 19–37, 42n., 66–7, 241n., 331. Le Vot, *Fitzgerald*, pp. 24–9, 33, 38, 49, 54–5, 59, 103. *Letters*, pp. 391–99 (to Shane Leslie). James R. Mellow, *Invented Lives: F. Scott and Zelda Fitzgerald* (London, 1985), pp. 25–8, 40–7, 59–60, 63, 74, 77, 195–97. Tony Buttitta, *The Lost Summer: A Personal Memoir of F. Scott Fitzgerald* (London, 1987), pp. 137–38. *This Side of Paradise* and its 'review' by Shane Leslie, *Dublin Review* (October–December 1920), also various volumes of memoirs by Leslie and his 'Some Memories of Scott Fitzgerald', *Times Literary Supplement* (31 October 1958; see also ibid., 14 and 21 November 1958, and 6 November 1959). It may have been of importance, psycho-medically, that Fay is believed to have been an albino.

24. Waugh's disclaimer might seem conclusive, but his quarrel with Edmund Wilson may have been reason to repudiate any suggestion of influence by Wilson's dead *protégé*, and another Wilson critique of Waugh was published in the *New Yorker* at the time of the diary entry. Waugh had severely personally censored Frederick J. Stopp, *Evelyn Waugh* (London, 1958), but had left unaltered this passage: 'The literary influences on the main, realistic current of his writing have been few, mainly those from which, in his first years as an author, he acquired some of his skill in narrative, economy and speed, in the conduct of dialogue and the devices of wit: "Saki", Fitzgerald, Hemingway, Wodehouse. These, though admitted by Mr. Waugh himself, are comparatively unimportant' (p. 212). The really obvious potential point of influence is Father Rothschild, in support of

which there is the odd legend, repeated in *D.N.B. 1971–1980* (Oxford, 1986), p. 207, that Rothschild was modelled on the Jesuit M. C. D'Arcy, despite denials from all parties and the clear fact that Waugh had never met him until after he had finished *Vile Bodies*; could it have been based on another 'Darcy', i.e. that embodying Fay in *This Side of Paradise*, with some remark of Waugh's to this effect being then assigned to the English priest? Rothschild certainly is not a normal Jesuit of fiction, as Waugh claimed, and he does seem to have *some* source, of which Fitzgerald's 'Darcy' seems the most likely ascription on its internal similarities (notably in Rothschild's famous speech explaining the Bright Young Things as compared to Darcy's advice to Amory Blaine). Waugh once more reasserted his ignorance of Fitzgerald as a young writer in *A Little Learning* (London, 1964), p. 181, in language which seems borrowed from the diary entry, and then he quotes Fitzgerald with an appositeness which sounds like the recall of an old favourite. We will probably never know.

25. The first coupling of the names of Mackenzie and Waugh to come to Evelyn Waugh's attention was, it may be, the review-article by Father Bede Jarrett, O.P., *Blackfriars*, II (1922), 716–23, discussing *Sinister Street* and Alec Waugh's *The Loom of Youth*; it had the curiously prophetic title 'Waughs and Rumours of Waughs' as a result of which it was very properly listed in the bibliography of *Ivlin Vo* (Moscow, 1981), p. 34, the choice ironies of which would probably not have amused 'Vo'. Evelyn Waugh would have been at Oxford when *Sinister Street* was being cited as an antecedent of his brother's book. See also Andro Linklater, *Compton Mackenzie* (London, 1987), p. 134.

26. Fay, 'The Genesis of the Super-German', *Dublin Review*, Vol. 162, 224–33. Harold Dean Cater, *Henry Adams and his Friends* (Boston, 1947), pp. cv, cxix.

27. Fay to Fitzgerald, 19 October 1918 (Bruccoli, *Correspondence of Fitzgerald*, pp. 33–4).

28. 'Stephen Fitz Fay Sr' (i.e. Fay) to Fitzgerald, 10 December 1917, 17 August 1918 (Bruccoli, *Correspondence of Fitzgerald*, pp. 23–4, 29–30).

29. As in n. 27.

30. Alan Margolies (ed.), *F. Scott Fitzgerald: St. Paul Plays 1911–1914* (Princeton, N.J., 1978), p. 13, and 'The Girl from Lazy J'. Fitzgerald to Arnold Gingrich, 7 February 1940 (*Letters*, pp. 619–20).

31. Fay to Fitzgerald, 22 August 1917 (Bruccoli, *Correspondence of Fitzgerald*, pp. 19–21).

32. Mellow, *Invented Lives*, p. 59. The incident is enlarged in *This Side of Paradise*.

33. See especially 'Interlude' in *This Side of Paradise*.

34. Fay to Fitzgerald, 17 August 1918 (Bruccoli, *Correspondence of Fitzgerald*, pp. 29–30).

35. Frances Newman, 'This Side of Paradise' (review), *Atlanta Constitution*, 13 February 1921, reprinted Bruccoli and Bryer (eds.), *F. Scott Fitzgerald in his Own Time: A Miscellany* (Kent, Ohio, 1971), pp. 401–3, attacks Fitzgerald's use of Mrs. Fane. Fitzgerald to Newman, 26 February 1921 (*Letters*, pp. 488–90) replies. Linklater, *Mackenzie*, pp. 17–30, shows how

well-founded Fitzgerald's rethinking was, however unintentional (despite his unsound views on Fitzgerald expressed at p. 134).

36. Ernest Hemingway, *A Movable Feast* (London, 1964), pp. 128, 131.

37. Cyril Sigourney Webster Fay, *The Bride of the Lamb and Other Essays* (New York, 1922) is a posthumous collection which gives some account of him. On Lydia H. Sigourney see the *Dictionary of American Biography*.

38. 'Interlude', *This Side of Paradise*.

39. So called because of his permanently unfulfilled desire to be present at a convention of the Sacred College of Cardinals for the election of a Pope; living before transatlantic air travel, he never reached the Vatican in time. See John Huston in Otto Preminger's tiresome film 'The Cardinal'. On Fay and his undoubted and apparently total acceptance by the experienced and accomplished Gibbons as emissary, see the authoritative John Tracy Ellis, *Life of James Cardinal Gibbons* (Milwaukee, Wis., 1952), II, 226–80.

40. Chanler, *Autumn in the Valley*, pp. 85–6. See also Chanler, *Roman Spring* (Boston, 1934), for an account of her background.

41. For Leslie, his notice (written by his daughter Anita just before her death) in *D.N.B. 1971–1980*, pp. 501–2, is inadequate. His *The Irish Issue in its American Aspect: A Contribution to the Settlement of Anglo-American Relations During and After the Great War* (London, 1918) conveys something of his attitudes and career at this time, as do his novels and his memoirs such as *American Wonderland* (London, 1936), *The Film of Memory* (London, 1938) and *Long Shadows* (London, 1966).

42. See references to *T.L.S.* under n. 23 above. Leslie claimed too much for his rôle in Fitzgerald's life, but he is right in making something of the social links then made with Cockran, at least more so than Arthur Mizener's reduction of *Gatsby* to a *roman à clef* of Great Neck 1922–24 in reply. The first sight of 'the rich' probably impinged very strongly on Fitzgerald with, as Leslie would say, long shadows.

43. *The Celt and the World* is not in the British Library, so small was its British circulation, but a second-hand copy was acquired some years ago by the National Library of Scotland, without whose providence this essay would not have been conceived. Fitzgerald's review was reprinted by Bruccoli and Bryer (and again I am deeply in *their* debt) in *Fitzgerald Miscellany*, pp. 115–16, where his review of Leslie's *Verses in Peace and War* is included on pp. 117–18, and of *The Oppidan* (*New York Tribune*, 14 May 1922), on pp. 134–35. Leslie's *The End of a Chapter* had important alterations between British editions of 1916 and 1929, and additional material in its U.S. edition of 1916.

44. *Fitzgerald Miscellany*, p. 134. Fitzgerald was still talking about Fay, Leslie, *The End of a Chapter* and *The Celt and the World* (now apparently as *Celts of the World*) in 1935 (Buttitta, *The Lost Summer*, p. 138).

45. *This Side of Paradise*, Sect. I ('Amory, Son of Beatrice'), subsection 'Preparatory to the Great Adventure'. Kuehl and Bryer (eds.), *Dear Scott/Dear Max: The Fitzgerald-Perkins Correspondence* (London, 1973), p. 20.

46. Le Vot, *Fitzgerald*, p. 33. Bruccoli, *Correspondence of Fitzgerald*, pp. 27, 30.

47. Reprinted in 1979 in Bruccoli (ed.), *The Price was High;* its omission

from earlier collections may have unjustly diminished its importance for students of Fitzgerald's psychology.

48. I have been able to compare Professor W. W. Robson's copy of the suppressed edition of *The Cantab* with the revised version (issuance of the original is still forbidden in British libraries). Fitzgerald knew of its suppression, but seems to have told Buttitta (*The Lost Summer*, p. 138) that it was because of action by Cambridge University (which, for once, was blameless).

49. Leslie included Wilde and Beardsley in his first (1925) edition of an anthology of Catholic poetry but withdrew their poems when it was reissued a quarter-century later. There are some signs that his spirit was broken by the prosecution of *The Cantab* and the threat of its condemnation by Cardinal Bourne.

50. *Fitzgerald Miscellany*, p. 117.

51. Mellow, *Invented Lives*, pp. 359–60. Sheilah Graham, *College of One* (London, 1967), p. 86. Fitzgerald taught Sheilah Graham to read; he can hardly have taught her to write. My thanks are due to Ms Betty Allsop for giving me the late Kenneth Allsop's impressions of Graham.

52. Bruccoli (ed.), *F. Scott Fitzgerald Poems 1911–1940* (Bloomfield Hills, Mich. and Columbia, S.C., 1981), p. 74. Leslie, *Masquerades* (London, 1924), pp. 11–23. The close of Leslie's story, reflecting on the Devil's origin in Heaven before his fall, may be very relevant to Fitzgerald; he was probably the last person with whom Fitzgerald conversed as a fellow-artist and fellow-Catholic.

> 'Frankly, then', said the Pope, 'the Devil is home-sick.'
> 'Damned home-sick', said the Grand Inquisitor.

53. Fitgerald's use of *The Celt and the World* should be considered in the context of his progress towards Spengler; see John S. Whitley's essay above.

54. Bruccoli, *Some Sort of Epic Grandeur*, p. 219. Mackenzie, *My Life and Times: Octave 6, 1923–30* (London, 1967), pp. 62–3.

55. Maxwell Geismar, *The Last of the Provincials: The American Novel 1915–1925* (New York, 1959), p. 287.

56. Bruccoli, *Some Sort of Epic Grandeur*, p. 163 and n. Nancy Milford, *Zelda: A Biography* (New York, 1970), p. 88. Sara Mayfield, *Exiles from Paradise*, p. 80. Mellow, *Invented Lives*, pp. 147–48. Mellow gives coherence to the matter by stating: 'In the novel, the problem is resolved when Gloria learns that she is not pregnant after all.' This is a reasonable inference, but in fact the question, to my mind, is not explicitly resolved. On the actual Fitzgerald marriage, there has been surmise by Sara Mayfield and others that Zelda had several abortions.

57. (London, 1904). For Leslie's response to him see his *Masquerades*, also A. J. A. Symons, *The Quest for Corvo* (London, 1934).

Notes on Contributors

ELIZABETH KASPAR ALDRICH, Visiting Professor at the University of Lausanne, has taught American literature at Yale, the University of Geneva, and the Claremont Graduate School. Her *American Hagiography*, a study of the formal properties and cultural uses of secular saints' lives, is forthcoming.

HAROLD BEAVER has just retired as Professor of American Literature at the University of Amsterdam. He has contributed five editions of Melville and Poe to the Penguin English Library. He has recently collected his essays on American literature in *The Great American Masquerade* (1985) for the Critical Studies Series, and published a study of *Huckleberry Finn* (1987) for the Unwin Critical Library.

HERBIE BUTTERFIELD is Reader in Literature at the University of Essex. He is the author of a study of Hart Crane, a monograph on Robinson Jeffers, and miscellaneous shorter pieces on, among others, Poe, Hawthorne, Longfellow, Melville, Henry James, Ambrose Bierce, Willa Cather and Hemingway. He is also the editor of *Modern American Poetry* (1984) in the Critical Studies Series.

OWEN DUDLEY EDWARDS is Reader in Commonwealth and American History at the University of Edinburgh, has studied and taught in various American universities, and written frequently about literary figures from a historical viewpoint. His publications include books and articles on P. G. Wodehouse, Conan Doyle, Mark Twain, Matthew Arnold, Sir Walter Scott and Anthony Trollope. He has books in the press on de Valera and on American presidential elections. He is currently at work on a new study of Macauley.

ROBERT GIDDINGS has published widely on film and media and especially on Smollett and Dickens. He is Senior Lecturer in the Department of Communication and Media at the Dorset Institute of Higher Education. He has edited volumes on Matthew Arnold, Tolkien, Dickens and Twain in the Critical Studies Series; contributed to collections in the series on Scott, Auden, Poe, Johnson,

Smollett and Le Carré; co-authored with Alan Bold *True Characters: Real People in Fiction* and *Who Was Really Who in Fiction*; written frequently for *New Society*, the *Listener, New Statesman*, and *Tribune*; and published his autobiography, *You Should See me in Pyjamas* (1981).

BRIAN HARDING teaches American literature at the University of Birmingham and is the author of *American Literature in Context* (II), 1830–1865 (1982). He has recently edited *Nathaniel Hawthorne: Young Goodman Brown and Other Tales* for the Oxford University Press's World's Classic Series (1987).

ANDREW HOOK is Bradley Professor of English Literature at the University of Glasgow. His American interests are reflected by his books, *Scotland and America 1750–1835* (1975) and *American Literature in Context* (III), 1865–1900 (1982) as well as by articles on Anglo-American relations.

A. ROBERT LEE is Senior Lecturer in English and American Literature at the University of Kent at Canterbury. He is editor of the Everyman *Moby-Dick* (1975) and of eight previous collections in the Critical Studies Series, among the most recent *Herman Melville: Reassessments* (1984), *Nineteenth-century American Poetry* (1985), *The Nineteenth-century American Short Story* (1985), *Edgar Allan Poe: The Design of Order* (1986) and *First Person Singular: Studies in American Autobiography* (1988). He is the author of a monograph *Black American Fiction Since Richard Wright* (1983) and recent essays on Richard Wright, Emily Dickinson, Mark Twain, Herman Melville, Robert Penn Warren, Harlem and Afro-American fiction and Stephen Crane. He broadcasts for B.B.C. radio and is a book-reviewer for the *Listener*.

JOHN S. WHITLEY is Reader in American Studies at the University of Sussex. He has published studies of William Golding and Scott Fitzgerald, edited an edition of Dickens's *American Notes* for Penguin Books and written essays on various detective-story writers. He is currently working on Dashiell Hammett and a further critical study of Scott Fitzgerald.

Index

Index

DATE DUE

PRINTED IN U.S.A.